The Commanders Who Kept Britain Great

The famed military excellence of the British won an empire with vast borders, where "the sun never set." With the onslaught of World War II, that empire was threatened on all fronts: in Africa, Asia, and worst of all, at home.

Imperiled by a German invasion, with armies tiny in comparison to enemy forces, the beleaguered nation stood its ground. The enemy had underestimated the courage of the British people and the brilliance and dedication of their leaders.

The British forces wrested victories from the enemy at the Battle of Salerno, in "Operation Crusader" in North Africa, and of course, at the Battle of Britain. Against what sometimes seemed insurmountable odds, the strategy, spirit and tenacity of the British commanders helped the Allies win the war—and kept the sun shining over Great Britain.

THE GREAT COMMANDERS OF WORLD WAR II
Volume II: THE BRITISH

BY CHARLES E. PFANNES AND VICTOR A. SALAMONE

ZEBRA BOOKS
KENSINGTON PUBLISHING CORP.

ZEBRA BOOKS

are published by

KENSINGTON PUBLISHING CORP.
475 Park Avenue South
New York, N.Y. 10016

Second printing: August 1985

Printed in the United States of America

TABLE OF CONTENTS

TO CHARLES AND CATHERINE SALAMONE:
FOR THEIR YEARS OF UNTIRING
LOVE AND SUPPORT

Preface

In Volume II of our Great Commander series we have spotlighted six British commanders. The first one is General Sir Richard O'Connor. Unfortunately for him, his career would be cut short when he was captured in early 1941, at the height of his ability. However, his dynamic leadership netted Great Britain its first major victory against the Axis foe.

Our second commander is Air Marshal Hugh Dowding. His conduct during the Battle of Britain would raise much criticism but the final result could not be doubted.

Field Marshal Sir Claude Auchinleck is spotlighted as our third selection. His brilliant leadership in the western desert from July 1941 to July 1942 would lay the ground work for eventual victory in North Africa, the honor for which would unfortunately fall to another.

Next we come to Field Marshal Sir Harold Alexander. His enthusiastic leadership would motivate his subordinates when at times all they had to go on was his inspiration. One of the great crimes of World War II was not having utilized Alexander as the chief British commander in the campaign for northwest Europe.

Our fifth selection falls to Field Marshal Bernard L. Montgomery. He was chosen not for his brilliant generalship but rather for his quality of leadership. Though his tactics on the battlefield were uninspired and predictable, his ability to inspire his men was contagious, thus netting Monty a slot as a Great Commander.

Lastly we examine the commanding ability of Field Marshal William Slim who in the face of retreat and humiliation trained and led his Fourteenth Army to eventual victory over the forces of Imperial Japan.

As in the first volume, there are many other commanders we could have chosen. In determining our choices we had to take certain points into consideration. First of all was the overall result the commander produced; secondly, the popularity of the man. Montgomery had to be chosen because it was expected, whereas O'Connor was chosen because we both felt his overall ability demanded his selection. Brian Horrocks, however, could have been chosen, but he wasn't, not because he lacked the quality of brilliant leadership, hardly! Rather there were others who had more illustrious careers, Auchinleck, Alexander, and Slim. Dowding might appear misplaced here, but we hardly feel wrong in having chosen him.

We would like to thank everyone at Zebra who have given us the opportunity to write this series. We would also like to thank our wives, Susanne and Lillian and our children for the patience to put up with their absent husbands and fathers.

Victor A. Salamone
Charles (Chuck) Pfannes
March 1981
Poughkeepsie, New York

Introduction

The secret that during almost the whole of the Second World War the radio communications of the German armed forces were decoded at Bletchley Park was kept for thirty years. The feats of cryptography, mathematics and electrical engineering which made the decoding possible were marvels without parallel.[1]

Few revelations concerning the Second World War have aroused so much excitement than the fact that for most of the war, the British codebreakers were able to read many of the secret communications of the German armed forces. Very few people during the war ever realized that the German Enigma Code was broken, especially the Germans. They considered their code totally secure, they had no reason to doubt it since it was such a complicated code containing almost an infinite variety of combinations.

It might seem strange that we have decided to write our introduction to the British commanders on the contribution of codebreakers. True, codebreakers were found in every country and many were quite successful. Except for the work of the American codebreakers under the capable leadership of William Friedman, the British codebreakers by far made the most important contribution to the winning of World War II. For that purpose alone we feel that a short introduction dedicated to the superb minds of these mathematicians and scientists is correct and proper.

Ultra was the codename given to the ability of reading the Enigma Code and the transcripts themselves. In approaching the topic of Ultra, the authors first of all will attempt to explain first, how it was broken, how the secret was kept, some potential dangers involved in its use and finally, a short bibliographical sketch of the current books published about Ultra. We will not go into the mechanics of how the code system operated. Totally unqualified to tread the path of advanced mathematics, we will refer the readers to the many fine books which precisely depict the mechanics involved.

Cryptanalysis is the ancient craft of intercepting and breaking ciphers of the secret communications of an adversary. There has been secret transmission of messages for as long as man has warred against his own kind. Some methods for passing these messages were relatively simple and easily broken while others were most complicated and virtually impossible to break. For every code, however, there were those who attempted to break it. The story of Ultra is one attempt to break an enemy's code by a heroic group of British codebreakers. This was not the first time, nor the last time codebreaking was utilized to help win battles. As long as man insists on pursuing his suicidal tendency of waging war there will be codebreakers.

Our story begins in 1934. Because of the many methods of presenting the facts behind the story one can only conclude that all the facts are not completely known. Subsequent revelations may be able to fill in the gaps in the story.

In 1934, the German government began to change its ciphers to a new system. The British Secret Service

(MI-6) was extremely interested in finding out just what this new code was. During the course of their investigations, they discovered that the German army's new cipher machine was known as Enigma.

Enigma was the brainchild of a Dutchman, Hugo Koch, who patented it originally as a "secret writing machine." He established a company to develop and market his invention but found himself unable to build the machine. Meanwhile, in Berlin, a German engineer and inventor, Arthur Scherbuis, was interested in building a cipher machine. In 1923 he purchased Koch's patent and constructed a machine and called it Enigma. His model was exhibited publicly for the first time at the Congress of the International Postal Union in the same year. The machine, however, was designed basically to protect secrets in the business world. The brochure accompanying Enigma stated:

> The natural inquisitiveness of competitors is at once checkmated by a machine which enables you to keep all your documents or at least their important parts entirely secret without occasioning any expense worth mentioning. One secret, well protected, may pay the whole cost of the machine.[2]

By 1928, with Scherbuis already in his grave, his successors made every effort to ensure that the invention brought the greatest possible profit.

Five years later, Adolf Hitler became the chancellor of Germany. Within the brief span of one year, all internal power was consolidated into his hands and he felt strong enough to proceed with his intention of rearming and reorganizing the Wehrmacht. A new German war machine would require a new cipher system. The search for this new system to protect their secrets was undertaken immediately. Enigma was one of the methods examined and it was given to Col. Erich Fellgiebel to evaluate. He found the machine to be inexpensive, durable, easy to transport, simple to operate, and easy to service. Most of all, he found that it produced cipher combinations in great abundance, so many combinations in fact that the system could reasonably be considered unbreakable. It was felt that it would not matter even if the enemy captured a machine, for the apparatus was useless without knowledge of the keying procedures. Fellgiebel's evaluation clinched matters; Enigma was officially adopted as the cipher system for the armed forces of the Third Reich.

From the moment it was determined that the Germans had adopted Enigma, a full scale attack on the system commenced by the Polish Secret Intelligence Service, followed in short order by the French and British.

The Poles had experimented with the commercial model of Enigma previously and so had some rudimentary knowledge of the system. But, they also knew that the Wehrmacht had modified and refined it for its own use. The Poles themselves had accomplished much but the threat of war disrupted their work. Luckily, before disaster struck, they shared their knowledge with the French and British.

The French had managed to penetrate the military version thanks to the work of Gen. Gustave Bertrand, a French cryptographer, and a German spy who sold the French relevant information about Enigma. France managed to build a replica of Enigma but relied on their spy to feed them the necessary data on the keying procedures. What they now needed was a machine capable of setting the keys simultaneously with the keys at German headquarters or wherever the message was being transmitted from. The British, capitalizing on the Polish and French knowledge, managed to develop one.

The key Englishmen responsible for the breakthrough were Alfred Dillwyn-Knox and Alan Turing. Knox was a mathematical genius and Turing one of the pioneers of computer theory. They were both attached to the Government Code and Cipher School at Bletchley Park. Throughout the war, Bletchley Park was the main headquarters for all codebreaking activities. It was a large, rather gloomy looking Victorian mansion near the London Midland and Scottish Railway, just outside the town of Bletchley, about forty miles north of London.

Knox and Turing already knew much about Enigma but realized they had to find out how the Germans had modified it and how the keying procedures were managed. In 1939, both men traveled first to Poland to consult with the Poles and determine what they knew of Enigma, then on to Paris before returning to Bletchley Park.

They had discovered that Enigma could produce an almost infinite number of different cipher alphabets merely by changing the keying procedure. Thus armed they went about building a duplicate machine feeling that it was the only way to penetrate the secrets of Enigma. They needed to build a machine that could:

> imitate or interpret the performance of each of the thousands of Enigmas that would come to exist in the Wehrmacht.[3]

The machine would also be required to have the ability to duplicate the constant changes of keying procedure that every major German command ordered each day and night. It would also have to possess the capability of making an almost infinite number of mathematical calculations at speeds far beyond human ability. Turing already had discussed in theory what must be built, something resembling a computer. Though different from a computer, the apparatus would work along the same principle.

Now, Turing and the rest at Government Code and Cipher School were therefore faced with this challenge. The machine took shape at Bletchley and when it was completed it was:

> A copper-colored cabinet some 8 feet tall and perhaps 8 feet wide at its base.[4]

This machine, though not quite the equivalent of the modern computer, was however, possessed with the capability of matching the electrical circuitry of Enigma. The creation was called a "bombe" and installed at Hut Three in Bletchley Park.

Throughout 1939, its performance steadily improved, but the first real signals of consequence came in the form of intercepts from the Luftwaffe sometime in April, 1940. From that time forward, the course of the war was in one way or another touched by Ultra, the new codename given to these high level decoded intercepts.

Though the first Ultras were not substantially beneficial, the potential of Ultra was enormous. Pause and ponder a moment on how valuable it would be to learn firsthand the high level decisions of the German High Command, or the plan of a commander in the field. The value of Ultra was incalculable. Something as valuable as this, however, required protection. Many important questions were raised about security. Who should know of it? How should it be used by the commander in the field? How could Ultra be put to use without revealing the fact that the code had been broken? If the Germans for one minute suspected that Enigma had been compromised, they would probably have changed their code immediately. The only way to protect the secret of Ultra therefore, was to limit its distribution and use.

Frederick W. Winterbotham became the head of a new, special secret agency made up of specially trained individuals whose job it was to distribute Ultras to commanders, to keep their chiefs of staff fully informed, and to coordinate the information of the various enemy units. These Special Liaison Units (SLU) were thus given the all-important assignment of insuring that Ultra was not abused; that some commander, general or admiral, be he British or American, did not use Ultra intelligence carelessly, ambitiously, or in such a manner that the enemy might detect that his signals were being read. So well did these SLU units operate that not once throughout the entire war did the Germans discontinue using Enigma. The secret was kept.

Was there a danger in using Ultra? Yes! There was a certain degree of risk involved when one totally relied upon it at the expense of other methods of gathering intelligence. Ultra was best used in conjunction with traditional, time-tested methods of gathering intelligence: reconnaissance, spying, wire tapping, etc. For example, Rommel frequently exaggerated his losses and requirements when sending messages over Enigma. By doing so, he hoped to prod Commando Supremo in Rome and the Fuhrer in Berlin into sending him additional supplies. Though Rommel always needed supplies, his exaggerated statements made the British think at times that they had "the Fox" by the tail when in reality, the Fox was ready to turn and bite, giving the British a nasty surprise on more than one occasion. Ultra therefore required substantiation by battlefield intelligence.

Another more dramatic example concerns the German Ardennes Offensive of December, 1944. Why did the Allies not know of the German preparation? Well, there were no Ultras and because of that, they decided that nothng was being planned. The lack of Ultras was due to the intense security measures instituted by Hitler. Very few German commanders knew of the plan and those who did were informed of their orders by conventional means of correspondence. If the Allies had paid more attention to the traditional means of obtaining information, the Battle of the Bulge would not have been as costly as it eventually was. Ultra was no substitute for traditional methods of garnering battlefield information. Too much reliance on Ultra could be just as dangerous as neglecting it completely, which also happened at times.

In conclusion, we would like to recommend some books that have come out on the subject of Ultra intelligence.

The most comprehensive study on the whole topic of codebreaking is David Kahn's *The Codebreakers*. Though it was written before publication of the first book on Ultra proper, its value is inestimable, especially for mathematically inclined people.

The first real book devoted to Ultra was written by F. W. Winterbotham in 1974 and called *The Ultra Secret*. This is the same man who commanded the Special Liaison Units. Unfortunately, he wrote this book before the official documents were released, and so for most of the book, he was forced to rely on his keen memory. The value of the book is however, untarnished by this handicap. As a precursor it has served its purpose admirably.

Following in the wake of Winterbotham's book is *Bodyguard of Lies*, by Anthony Cave-Brown. Though the book covers in depth the deceptions practiced on Hitler by the Allies in their cloaking of the D-Day objective, Ultra knowledge is interspaced throughout the huge and valuable work.

In 1977, Patrick Beesly published *Very Special Intelligence* which expounded in detail the use of codebreaking in the naval war against Germany.

The publication of Ronald Lewin's fine book, *Ultra Goes to War*, came in 1978. This is the first account of Ultra garnered from official documents that were finally released after the expiration of the thirty year statute of limitations. Lewin reverses some of what Winterbotham says and gives a totally fascinating account of Ultra's role in the war. In the same year,

The Wizard War, by R. V. Jones reached the bookstands and provided the reader with a deep insight into the world of the scientist at Bletchley Park. Ultra is among the many fascinating topics discussed in this large book.

In 1979, two additional books were released on Ultra; Josef Garlinski's *The Enigma War*, and Ralph Bennett's *Ultra in the West: The Normandy Campaign of 1944–45*. Garlinski's work is a superb treatise on the background and breaking of Enigma. His sketches actually make Enigma understandable to the nonmathematician. Bennett's book is quite interesting on Ultra's use near the end of the war.

So much is yet to be revealed about Ultra. No study of World War II could be complete without knowledge of its existence and its effects. The British government is presently working on a three volume *History of the British Intelligence in the Second World War*. The authors look forward with eager anticipation to its completion.

General Sir Richard O'Connor

Chapter 1

October, 1940—France lay prostrate and soundly defeated by the slashing drive of General Guderian's panzers, the Battle of Britain was in full sway and the "gallant few" were tenaciously protecting their homeland, the British Middle East Command was confronted by Vichy stirrings in Syria and Palestine, Gen. Sir Alan Cunningham was waging a bitter struggle against the Italians under the Duke of Aosta in Ethiopia and Eritrea. On top of this, a huge Italian host, commanded by Marshal Rudolfo Graziani was advancing into Egypt and making menacing gestures towards the Suez Canal and the home of the British Mediterranean Fleet, the great naval base at Alexandria.

Sir Archibald Wavell, British commander in chief of the Middle East, found himself harried on all sides by hostile forces and relentless pressure from the politicians back home. Fortunately, this imperturbable man was a keen judge of talent, a trait that was reflected in his selection of subordinates. Early in June, Wavell had ordered the commanding officer of the District of Southern Palestine to assume the post of G.O.C. Western Desert Force, subordinate to Gen. Henry Maitland ("Jumbo") Wilson, commander in chief of Egypt. This selection proved to be one of the most astute and beneficial appointments that Wavell ever made during a distinguished and brilliant career. Though few could have forseen it at the time, the new commander, Sir Richard O'Connor was destined to conduct perhaps the most amazing and brilliant operation in the long and glorious history of the British Army.

Dick O'Connor was a small, thin, quiet warrior whose unassuming personality cloaked a keen, energetic military brain. This future hero was born in 1889 and educated at Wellington College before completing his studies at Sandhurst, the British military academy. During World War I he distinguished himself by his bravery, earning a D.S.O.* and Bar, the Italian medal for valour, and frequent mention in dispatches.

Between wars, he served in the War Office where he came in frequent contact with many of the men who were later to lead England during World War II. In 1936, he was sent to India in command of a brigade on the turbulent Northwest Frontier, a position he held until 1938 when he took up his post in Palestine. During his Indian days he was stricken with a severe case of rheumatism which placed his entire military career in jeopardy. The affliction soon became so acute that an army board recommended his retirement on the grounds of failing health. Undaunted but determined, O'Connor sought treatment from a famous Eastern physician known for his revolutionary techniques and treatment of famous celebrities. When completely cured, O'Connor

*Distinguished Service Order

demanded a review of his case. The findings of the medical board was unanimous; the British general was completely cured and a recommendation for continuance of active duty swiftly followed.

In June, 1940, O'Connor was routinely going about his duties in Palestine when the wire came from Wavell ordering his transfer to Egypt. His initial reaction was so typical of the man. Why me? Wasn't Henry Wilson capable of dealing with events in Egypt? Although Jumbo Wilson was a very capable administrator and military governor, he was simply not cut out for command in the field. Wavell had perceived this and decided to establish a separate command within a command. The result was the establishment of the Western Desert Command, and who better to command it than his old friend and former pupil, Dick O'Connor.

O'Connor's arrival in Egypt on June 8 produced little fanfare and no promises. He found the body of his command to consist of a corps made up of the proud Fourth Indian Division and the Seventh Armoured. The latter were the famous "Desert Rats" whose nickname was derived from the red Jerboa, a ratlike desert creature, painted on the side of their tanks. Both units were seriously understrength and acutely lacking in both armour and transport.

O'Connor wasted little time in organizing his command and making his presence known to the advancing Italians, who were commanded by Marshal Balbo.* Immediately upon declaration of war by Italy on June 10, O'Connor dispatched a raid into Italian

*Balbo perished on June 28 when his aircraft was (accidently?) shot down by his own troops. He was succeeded by Marshal Rudolfo Graziani.

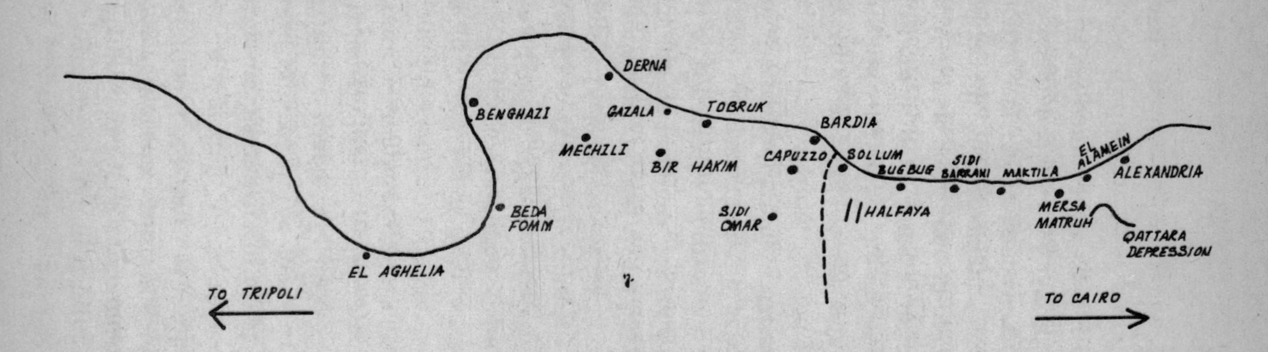
MEDITERRANEAN SEA
DERNA
BENGHAZI
GAZALA
TOBRUK
BARDIA
MECHILI
BIR HAKIM
CAPUZZO
SOLLUM
BUGBUG
SIDI BARRANI
MAKTILA
EL ALAMEIN
ALEXANDRIA
BEDA FOMM
SIDI OMAR
HALFAYA
MERSA MATRUH
QATTARA DEPRESSION
EL AGHELIA
TO TRIPOLI
TO CAIRO

MAP 1

held Libya and on the night of June 11, the first skirmish took place when a small British detachment ambushed an Italian formation near Capuzzo, taking the entire group prisoner. Still confident, O'Connor ordered his raiders to probe the area of Sidi Omar which, when sighted, proved to have been abandoned by the alarmed and cautious Italians. (See Map 1)

Heartened by his success, O'Connor decided to attack Capuzzo, an Italian position strategically located on the Libyan frontier. After a brief but fierce fight the Italians surrendered to a detachment of the Seventh Hussars.

These nuisance raids continued until late in June when the Italians decided to bring in reinforcements. Until that point, far-ranging British patrols had boldly attacked enemy convoys motoring along the coastal road between Bardia and Tobruk.

Although the June raids had achieved little in the way of territorial gains, the British command did receive invaluable information—an answer to the very question that was foremost in British minds—What was the state of the Italian army and the quality of their troops?

Though Mussolini had long dreamed of a new Roman Empire, the Italian legions in North Africa, much like the British, were seriously understrength. A large portion of their overall command consisted of Libyan troops who proved totally unreliable and unwilling to die for the glory of Italy. The Italian infantry units, although brave, were inadequately trained and their equipment, though plentiful in contrast to that available to the British, was of dubious quality. Indeed, many of the Italian tanks rode into battle with sandbags protecting the crews from the gaps in the seams of the armour. Only the artillery formations consistently demonstrated a quality performance.

The Italian soldier has been much maligned for his lack of fortitude during battle. In fact his lack of aggressiveness has been the butt of ethnic humor for many years. This reputation is totally undeserved and has been unfairly attributed to all but a small minority. The Tunisian station was a relatively calm one that lulled men into a peaceful sense of being out of combat. Furthermore, the Italian soldier was lacking in motivation. Not only was inspirational leadership completely missing, but the reasons for going to war were relatively vague and unpopular. After all, wasn't it Germany's war? By far the weakest section of the Italian army was its officer corps. These leaders treated army life as a sport to be enjoyed. A distinct caste system developed which saw the enlisted man forced to live off field rations while the officers basked in the lap of relative luxury that included tinned delicacies, gourmet food, traveling brothels, and the finest of accommodations.

In order to gain a more respectful opinion of the Italian fighting man, one need look no further than the Ariete and Trieste Divisions that fought under Rommel. Although hardly comparable to Caesar's legions, these two units, when sprinkled with German officers, proved themselves among the finest warriors of World War II.

Compounding the Italian situation in 1940 was the newly appointed commander, Rudolfo Graziani. Where Balbo was confident, Graziani was anything but; in contrast to Balbo's bombast was Graziani's reserve and quiet manner; and while the former was cocky and an inspiration to his troops, Graziani had little faith in his units and openly voiced his contempt causing a decline in morale. Finally, Balbo was a brave man while Graziani repeatedly demonstrated timidity and excessive caution.

Under prods, pleads, and eventually demands from Mussolini, Graziani finally agreed to move forward into Egypt. On September 13, 1940, his army entered Egypt on a narrow front along the coast, heading towards the Nile. After four days and sixty miles however, Graziani halted to regroup and consolidate his gains near Sidi Barrani even though he was still almost a hundred miles from O'Connor's main force at Mersa Matruh. The unanswered question was why had Graziani halted since it was obviously improbable that O'Connor would have been able to stop him?

The British had available approximately thirty-six thousand men in comparison to the Italian's two hundred fifty thousand. Reinforcements were however, on the way to O'Connor but it was questionable if they would arrive in time to be of any assistance. Therefore, it was imperative to the British to deceive the Italians about their military strength. Deception was used to simulate a greater force than was actually available, hoping that it would exercise a strong influence on the timid Graziani. Using hundreds of cruiser tanks made of inflatable rubber, artillery guns, and trucks, the British fabricated a powerful army in the field. They then recruited hordes of Arabs with camels and horses who dragged devices behind them raising great clouds of dust, which when observed from a high altitude, gave the appearance of a huge advancing army. Photographic evidence and intelligence reports substantiated Graziani's fears and convinced him to halt his columns, dig in, and construct fortified positions along the Alexandria road. Ssee Map 2)

For over two months the adversaries eyed each other across the vast expanse of sand with both sides apparently reluctant to take the initiative and precipitate battle. But while Graziani was making excuses for his lethargy and caution to Mussolini, the British were daily growing in strength and making their preparations.

Both the Fourth Indian and Seventh Armoured Divisions were brought up to full strength and trained constantly. Meanwhile, Wavell had directed O'Connor to submit a plan for dealing with the Italian menace. It took O'Connor's staff less than two weeks to conceive a suitable plan which was quickly approved by Wavell. Field Marshal Sir John Harding, who at that time was serving as O'Connor's chief of staff, had this observation of the plan:

> Although he had the wise advice of Field Marshal's Wavell and Wilson to aid him, the plan of battle was hatched in General O'Connor's brain. The tactical decision on which success or failure depended were his and the grim determination that inspired all our own troops stemmed up from his heart. It was his skill in calculating the risks and his daring in accepting them that turned what might have been merely a limited success into a victorious campaign with far reaching effects on the future course of the war.[1]

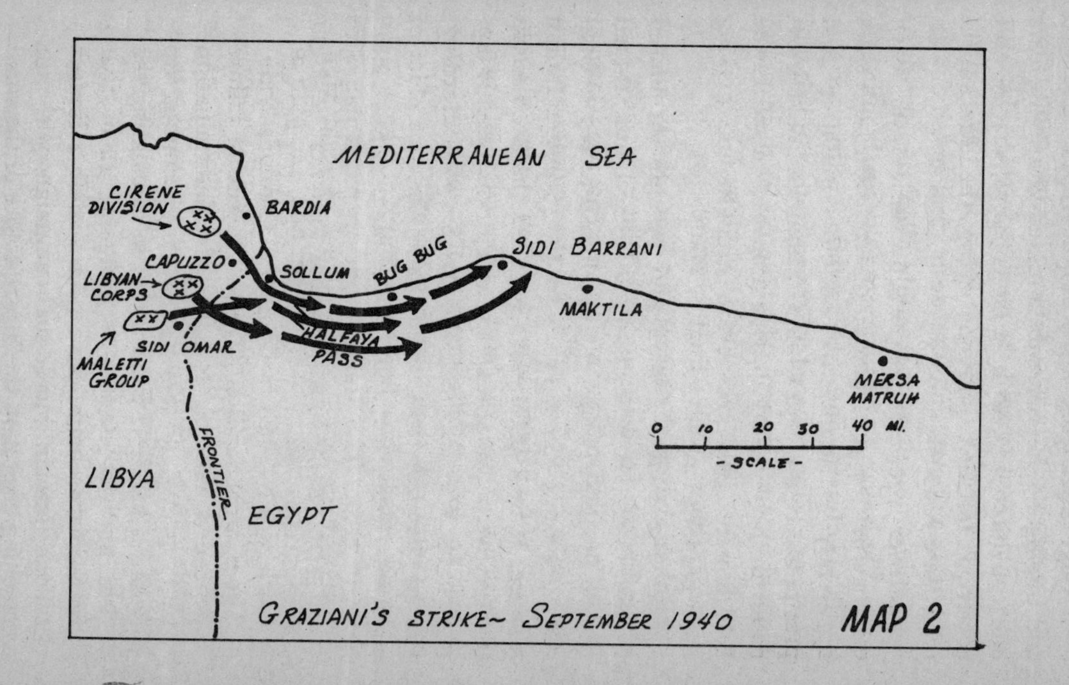
MEDITERRANEAN SEA
CIRENE DIVISION
BARDIA
CAPUZZO
SOLLUM
BUG BUG
SIDI BARRANI
LIBYAN CORPS
MALETTI GROUP
SIDI OMAR
HALFAYA PASS
MAKTILA
MERSA MATRUH
0 10 20 30 40 MI.
- SCALE -
FRONTIER
LIBYA
EGYPT
GRAZIANI'S STRIKE~ SEPTEMBER 1940
MAP 2

Thus was set the stage for one of the most remarkable feats of arms of the twentieth century.

O'Connor's plan was codenamed "Operation Compass." Reluctant to split his meagre forces, O'Connor discarded Wavell's suggestion for a five day raid on both Italian flanks simultaneously, and opted for an enveloping movement that would allow the British to attack the Italian formations from the south and rear, sowing confusion and panic while cutting off the avenue of escape. These tactics were later studied and adopted by another general whose use of them would earn him the name of "The Desert Fox."

Preparations were finally completed in early December and on the seventh of that month, all was in readiness. To disguise British intentions, Wavell himself participated in an elaborate charade. Cairo of 1940 was a hot bed of spies. All the comings and goings of the British officers, even their slightest movements, were diligently reported and swiftly relayed to Axis intelligence stations whose personnel could then draw their own conclusions.

Those conclusions however, could not have been more in error. The Italians, and in particular Graziani, were totally convinced that they were seriously outnumbered. Reports emitted from Cairo which greatly distorted the actual strength of the British coupled with the inflatable decoys planted by O'Connor's deceptive groups, helped to distort Graziani's appreciation of the situation. Usually it is part of battlefield intelligence to exaggerate. Therefore, battalions became brigades, brigades, divisions, and so on. Poor Graziani, with such a woebegone, motley collection of soldiers, how could he be expected to defeat a more powerful force of well-trained and professional soldiers.

In fact, just the opposite was true. The Italians outnumbered the British in men at an almost seven to one ratio, in guns, over two to one, and in fighter planes, four to one. Only in the area of armour did the British possess overall superiority, not only in quantity but in quality.

Therefore, during the day of December 7, Wavell took extreme care not to arouse suspicion. In the afternoon, he was noticeably visible attending the races at Cairo's race track and that night hosted a relatively conspicuous dinner party for a number of his officers.

While this careful smoke screen was being laid over Cairo, O'Connor's preparations were nearing final completion. While Wavell's dinner party was in full swing, the British offensive began. An officer of the Seventh Armoured Division recounts the jump off:

> Just before dusk we started the move forward. I can vividly remember watching the tanks ahead with their hulls hidden in drifting clouds of dust, but with each turret standing out clear and black against the fading western sky, each with two muffled heads emerging and two pennants fluttering above from the wireless aerial. Late at night we halted for refueling and a few hours of sleep—daylight revealed a wonderful sight, the whole desert to the North covered with a mass of dispersed vehicles—tanks, trucks and guns all moving westward, with a long plume of dust rolling out behind.[2]

Due to the relatively large distance that separated the opposing forces, it was some time before battle was joined. However, by the morning of December 9, the British formations were in place and poised to strike. Total surprise favored the British from the outset. The unsuspecting Italians were just starting what they expected to be merely another routine day, when without warning, the battle burst upon them. (See Map 3)

The Italian camp at Nibeiwa was blasted awake by the artillery of the Fourth Indian Division. Before the stunned enemy could man their positions, an armoured company of the Seventh Royal Tank Regiment blasted its way through the outgunned Italian tanks at the western edge of the camp. The British tankers, attacking from an unexpected position, burst into the center of the Italian camp firing in all directions. General Maletti, the Italian commander, was killed while manning a machine gun. The British infantry, following on the heels of the armoured breakthrough, rounded up over two thousand prisoners and over thirty tanks.

North of Nibeiwa stood two additional camps known as Tummar East and Tummar West. The Royal Tank Regiment hardly paused to catch their breath at Nibeiwa before setting off for the latter camp. Using the same tactics that had earlier proved successful, Tummar West fell by late afternoon and the eastern camp came under attack. Here the Italians offered a stiffer resistance and not only foiled the initial British assault but actually counterattacked. Fortunately, the firepower of Beresford-Pierse's Fourth Indian Division proved superior and thwarted the Italian attack. With that, the back of the Italian resistance was broken and Tummar East

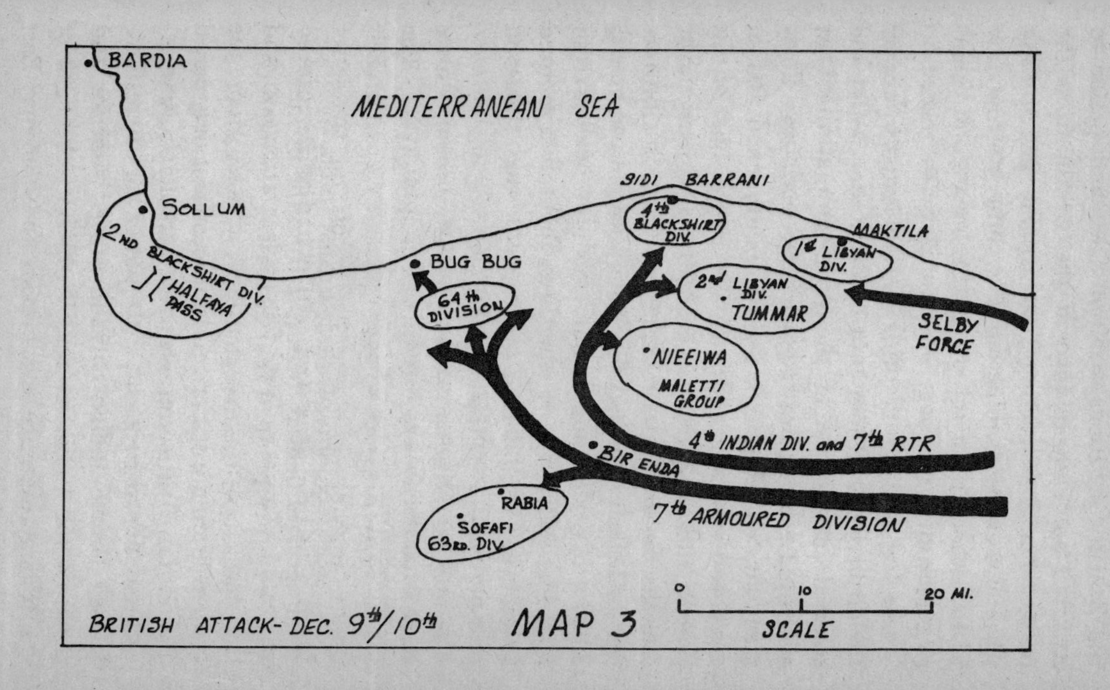

BRITISH ATTACK- DEC. 9th/10th

MAP 3

fell early in the following morning.

While the battle raged twenty miles deep in the desert, an ad hoc infantry formation known as the Selby Force, headed along the coastal road towards the Italian camp at Maktila. The camp however, was alerted and evacuated the position, leaving the British to punch an empty bag. Undaunted, Selby pushed his troops beyond towards Sidi Barrani, where he was halted by the stiff resistance of the Italians, who had made excellent use of the protection afforded by three previously prepared defensive positions. These positions however, were unable to withstand attacks from two quarters and with the appearance of the Fourth Indian Division, the heart went out of the Italians. By dinner time of the next day, Sidi Barrani was in British hands. A jubilant officer of the Fourth Indian Division proudly informed his headquarters that his unit was now guarding about five acres of prisoners. The Italians had been thoroughly routed. The only enemy remaining in Egypt was being marched eastward to prisoner of war camps. Correspondent Alan Moorehead was witness to this spectacular event and he vividly recalls:

> A great column of dust turned pink by the sunset light behind them rose from the prisoners' feet as they plodded four abreast in the sand on either side of the mettaled track. They came on, first in hundreds, then in thousands. No one had time to count them—six, possibly seven thousand all in green dirty uniforms and cloth caps. Outnumbered roughly three hundred to one, a handful of British privates marched alongside the two columns.[3]

During the battle, O'Connor had been everywhere, visiting various brigade headquarters, making suggestions to various commanders in the field, and issuing instructions to the Seventh Armoured Division under the temporary command of General Caunter.*

What of the Seventh Armoured? Where were the Desert Rats during the battle for the Tummars and Sidi Barrani? It should be recalled that both divisions had begun the advance westward together, with the Fourth Indian Division nearest the coast. South of Nibeiwa, the Fourth turned north and attacked the Italians from inland while the Seventh continued in a wide arc towards Bug Bug where marched the Italian Sixty-fourth Division confidently moving towards Sidi Barrani. Thus, while the two Libyan divisions and the Blackshirts were being routed in turn, the Desert Rats were taking on the Sixty-fourth and cutting the Sollum-Sidi Barrani road, preventing an Italian retreat and stopping reinforcements from reaching the latter town.

One of the few who did escape was the Italian commander, General ("Electric Whiskers") Bergonzoli. The pursuit of this legendary and colorful character provided one of the lighter episodes of the campaign and eventually came to obsess the British troops.

O'Connor's euphoric state during the battle was short lived, for at the height of the battle he was informed by Wavell that the Fourth Indian Division was being withdrawn for General Cunningham's use in Eritrea. In return, the Western Desert Force was to receive the Sixth Australian Division. It proved small

*The actual commander of the Seventh Armoured, Gen. Milo O'Moore Creagh was back in Cairo undergoing treatment for a seriously abscessed tongue.

consolation, for the Indians were by now battle hardened members of a closely knit, proven team, whereas the Australians were relative newcomers to the desert and had seen little or no action.

Nonplussed, O'Connor refused to rest on his laurels. Although he had accomplished what he had originally set out to do—conduct a short raid aimed at driving the Italians out of Egypt—he was not satisfied. O'Connor's offensive spirit would not allow him to let go now that he had taken a bite of victory.

Therefore, he pushed fresh units of the Seventh Armoured Division along the coastal road in hot pursuit of the fleeing enemy. After obtaining Wavell's approval for a further advance, O'Connor ordered his remaining units to press the advantage despite having to send the Fourth Indian Division back to Egypt, which effectively halved his force. Beresford-Pierse's division's feelings were somewhat soothed by the fact that they took with them over thirty-eight thousand Italian and Libyan prisoners.

The Seventh Armoured Division dutifully followed in the wake of the retreating Italians along the coastal road towards Sollum and Bardia. Unfortunately, the pursuit was relatively slow although conducted in spirit. As previously mentioned, the British learned early in the game to respect Italian artillery skill and determination. Time and again the Desert Rats were forced to halt in the face of heavy artillery fire at Capuzzo, Halfaya, and Sollum.

Meanwhile, Sollum had been shelled by the battleships of Adm. Andrew Cunningham's Mediterranean fleet during the latter stages of the Sidi Barrani battle. Thus, when O'Connor's forces reached that town, they found it totally abandoned by the Italians, who had elected instead to make a stand at Bardia. O'Connor had hoped that the enemy would treat Bardia in the same fashion as they had Sollum. This however, was not to be. Mussolini himself expressed a desire to halt the British at Bardia and fired off an inspirational message aimed at boosting morale. Apparently it had some effect, for the always eloquent "Electric Whiskers" promptly replied:

> I am aware of the honor and I have today repeated to my troops your message—simple and unequivocal. In Bardia we are and here we stay.[4]

By the first day of 1941, the Australian Sixth Division had melded nicely with Western Desert Force, which on this date was redesignated XIII Corps and made directly subordinate to Wavell, easing Wilson out of the chain of command.

Satisfied that the Aussies were ready, O'Connor set the date for the attack on Bardia for early morning, January 3. First though, he allowed Admiral Cunningham to deliver a New Year's gift to the city.

The Italians were apparently content to allow the Mediterranean Fleet to roam at will. On New Year's Day, Cunningham paraded his entire battle squadron back and forth outside the port of Bardia, adding a fiery and deadly display to Bergonzoli's New Year celebration. What fanfare. All the queens of the fleet attended; Barham, Valiant, and the magnificent Warspite, famous names all, rained death and destruction into Bardia.

During the night of January 2, O'Connor ordered tanks and trucks driven back and forth in front of the city to give the impression of overwhelming strength.

How far this was from the actual truth. Very few runners remained of the tanks available to the Royal Tank Regiment accompanying the Australians. As for the Seventh Armoured Division, O'Connor had other plans.

Early on the morning of January 3, the Australians went "over the top" preceded by the Royal Tank Regiment. General Mackay, commanding the Australian force, launched a three-pronged attack on the perimeter defenses. The tanks supporting the infantry destroyed most major strongholds quickly and a precise, step by step advance was made. Those strongholds that refused to yield to the armoured bombardment were subsequently destroyed by infantry using mortars and grenades. By and large however, it had been a walkover. On January 5, Bardia surrendered and with it were captured over forty thousand more prisoners. As an indication of the disparity between the British and their enemy, the total Australian casualty list including killed, wounded, and missing, amounted to less than five hundred. Bardia proved a resounding victory for the previously untried Aussies and a tribute to the fighting ability and spirit of these magnificent warriors.

Shortly after the attack began General Creagh took his Seventh Armoured Division off towards Tobruk. By January 6, that city was surrounded and those refugees that had escaped Bardia were rounded up and sent off to join their comrades in P.O.W. cages. Once more however, the list of prisoners was void of the name of Bergonzoli.

Wavell now directed O'Connor to take Tobruk, but the commander of XIII Corps had anticipated the order by sending Creagh off to investigate the town in anticipation of Wavell's approval.

By January 20, all was in readiness as the Australians arrived in the line and began probing the defenses. Once more O'Connor directed Creagh to establish barriers west of the city, and early on the next day, the Australians attacked. The defensive positions immediately inside the Tobruk perimeter fell quickly to the fierce determination of the Australians. Once these positions fell, the rout set in. The bewildered Italians began surrendering in droves and by early the following day, the battle was for all intents and purposes over. The final surrender of Tobruk took place on January 22. Besides an abundance of supplies, another horde of prisoners went into the P.O.W. camps. The disappointed Australians however, were unable to view the general whose whiskers were reputed to give off electric sparks. The wily Bergonzoli was not to be found.

All in all it had been an amazing string of victories, with over one hundred thousand prisoners taken as well as the ports of Bardia and Tobruk. Through these ports O'Connor's advance could be supplied, owing to Cunningham's mastery of the Mediterranean. Had these ports not fallen, it is doubtful that O'Connor could have proceeded, for his supply line stretched hundreds of miles through the desert back into Egypt.

As O'Connor was making preparations to commence the battle for Tobruk, Wavell was considering the importance of Benghazi, west of Tobruk. After a lengthy discussion with his advisors and intelligence people, the commander in chief acceded to O'Connor's request that the advance be allowed to continue. Wavell was however, quick to point out that all further offensive action was subject to the demands of other theatres. Unfortunately, Churchill had offered assistance to the Greeks who, even now, were under attack from Italy. O'Connor received a brief reprieve when Greece refused Churchill's initial offer. But, as Wavell was quick to add, from now on it would be a day to day thing.

Before an assault on Benghazi could take place however, Derna would have to be secured. This would prove a tall order for XIII Corps, for Derna was situated in a natural defensive position. Furthermore, it was protected on one side by the sea and on the other by the heavily fortified Italian camp at Mechili.

O'Connor once more set the wheels of advance in motion. Creagh and his Desert Rats were ordered to take Mechili while the Australians were given responsibility for Derna itself. As in previous battles, Mackay's division would find itself supported by the armour of the Royal Tank Regiment. Unfortunately, this unit was down to very few runners. The constant advances and the punishing desert terrain had taken its toll.

Nevertheless both divisions set off for their respective objectives in high spirits. Creagh split his two brigades, sending the Seventh south of Mechili and the Fourth to the north in an enveloping formation. Creagh's advance was delayed by a spirited but brief counterattack launched by the Italian commander at Mechili, the bold General Barbini. Although the British managed to fend off the attack with relative ease, the encounter served its purpose in that it allowed the quarry to flee. Thus, when the British advance arrived at Mechili, they found the position abandoned. Barbini had marched his units out the previous evening and arrived safely at Derna the following day. Consequently, Creagh's attack hit a hollow shell and he was severely reprimanded by O'Connor for allowing the Italians to get away. General Caunter of the Fourth Armoured Brigade shouldered the bulk of the blame, for it was his assignment to block the northern escape route. Barbini's harassing attacks however, had been primarily directed at Caunter, thus slowing his progress.

Although Barbini had been allowed to escape, the temporary setback failed to give a respite to Derna. On January 30, the Australians easily shouldered aside the opposition there and once more the Italians were forced to flee in the direction of Benghazi where Graziani had elected to make a stand. Before resuming the offensive, O'Connor was forced to reequip and resupply his forces. All units were operating considerably understrength due to the harsh conditions imposed by life in the desert.

Dick O'Connor now made one of the most momentous and brilliant decisions of the entire war. There was little or no precedent established for the action and as far as O'Connor was concerned it was a calculated risk at best. Guderian's triumph in France was still relatively fresh and unchronicled, and the great tank battles in Russia were yet on the horizon. Thereupon, the XIII Corps commander had not the opportunity to study these campaigns. He admittedly however, had studied the campaigns of Stonewall Jackson, whose tactics demanded rapid movement and appearances at the least likely places. Consequently, O'Connor decided to cut the Italian retreat by sending his armour overland through the desert to an area south of Benghazi. If successful, this maneuver would seal off the Cyrenaician Bulge and cut off the avenue of escape for all Italian units operating in Cyrenaica. Failure would allow Graziani to extradite his army safely to Tripoli. Adding to the urgency of the situation was the fact that Graziani had already decided to evacuate the very area to be contested. Unlike Montgomery later on, who was always content to merely follow his beaten enemy, O'Connor was determined to make victory total and final. Before authorizing such an ambitious maneuver, O'Connor's extreme sense of loyalty dictated that he obtain the approval of Wavell. The commander in chief was so pleased with O'Connor's performance and handling of the campaign to date that little or no convincing was necessary. Approval for the plan was immediately granted.

On February 4, after being reinforced and replenished, Creagh took his Seventh Armoured Division off into the unknown and uncharted desert. He later commented:

> Off we went across the unknown country in full cry. It was definitely exciting and the division pushing on and on across the desert was a stimulating sight. Some of this desert was very rough and slowed us up; so I went a wheeled column ahead which was faster than the tracked tanks. This column was to get on to the coast road and hold up any retreating forces until the main body of the division could go into action.[5]

That evening O'Connor and General Dorman-Smith set off to follow Creagh's Desert Rats. The Irish

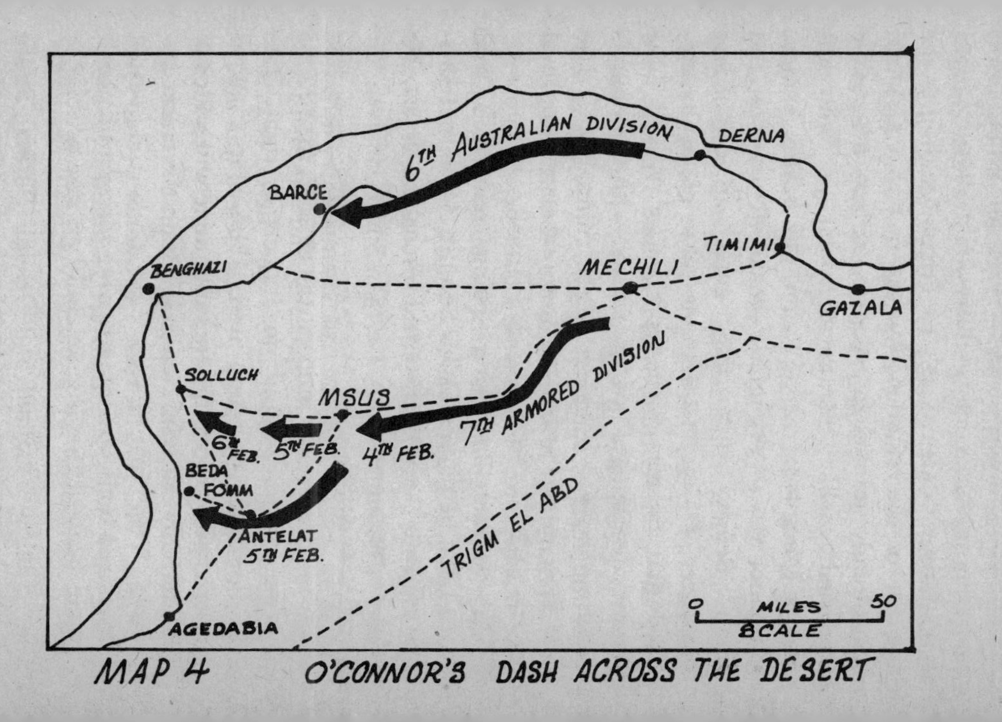

MAP 4 O'CONNOR'S DASH ACROSS THE DESERT

fighting spirit of O'Connor and Creagh was definitely up. (See Map 4)

The going was terrible. Tracked and wheeled vehicles alike broke down from the rugged terrain and incessant dust. Machinery of war littered every mile of the way and by late afternoon the Eleventh Hussars, leading the way, were still over fifty miles from the coast.

O'Connor's chief of staff, General Harding, now rushed to Creagh's headquarters with the news that the Italian retreat had begun. Urgency now replaced caution and speed became dictator. Consequently, early the next morning, the Eleventh Hussars were dispatched posthaste in a mad dash toward the coast. That unit reached the coast around mid-morning and its commanding officer reported that the Italians were nowhere to be found. He then decided to take his unit on to explore the area around a little whistle stop known as Beda Fomm.

Meanwhile, after an adventurous night in the desert, O'Connor and Dorman-Smith arrived at Creagh's headquarters. The news seemed encouraging, with the advance units on the coast in the process of being reinforced and no Italians in sight. The relief however, was short lived. Within an hour of positioning his forces, Colonel Combe, commander of the Eleventh Hussars reported Italian trucks approaching his thin screen. O'Connor's trap had sprung shut with less than sixty minutes to spare. Combe, reinforced by a battery of artillery, rudely halted the Italian flight. The initial convoy, caught completely unaware out in the open, was systematically destroyed.

Meanwhile, the tenacious Australians were advancing hard along the coast road driving the Italians before them. Mackay's division, like a terrier who once into the attack refuses to let go, was smashing aside all Italian rearguards. This advance had far reaching consequences further south at the hotly contested area of Beda Fomm. All the Italian attention was focused on their rear, for the Australians were making their presence felt. Never in their wildest dreams did the Italian commanders anticipate the presence of the Seventh Armoured Division at their front.

But the entire Seventh Armoured was not in place. The impossible terrain had delayed all but the leading elements of Creagh's formation. Consequently, Combe's thin screen was in imminent danger of being shattered as unit after unit of the Italian army, streaming down the road from Benghazi, stumbled onto the British roadblock. The Italians attacked in desperation, seeking escape from the rampaging Australians and safety in the relatively secure area of Tripoli. Throughout the day, Combe's troops held and by evening the front had stabilized somewhat.

February sixth would prove the critical day. The question still remained, could O'Connor's screen hold? Certainly not unless support was forthcoming. But the Fourth Armoured Brigade was still not in position, having been delayed by the terrain and lack of fuel.

The day dawned gray and rainy. The Italian Tenth Army, more desperate than ever, sniffing safety beyond Beda Fomm, prepared to launch a concerted attack. Shortly after the attack was underway,

Caunter hit their flank. The effect was devastating. The Italian line stretched for miles back into the desert and was fair game for the marauding British tankers who poured a withering fire into the flanks of the enemy.

But the Italians resisted with determination. Each man was conscious that safety lay just a few miles over the sand dunes. Therefore, with a grim determination despite heavy losses, the Italians fended off attack after attack by the outnumbered British. Late in the day, leading patrols of the Sixth Australian Division began nipping at the rear of the Italians, adding to the panic that was beginning to plant its seed in the ranks of the Italian soldier. Only the advent of darkness quelled the fray and brought relative calm to the battlefield. The next morning, February 7, would be decisive.

General Bergonzoli decided to make one final effort. Concentrating his forces early the next morning, he attempted to break through between the coastal road and the sea. The valiant attack broke its back against the dug in British and the superb maneuvers of Creagh's armour.

With the failure of this final attack, the British roaming up and down the Italian line at will, pouring deadly fire amongst the masses huddled along the length of the column, and the Australians attacking the rear in strength, Bergonzoli decided it was time to surrender.

Meanwhile, events had preceded him. One white flag, then another waved from the Italian positions. Soon it became infectious; throughout the entire army white flags were displayed everywhere. Unit after unit threw down their arms and surrendered. Victory was complete.

Finally, the man with the famous whiskers was in British captivity. His simple statement to his captors summed it up nicely. "You got here too fast today."[6] Unfortunately for the unhappy Australians, Bergonzoli was hustled off to Cairo, disappointing the men of Mackay's division, who had chased the elusive general across miles of desert and were now denied the pleasure of viewing the man whose beard was reputed to give off electric sparks.

All in all it had been a remarkable feat of arms. In two months O'Connor had led his army over five hundred miles and conquered all of Cyrenaicia. His thirty thousand men had defeated an entire army over three times its own size, had captured over one hundred and thirty thousand prisoners, losing less than two thousand of their own in killed, wounded, and missing, and had given England a spectacular victory at a time when one was so desperately required. But the decision to advance overland toward Beda Fomm was the momentous point of the entire campaign. This maneuver had no precedent and no one was sure it would have succeeded. Certainly not the Italians. They simply did not expect this maneuver. Only O'Connor (and Creagh) were willing to risk all on one cast of the dice. Wavell, back in Cairo, was willing to permit the advance based solely on O'Connor's previous record of success.

Mysteriously, throughout the entire advance, Churchill remained uncharacteristically quiet regarding O'Connor's feats. The Prime Minister, who was so quick to lavish praise on successive victorious commanders, was strangely silent to the achievements of O'Connor. The only praise forthcoming was a short telegram to Wavell suggesting that O'Connor and Creagh be congratulated. The question remains unanswered why Churchill, who demonstrated unabashed eagerness to champion Montgomery later on, remained so silent to O'Connor's spectacular victory.

With Beda Fomm brought to a successful conclusion, O'Connor requested permission for an advance in strength on Tripoli and complete his victory with the conquest of Tripolitania. Unfortunately, Greece picked this moment to accept the British offer of help and this assistance could only come at the expense of Wavell's desert command. As a result, O'Connor's command was stripped and its commander ordered to Cairo for a much needed and well earned rest. In his place came Sir Philip Neame, an old friend of O'Connor's but a general completely devoid of experience in handling armour and totally unfamiliar with conditions in the desert.

O'Connor's amazing victory had one other far reaching effect. Less than a week after British patrols probed as far as El Agheila, a German delegation headed by a young general named Erwin Rommel arrived in Tripoli.

On March 31, Rommel launched an attack against the British forces waiting and watching for the next Axis move. In the face of Rommel's brilliant conduct of the battle, Neame was forced to give ground and soon the British position became critical.*

As reports of the serious turn of events became

*See Volume I, Chapter 3

known, Churchill cabled Wavell expressing his dire concern.

> Have you got a man like O'Connor or Creagh dealing with the frontier problem?[7]

Although he had virtually ignored the two generals after their amazing string of victories, the Prime Minister had no reservations about calling for them in his time of need. Unfortunately the answer to his question was a firm no! O'Connor was back in Cairo and a seriously ill Creagh had been invalided home. Wavell's solution was to go forward himself and see firsthand what could be done to salvage the situation. His observations displeased him greatly.

> I soon realized that Neame had lost control and was making no effort to regain it by the only possible means, going forward personally. I wanted to go forward myself but no suitable aircraft was available and no one seemed to have much idea where our own troops or the enemy were. I sent a message for Dick O'Connor to come out and take over from Neame.[8]

Probably out of loyalty to his old friend Neame, O'Connor received Wavell's message with a great deal of dismay.

> "I thought the chief was misjudging Neame. I therefore decided I would ask the chief to reconsider my replacing Neame and to consider as an alternative my remaining with him for a few days, but ultimately returning to organize the defense of Egypt. The chief agreed to this proposal provided I remain until the situation had stabilized."[9]

O'Connor rushed forward but he was totally uncomfortable and felt extremely awkward at having to look over Neame's shoulder. Only his deep admiration for the latter made O'Connor's task easier. Immediately upon arriving at Neame's headquarters, O'Connor drew the following conclusions.

> Neame's use of the Second Armoured Division seemed to be eminently sound.* It seemed to me that the situation was definitely more serious than the chief believed.[10]

On the evening of April 6, Neame and O'Connor left their headquarters to travel to their rear headquarters at Derna. Enroute, they became lost and stumbled into a German patrol which led them into captivity. Their top corps commander, Gambier-Parry soon followed.

In one fell swoop, Rommel had completely eliminated the senior British command and soon eliminated all the earlier conquests of O'Connor's which had been so expertly achieved at the expense of the Italians.

During their period of captivity in Italy, O'Connor and Neame, in company with other captured generals, were constantly plotting their escape. The ringleader of this conspiracy was primarily Neame. On their fifth attempt, organized and commanded by Neame, they were successful and reached Allied lines in December of 1943.

Unfortunately, during O'Connor's absence, a new star had risen on the British horizon, Bernard Mont-

*Neame had been severely criticized by Wavell for his use of this formation.

gomery. Writing after the war, General Galloway summed up the two differing personalities.

> The difference between O'Connor and Montgomery was that O'Connor detested publicity while Monty lived on it—not only lived on it, but began it.[11]

After a suitable period of recuperation, O'Connor was given command of VIII Corps in Montgomery's army during the bitter battles around Caën. Shortly after the German stranglehold was finally broken, O'Connor was reassigned as general officer commanding the eastern command in India until 1945, when he took over command of the Western Army in the same theatre until 1946. His long overdue appointment to lieutenant general was finally approved in 1945. Recalled to England in 1946, he served as adjutant general until his retirement from the army in 1948.

At the very zenith of his success, fate cruelly snatched O'Connor from the stage of history. Historians can only speculate what may have transpired had O'Connor been allowed to continue in command in North Africa. Would Rommel have soared to such fame? Would there have been a place for Montgomery? What would the effect on Sicily, Normandy, and France have been had O'Connor's aggressive spirit been present in place of Montgomery's excessive caution. Unfortunately history will never know. But it is tantalizingly tempting to speculate.

Air Marshal Hugh Dowding

Chapter 2

A majority of the many individual battles of World War II were but stepping stones toward a final objective—ultimate victory. A few influenced the course of events more dramatically than others and can properly be classified as turning points; for example, France in 1940, Midway, Stalingrad, Kursk, and El Alamein to mention the most prominent. One battle, however, stands alone for the decisive influence it had on the course of subsequent history. The Battle of Britain.

In the summer of 1940 England stood alone against the Nazi horde that had overrun Europe in a series of quick devastating campaigns. In the brief span of one year, Norway, Poland, Denmark, France, and the Benelux nations found themselves conquered and firmly under the domination of Hitler's triumphant legions. From the North Cape to the Pyrenees; from the borders of the Soviet Union to the English Channel, Germany reigned supreme, and for all intents and purposes, unchallenged. Only England remained to impugn Hitler's effort at total European domination. The British people, secure in their "Island Fortress," which had successfully thwarted would be conquerors for over nine centuries, resolved to fight on.

Traditionally England relied on her fleet for protection and once more the Nation's Pride was being relied on to protect its homeland, especially since the army had been ignominiously ejected from the continent via Dunkirk and forced to abandon the bulk of its arms. Only a mere handful of visionaries realized that it would not be the Royal Navy that would play the decisive role in the defense of the British Isles. Instead, the job would fall to the fledgling junior service, the RAF,* that renowned few of Fighter Command, under the inspired, brilliant, and dedicated leadership of Sir Hugh Dowding. However, to appreciate the contribution of that handful of pilots who managed to keep the Germans at bay, prevent defeat, and hand England the breathing space she so desperately required to maintain the struggle, we must examine the man (Dowding), the service (the RAF), and the branch (Fighter Command) and treat them as one.

Hugh C. Dowding was born in April of 1882 at Dunfries, Scotland, on the Solway Firth. His family, however, was not of Scottish origin. At the time of his birth, Hugh's father was headmaster of a preparatory school in that area. Instead, Dowding's family roots were firmly entrenched in the western portion of England but because of the accident of his birthplace, Hugh was forever after referred to as a Scotsman.

After an early education at St. Ninians he continued his studies at Winchester. There he made the acquaintance of another future distinguished English military hero, Archibald Wavell. Upon completion of his elementary studies Dowding opted for a military

*Royal Air Force

career, and after passage of the required examinations, entered the Royal Military Academy in the fall of 1899. Wavell has since stated that Dowding admitted to him that the only reason for selecting a military career was to avoid having to study Greek.

At the turn of the century England found herself embroiled in the Boer War in South Africa and therefore, the course of study at the Royal Military Academy was shortened from the normal two years to one. Accordingly, in 1900, Dowding found himself commissioned a 2nd lt. of artillery and set off for Gibraltar and his first command. The following year his company was sent to Ceylon and shortly thereafter to Hong Kong. In the spring of 1904, in response to an earlier request, Dowding was transferred to the mountain artillery in India. From the very beginning of his commission, Dowding's independent spirit and refusal to unilaterally accept the orthodox exerted itself. Consequently he ran afoul of his new commanding officer, who refused to endorse Dowding's application for Staff College.

In 1910 after a change in commanding officers, Dowding set off for Camberley and the two year course at the Royal Staff College. For the most part, Dowding enjoyed the curriculum but expressed dissatisfaction with the way the course emphasized independent thinking but discouraged its use. However, by this time Dowding considered himself to be somewhat of a nonconformist anyway and refused to have his independent spirit dampened by the conformists and traditionalists that abounded at the Staff College. A year after completion of the course, he was posted to command one of the school's exercises which involved the use of airplanes.

> While at the Staff College, Dowding had been dubbed with the nickname of 'Stuffy' that was to stay with him for the rest of his life. His fellow students found that he had a strong inclination to stand apart from their antics. Not that he disapproved of them or of what they got up to. He did not. But he could not bring himself to become whole-heartedly one of them or their way of expressing themselves. He was too critical of his own behavior.[1]

Dowding soon realized the value of the plane as an instrument of war and incorporated it into his teachings. In addition, because he wished to be well versed in all aspects of his command, he resolved to learn how to fly. After a course of instruction in flying he financed himself, Dowding earned his flying certificate. After completing yet another course at the Royal Flying Corps School he considered himself a qualified pilot at the age of thirty-two. However, Dowding's father voiced such stringent objections over his son's intentions that Hugh, who had a strong sense of family duty, decided to return to the artillery.

His setback was short-lived. In August of 1914, World War I began and the RCF* found itself desperately short of qualified flyers. Consequently, as a member of the RFC reserve, he was called to active duty with that branch of the service and posted to Farnborough which was commanded by Hugh Trenchard, one of Dowding's former instructors at Upavon.

Royal Flying Corps

Immediately, Dowding found himself at odds with his new commanding officer. The friction between Dowding and Trenchard continued for many years. Dowding began agitating to be sent to France and active duty. Eventually, after pestering Trenchard regularly, Dowding got his wish, but Trenchard sent him off instead as an observer, not a pilot, which in those days amounted to an insult.

While in France, Dowding found himself fascinated with the technical aspects of flying and in particular, wireless communication. His interest soon led him to be returned to England early in 1915 to continue work on wireless experiments.

> I was the first person certainly in England if not in the world, to listen to a wireless message from the air. We could have fixed up two-way communication too if we had not received a directive from the War Office that radio-telephonic communication between air and ground was not considered practical.[2]

So much for the highly vaunted independent and forward thinking method encouraged at Staff College.

In the summer of the same year, Dowding returned to France as squadron commander. His unit was one of those constituting a wing commanded by none other than "Boom" Trenchard himself. From the outset one could see that the command situation could do little but bode ill for Dowding. He and Trenchard never managed to solve their differences and for many years thereafter, the latter remained one of Dowding's greatest antagonists.

Today, as we observe huge machines passir

overhead at supersonic speeds it is difficult to imagine the conditions and machines that were predominant in World War I. By modern standards, those early days of aerial combat can only be described as primitive at best. Flying two-man machines with open cockpits, pilots were obliged to maneuver their planes close enough to the enemy to allow him or his observer to open fire with either handguns or carbines. Eventually, technology began to gradually close the gap and the biplanes were fitted with their own fixed armament. Although basic tactics continued to stress man against man in the skies, these new developments were a foretaste of the shift in emphasis to machine versus machine.

Consequently, the air war in Europe was, in effect, a series of individual duels. As parachutes were yet to arrive on the scene, this type of warfare was particularly brutal. Instead of focusing on the machine, the accepted method of combat called for opponents to concentrate on the destruction of the enemy pilot. As a result, many of those early airmen died a horrible death.

Dowding's troubles with Trenchard continued to mount and plague him. Shortly after a particularly bitter disagreement over some newly acquired replacement propellers, Dowding found himself promoted to lt. colonel and once more transferred home to England to command the administrative wing at Farnborough, home of the Royal Flying Corps.

In the spring of 1916, he returned once more to France and found himself again under Trenchard's immediate command. Indeed, it seemed as if the destinies of the two were irrevocably entwined. During the Battle of the Somme, the RFC suffered heavily and squadrons found themselves manned by exhausted pilots. Concerned over the high rate of casualties, Dowding suggested to Trenchard that squadrons be rotated, thus allowing for brief periods of rest and relief from the constant pressures of daily sorties. A terrible row erupted with Trenchard accusing Dowding of being a "Dismal Jimmy." Trenchard refused to be swayed and made up his mind to rid himself of Dowding's influence once and for all. As a result, the latter was promoted to colonel and sent home to a training command.

Although Dowding was now isolated from Trenchard's direct control, the two remained at odds; their now legendary squabbles continued unabated. Dowding complained that too many qualified instructors were being withdrawn and sent to France, leaving few experienced men to train the badly needed replacement pilots. The resulting fury alienated the two antagonists for nearly a decade.

Nevertheless, despite seething problems inherent in the RFC and the open hostility of Trenchard, Dowding thrust himself into the job with vigor and soon became recognized as an authority on training. Midway through the year 1917, he was promoted to brigadier general at the relatively early age of thirty-four. Unfortunately, shortly after his promotion, Dowding lost his command on the whim of the air minister. (Politics played an important role in determining which officer held which post.) From Training Command headquarters, he was reassigned as chief of staff to the RAF area at York.

With the war's end, Dowding suddenly found

himself one of the senior officers in the RAF. Just as suddenly, he received a letter from the Air Ministry informing him that he was to be reassigned to the army. Though demobilization and scarcity of suitable positions were cited as the official reasons, it was obvious that Trenchard's influence was behind the entire affair. Dowding was quite naturally, appalled. He had risen rapidly through the ranks of the RAF and his expertise lay in that field. He was hardly qualified to return to the army as a general of artillery. In defense of Trenchard, however, Dowding could be just as obstinate and inflexible as the man who would later come to be known as the "father of the RAF." Try as he might, Dowding was unable to convince the authorities that their decision was totally erroneous. Fortunately a mutual friend, Adm. Sir Vyell Vyvyan, managed to impress upon Trenchard that it was folly to allow personal prejudices to influence the future of a man such as Dowding who had so much to offer the future of the still relatively new RAF.

The postwar years found Dowding holding a variety of commands. The first one was as commander of Number One Group, with responsibility for control of many of those airfields that would later play so prominent a part in the Battle of Britain, including Biggin Hill, Hawkhinge, and Manston. During this period Dowding was also to make the acquaintance of some of those who would later fight by his side as comrades-in-arms and critics. Trafford Leigh-Mallory, Keith Park, and Sholto Douglas, along with Charles Portal and Arthur Tedder came under the influence of Dowding's teachings and leadership.

In 1925, while Trenchard was fighting dearly for

the very existence of the RAF, Dowding was selected to become chief of staff to the air vice marshal in Iraq. However, the following year he was recalled to England to become director of training under Trenchard who by now was chief of the air staff. Much to his surprise, Dowding found that he could work side by side with Trenchard in complete harmony. Finally, one afternoon Trenchard called Dowding and told the latter:

> Dowding—I don't often make mistakes about people. I made one about you.[3]

From that time forward, the two were able to work in unison for the betterment of the service as a whole. Trenchard began to rely more and more on Dowding's advice and handed him responsible commands. He was sent to Palestine in 1929 when unrest in that area demanded increased British attention. In addition to his duties as air officer commanding, Dowding was instructed to act as the eyes and ears of Trenchard. So effectively did Dowding carry out this assignment that Trenchard frequently wrote glowing tributes to Dowding's achievements.

At the end of 1929, Dowding returned from Palestine and assumed the position of air officer commanding Inland Area. This command lasted less than a year as Dowding was shortly appointed air member for supply and research. This new command was obviously designed to take full advantage of Dowding's technical expertise. Not only did he find himself responsible for procurement, but development as well and it was here that he was to make his first significant contribution to the Battle of Britain.

With Dowding's encouragement, two new fighter planes were developed and eventually accepted for use by the RAF. Although not originally designed for military use, but instead as experimental planes, Dowding quickly recognized their potential and saw that a few modifications could equip these revolutionary machines easily for such use. At his urging, the Air Ministry placed the first order with Hawkers in 1936, and a year and a half later, the first Hurricanes came into service. In addition, in June 1936, once more at Dowding's recommendations, the Supermarine Company was rewarded with an order for just over 300 of their new planes. A year later, the plane that was destined to become famous throughout the world as the hero of the Battle of Britain was delivered to the RAF. The Spitfire went on active duty.

Meanwhile, Dowding's command was split when it was found to be too large and unwieldy. Thus he found himself responsible solely for research and development, while an old friend from his Indian days and fellow squadron commander from World War I, Cyril Newell, was elevated to handle responsibility for supply and procurement.

As air minister for research and development, Dowding was to make his second significant contribution to World War II. An early warning system was being sought by England. When Dowding heard of the successful experiments of a team of scientists with RDF (Radio Direction Finding), which would later become famous as radar, he made it his business to find out more about the project. Once more, he was quick to recognize the potential of a new weapon and threw his wholehearted support behind the further development of this remarkable invention. His foresight later paid handsome dividends as radar played one of the most important roles in the Battle of Britain. By 1940, thanks to Dowding's ability for independent thinking and willingness to try something new, Britain was to have available an entire chain of RDF stations on the Channel coast.

Thanks to the earlier machinations of Trenchard and the dedication and determination of those who followed in his wake, by the end of the 1930s, the RAF was on secure grounds as a separate service. The junior service was divided into three distinct operational commands: Fighter Command, Coastal Command, and Bomber Command. All three competed intensely for the meager funds available, with Bomber Command receiving priority. During the years following World War I, air strategists such as Douhet and Mitchel encouraged development of the world's air forces with the theory that "the bomber will always get through."

After Bomber Command, Coastal Command was considered to be of next importance. With England strictly a maritime nation, the protection of the sea lanes in and around the British Isles warranted attention. Consequently, Fighter Command was the poor sister of the RAF. It was to the command of this last that Dowding found himself posted as the first commander in chief in the spring of 1936. Typically, Dowding arrived at his headquarters at Bentley Priory on July 14, 1936, with no fanfare and was unannounced. One might gain a clearer insight into the character of the man by recalling Peter Wykeham's words.

Dowding arrived at the gate sharp at nine o'clock in the morning. No staff was present and he was greeted by Sgt. Cornthwaite, the N.C.O. in charge of the orderly room. Together they explored the Priory and grounds. When the tour was over, the new Commander-in-Chief selected a room looking south that contained some office furniture, and told Cornthwaite to put his name on the door.[4]

Dowding refused to allow himself to be disappointed by having been assigned to Fighter Command. With typical enthusiasm he immersed himself completely in his new assignment. Unfortunately, he did so with the impression that he was to become the next chief of air staff.

Early in 1936, the chief of air staff, Edward Ellington, led Dowding to believe that he would be Ellington's logical successor. This was hardly a surprise, for Dowding was the senior officer available for the position. Though he had not originally sought to be top dog in the RAF and his low-key and unspectacular approach to objectives prevented him from participating in back room politics, his seniority alone rated considerably. However, he could be rather vocal in his protestations when he failed to receive that which he deemed to be his just due, and as a result, over the years had antagonized too many influential people.

Accordingly, although he later expressed relief at not receiving the command, he was obviously disappointed when, on February 3, 1937, he received a letter from Ellington announcing the selection of Newell to become the next chief of air staff. The letter was apologetic in nature and in it, Ellington denied that he had any influence in the selection of a successor. Rightly, Dowding now became concerned about his future employment as his advancing years precluded any hope he might entertain of eventually becoming chief of air staff. As a result he answered Ellington's letter with one of his own that expressed contempt for officers who complained about being passed over for promotion and offered to resign should that be the wish of the incoming chief, Newell. Dowding was always ready to take up the pen and respond to those friends and critics despite the need for discretion. Later, this correspondence would come back to haunt him, for in many instances, even though he obviously failed to realize it, his manner could be abrasive and curt. Nonplussed at having his resignation refused, Dowding went about turning Fighter Command into a force able to defend England from potential enemies.

The development of radar and subsequent construction of radar stations had given England the eyes with which to warn her of imminent danger. How best to take advantage of these eyes now began to consume much of Dowding's attention. Thanks to his earlier foresight, he now had not only radar, but two new fighter models as well. Still, a link in the chain appeared to be missing. How best could he connect these two?

The radar stations were linked to Fighter Command headquarters at Bentley Priory via phone or landline. From there, Dowding established a system whereby the incoming information was sorted out in a "filter room" and when the course and strength of enemy attacks was assessed, the information was then passed on to Group headquarters thence to the various sector stations at the airfields where the fighters were based. Thus was the first piece of the puzzle put in place. England now possessed an efficient and smoothly operating defensive system. This system became a highly guarded secret and jealously guarded system which would later completely baffle the Luftwaffe. All that remained was the forging of the strategy that could best take advantage of the elaborate system designed by Dowding and his staff.

Fighter Command was divided into four groups. Number Ten Group was responsible for defending the southwest portion of England, Number Eleven Group had responsibility for that area in closest proximity to France. Its area included Portsmouth, Southampton, the Thames Estuary and London, stretching as far west as Bath. North of this group, Number Twelve Group was responsible for the defense of the industrial heartland of the Island. On an east-west axis running from just north of Hull, Number Twelve's area included the key manufacturing cities of Manchester, Sheffield, Liverpool, and Birmingham among others. Finally, Number Thirteen Group was given the task of defending all of Scotland and the remaining portion of England on Number Twelve Group's north flank.

Although the final selection of commanders for the groups was the sole province of the Air Ministry, Dowding appeared satisfied with the men who held the key commands. He was not one to arbitrarily sack commanders just to place his own men in key positions. Leigh-Mallory commanded Twelve Group from

1937 onward, Quentin Brand had Ten Group and Thirteen Group was in the hands of Air Vice Marshal R. E. Saul. The key group, Eleven, was commanded by Air Vice Marshal E. L. Gossage whose term was due to expire in a few years.

The two years immediately preceding the outbreak of World War II were utilized by Dowding to mold Fighter Command into an effective and highly efficient fighting force. Foremost among his accomplishments was the integration of the communications network of radar stations, Fighter Command Operations Center, and Group and Sector controllers. In addition, Dowding continued to battle the Air Ministry over those items which he felt to be absolutely essential.

He frequently condemned what he considered the Air Ministry's lack of foresight and in some instances, sheer stupidity. Dowding clamored for the construction of all-weather airfields, for the winter months gave evidence that on many days the present fields became unsuitable for flying owing to poor, muddy, conditions. Accordingly, he demanded that the fields be provided with concrete runways. In its infinite wisdom, the Air Ministry repeatedly rebuffed these requests and Dowding was reduced to experimenting with various types of grass in search of the one most suitable for runways. It was not until shortly before the outbreak of the war that concrete construction was finally authorized. Unfortunately, by then it was too late and during the Battle of Britain many of the fighter squadrons continued to fly from grass covered airfields.

Dowding also railed at the lack of any organized

plans for the mobilization and use of an observer corps. His radar stations were situated on the coast and an enemy flying over them was lost to view for these stations could see in only one direction. Therefore, the need for an observer corps to track the course of incoming flights was paramount.

Probably the most famous and oft quoted clash between Dowding and the Air Ministry, however, concerned the installation of bulletproof canopies in the fighter planes. Once more the Air Ministry concluded that Dowding was being unduly pessimistic and refused repeated requests to consider the matter. Dowding finally won the day when he asked why, if gangsters in Chicago could ride behind bulletproof glass, couldn't his fighter pilots be afforded the same protection?

Dowding's strategic plans for Fighter Command came under fire early from a variety of critics. With the then prevailing attitude that "the bomber will always get through," many in the RAF thought only in terms of offense. Although obstinate and frequently over zealous in attempting to have his theories accepted, Dowding could also be most perceptive. He felt that the primary concern of Fighter Command was "security of base" and as such, defense was the key. This by no means meant that offense was to be ignored. It was simply a matter of placing the emphasis in the proper place.

On June 28, 1938, another significant event took place. Keith Park, who later died at Tangmere, arrived at Bentley Priory to become Dowding's senior staff officer. Park's arrival brought together the team that was to win the Battle of Britain.

Keith Park was an amiable New Zealander who had begun his military career as a gunner in the army. During World War I he was wounded at Gallipoli and again, more seriously, during the Battle of the Somme. After his second wound he made up his mind to join the RFC and gradually rose in the ranks. Shortly after the Great War he served as squadron commander under Dowding and later attended the Staff College before a tour of duty in the Middle East. By the time Dowding took over Fighter Command, Park had gained the reputation as an authority on the use of fighters and was ideally suited both in expertise and temperament to work with Dowding.

Meanwhile, in July of 1938, Dowding received word from Newell that his services would shortly be no longer required. In effect, this meant that Dowding was to be retired at the age of fifty-eight. Although shocked and disappointed, Dowding refused to let this latest turn of events erode his dedication and intensity. But although he continued his efforts to improve the efficiency of Fighter Command, he nevertheless began to make plans for his retirement.

Three months prior to the anticipated retirement, as war clouds gathered over the continent, another letter was received from Newell in which he stated that the Air Ministry had decided to ask Dowding to postpone his retirement until March, 1940. Although he felt that he was being treated in somewhat of a cavalier fashion, Dowding complied and agreed to stay on.

Yet another ominous foretaste of things to come revolved around Trafford Leigh-Mallory, commander of Twelve Group. This officer was intensely ambitious and would stop at nothing to obtain that which he considered his due. Leigh-Mallory was disappointed that he had not been appointed commander of the crucial Eleven Group, which obviously was to be in the forefront of any battle fought over the British Isles or the English Channel. Dowding always demanded loyalty from his subordinates and his style of command usually earned this loyalty. From Park, Brand, and Saul this loyalty was faithfully forthcoming. But from Leigh-Mallory all he received was betrayal and back-stabbing. Keith Park has recorded a conversation he had with Leigh-Mallory during the spring of 1940:

> Leigh-Mallory came striding into my office at Headquarters one day after an interview with the C.-in-C. He was very angry and he made a rude comment about what he called Dowding's obstinacy. He said that he would move heaven and earth to get Dowding sacked from his job. I was very annoyed at this, and I told Leigh-Mallory so. Although at that time I was only an Air Commodore and he was an Air Vice-Marshal, I told him just what I thought of such a remark and his obvious disloyalty.[5]

This then was the state of affairs as the RAF and Fighter Command prepared to take on the mightiest airforce in the world—the German Luftwaffe. However, after a swift German victory over Poland the war settled down to a stalemate and the winter of the "Phoney War" was spent by Dowding in preparation for his forthcoming retirement.

At the beginning of March, 1940, Dowding requested Newell make the former's successor known as it seemed only proper that the new chief of Fighter Command receive a briefing from his predecessor. No reply was forthcoming so Dowding packed his bags and prepared to leave. On the day before he was to become a civilian, the long awaited letter arrived from Newell but contained a surprise. The chief of air staff once more requested that Dowding put off his retirement until July 14 of that year. Dowding agreed but was justifiably disturbed by what seemed to him a lack of courtesy on the part of the Air Ministry.

Given this brief reprieve, Dowding responded by changing commanders at Eleven Group. Instead of Leigh-Mallory who had openly advanced his own cause and lobbied vigorously for the position, Keith Park was sent off to head this critical command. Dowding held no animosity towards Leigh-Mallory and was completely unaware of the latter's feelings towards him. Therefore, personalities did not enter into the selection of Park over the commander of Twelve Group. Instead, Dowding felt that it was a sensible choice, as Park was acknowledged as an expert in fighter tactics while Leigh-Mallory's field of expertise was support of ground troops, a field in which he had few peers. Furthermore, Park had been broadly exposed to Dowding's system of command and few knew more about Fighter Command's day-to-day operation than did Park. All in all, at the time, the selection of Park appeared to be totally justified. Subsequent events would prove the selection to be one of the most astute of the entire war.

On May 10, Germany launched the long awaited attack in the west. As the Anglo-French forces were driven steadily back the rate of loss among fighter planes climbed at a disastrous rate. Time and again Dowding was ordered to dispatch squadrons to France as replacements for those lost in action, consequently the number of squadrons available for defense of the homeland declined at an alarming rate.

Dowding's entire defensive plan for England was based on the premise that fifty-two fighter squadrons would be required if he were to guarantee safety. However, by May 15, thanks to the alarming rate of loss in France, Fighter Command found itself reduced to thirty-six squadrons, nine of them equipped with obsolete aircraft. In spite of this, Churchill, an avowed Francophile, readily yielded to the pleas of French Premier Reynaud and agreed to send an additional ten squadrons to France. When he heard of this latest request, Dowding was beside himself. Already he had lost over two hundred Hurricanes in France. He urgently requested the Air Minister, Sir Archibald Sinclair, to allow him to address the War Cabinet which was meeting daily. Although the request was highly irregular, Sinclair made the necessary arrangements.

That evening, the War Cabinet met for their fourth session of the day. Present were cabinet ministers, chiefs of staff and others whose positions demanded attendance. Dowding arrived and was seated in close proximity to Churchill himself. Shortly, he was invited to state his case. Normally Dowding's dour manner justified the attitude of those who still regarded him as somewhat pessimistic or a

"Dismal Jimmy." However, on this occasion his manner was eloquent; but he soon felt that his arguments were falling on hostile ears. No assistance was provided by Sinclair or the chief of air staff, Newell, whose duty it was to support his subordinate. Throughout the session both sat in silence. Finally Dowding rose, grasped a hastily prepared graph, walked over to the Prime Minister's chair and placed the paper in front of him. He then stated:

> The red line shows the wastage of Hurricanes in the last ten days. If the line goes on at the same rate for the next ten days, there won't be a single Hurricane left, either in France or England.[6]

With that, the mood of the conference seemed to shift and Dowding left confident that his arguments had won the day. Unfortunately, although visibly moved by Dowding's effective presentation, upon adjournment of the meeting Churchill ordered two more squadrons to France immediately. Although he was dismayed by the turn of events, Dowding had little choice but to obey. However, his arguments had not fallen on deaf ears. The following day, during a visit to France, Churchill sent a dispatch ordering the transfer of still another ten squadrons to France. This request was flatly denied by the War Cabinet. Dowding's arguments had indeed made an impression.

Fighter Command was still obliged though, to provide protection for the hard pressed BEF* fighting in

*British Expeditionary Force

France. Dowding agreed to a compromise whereby Hurricane squadrons would be dispatched to France during daylight hours and use French airfields, but each evening they were to return to England. Historians credit this stand of Dowding's as one of the turning points of the war, and rightly so. His determined stand, unsupported by his superiors, insured the availability of adequate strength to stave off certain defeat.

But it was not the lack of planes themselves that plagued the head of Fighter Command. Lord Beaverbrook, newly appointed minister of aircraft production, eventually managed to devise a method whereby replacement aircraft were available in more than sufficient quantity. Consequently, it was the loss of experienced pilots that was the prime concern to Fighter Command. A pilot killed or forced down over enemy held territory remained lost forever to the RAF. Although machines could be replaced, experienced flyers were not as readily available.

By the last week in May the German advance spearheads had compressed the BEF and large portions of the French army into a small defensive perimeter around the port town of Dunkirk. In an effort unparalleled in history, Operation Dynamo was launched to rescue as many soldiers as possible. Instead of allowing his successful armies to finish the job, Hitler acceded to Goering's boasts and handed responsibility for eliminating the Dunkirk pocket to the Luftwaffe.

As the evacuees queued up on the beaches to await shipment to the United Kingdom, Stukas of the Luftwaffe pounded the Dunkirk beaches unmercifully.

Overhead, the outnumbered pilots of the RAF gamely attempted to thwart the Luftwaffe attacks. The latter clearly held the advantage. As the RAF pilots attacked the bombers, they in turn were set upon by swarms of ME 109s operating from nearby captured French airfields. Goering's pilots were able to fly their mission, land, refuel and rearm, and return to the fray with relative swiftness. On the other hand, the RAF pilots were handicapped by the fact that their actual operational time over the beaches was comparatively short because much of their precious fuel was used in reaching the target area. In addition, Dowding was unable to commit all of his already depleted squadrons, as he was forced to husband resources for the defense of England itself. Consequently, the man on the ground formed the mistaken impression that the RAF was not pulling its weight. Augmenting this impression was the fact that many of the dogfights were fought far from the beaches themselves and thus out of sight of the beleaguered ground troops.

Pilot Al Deere of Fifty-four Squadron was made acutely aware of the animosity directed towards the RAF. On May 29, his squadron set off on its final flight over Dunkirk after having received word that they were to be relieved the next day by Forty-one Squadron. It was Dowding's policy to keep rotating squadrons as the strain placed on his pilots taxed human endurance to its fullest. This was a tactic Dowding adopted after seeing tired, worn out pilots suffer heavily during the Battle of the Somme in World War I. From that point forward, he was determined to rotate squadrons in order to insure a steady stream of fresh pilots whenever possible. Over Gravelines, Deere found himself involved in a dogfight during which his plane was badly damaged. He was forced to crash land on the beach. Deere then made his way inland and managed to join the horde of refugees making for Dunkirk. Upon arrival at the port he was amazed to find the scene which now confronted him. Everywhere there were abandoned arms, long lines of troops awaiting transport, but for all the carnage, discipline appeared to remain intact. Deere then attempted to get aboard a destroyer. He introduced himself as a member of the RAF to an officer directing traffic on the beach. The pilot explained that he required passage so that he could return to active duty immediately. Such was the reputation of the RAF that the officer's retort was:

> I don't give a damn who you are. For all the good you chaps seem to be doing you might as well stay on the ground.[7]

Nevertheless, Deere managed to get aboard and make his way to the ship's wardroom where he received a cool reception. Puzzled, he asked: "Why so friendly? What have the RAF done?"[8] The reply shocked him: "That's just it, what have they done?"[9] Bitterly, Deere managed to make his way back to his squadron.

By June 4, it was all over. Men like Deere, Bob Tuck and Douglas Bader had flown their hearts out and taxed themselves to the limit, but in vain. However, without doubt the casualty rate would have been much higher had it not been for the valiant effort of Dowding's pilots.

With France now defeated and the Germans in

possession of bases a few miles across the English Channel, the British were acutely aware that their turn was next.

On the other side of the channel, Hitler and his commanders were themselves aware that before an invasion could even be considered, the RAF would have to be driven from the skies. The French collapse had been so rapid that the Germans had been unable to plan beyond that point. Consequently they were ill-prepared to launch an invasion.

In the cities and countryside of England, the German predicament was unknown. Any moment now, the British expected German troops to swarm ashore on the East Coast; but a full month of anticipation and waiting passed before the next concentrated German move.

During the month's respite, Dowding busied himself refining the system that he had so diligently put together. Radar stations, Group headquarters and sector stations were all checked and rechecked thoroughly for their state of readiness. Staffs were briefed and rebriefed until Dowding and his Group commanders were confident that everyone thoroughly understood their roles. At the various airfields, squadron leaders worked diligently to insure a high degree of efficiency and readiness in their squadrons.

At 242d Canadian Squadron, Douglas Bader, "he of the tin legs," arrived in late June to take up his appointment as squadron commander. Morale was low after the debacle of France and he found that most of the squadron's tools and equipment had been left behind during the hasty departure from the continent. After several frustrating attempts to obtain replacements via proper channels, Bader sent off a wire to Fighter Command headquarters.

> 242 Squadron now operational as regards pilots but non-operational, repeat non-operational as regards equipment.[10]

Bader's immediate superior, Leigh-Mallory, commander of Twelve Group, called him in and told him that because of his audacity he could expect a summons from Fighter Command. Sure enough, a few days later the summons came.

When Bader was ushered into Dowding's presence he was asked to explain his signal. Bader explained that he had made every attempt through proper channels until it was clear that he was getting nowhere and his squadron was suffering. Dowding then showed Bader a report from the supply officer which indicated that Bader's manner and attitude had left something to be desired. Bader responded by informing Dowding that the supply officer had attempted to intimidate him by stating that the commander in chief was furious. "Oh, he said I was furious did he?"[11] said Dowding, and summoned the officer in question. The officer was then asked if he had indeed informed Bader that the commander in chief was furious. The officer pleaded guilty. Dowding then said:

> I will not have any officer taking my name in vain or predicting my emotions. Your job is—or was—to help squadrons in the field. You will be off this headquarters in twenty-four hours."[12]

Such was Dowding's style of command and Douglas

Bader's first exposure to his commander in chief. The episode had a lasting impression on Bader.

Besides making sure that his entire command was operating at peak efficiency, Dowding was also concerned about the state of adequate replacements for those losses that inevitably lay ahead. In this area, he need not have been concerned with aircraft for Lord Beaverbrook had recently been appointed minister of aircraft production and proved to be absolutely brilliant in this role. After the battle, Dowding would acclaim Beaverbrook:

> The country owes as much to Beaverbrook for the Battle of Britain as it does to me.[13]

Despite different backgrounds and diametrically opposite personalities, the two became staunch friends. Beaverbrook's response to Dowding's praise was:

> London has many lamp posts. Hitler has reserved one for me and that is where I would have been hanging if I had not procured the fighters.[14]

Finally, Dowding called in his Group commanders, Brand, Saul, Park, and Leigh-Mallory and stressed the importance of emphasizing the defensive. For the present, Bomber Command's fleet of bombers would have to assume responsibility for any offensive action. Fighter Command's role was to be purely defensive in nature. Security of base was to receive the highest priority. Dowding went on to state that he would not involve himself in the day-to-day operation of the groups. Instead, he was responsible for the strategic decisions and the operation of Fighter Command itself. Therefore, Group commanders would be responsible for devising their own tactics but cooperation between Groups was essential. The latter was to be stressed at all times. Dowding was determined to leave Fighter Command in top form for his successor.

On July 5, Newell again sent a letter to Dowding asking that he once again postpone his retirement beyond July 14, this time till the end of October. Although Dowding readily agreed, for he was not anxious to miss the forthcoming battle, he was nonetheless irritated by still one more shift (the fifth) in the attitude of the Air Ministry. Newell's letter stated:

> I am writing to ask if you will again defer your retirement beyond the date which I last gave you of July 14. Under present conditions I should be more than loathe (sic) for you to leave Fighter Command on that date, and I would be very glad if you would continue in your appointment as Air Officer Commanding-in-Chief until the end of October. If, as I sincerely hope you will be, you are willing to accept the extension, an official letter to this effect will be sent to you in due course, and I will also write to you regarding your successor.[15]

Another letter arrived, this one from Sir Archibald Sinclair, Secretary of State for Air:

> I can only say that the Chief of the Air Staff consulted me before asking you to retain your command until October, and that it was my wish that you should remain in command of our Fighter Squadrons, upon whose success in defeating the German attack upon our munition factories during the next three months will

almost certainly depend the issue of this war.[16]

On July 10, the opening moves by the Luftwaffe in the Battle of Britain were made. German dive bombers, escorted by fighters, attacked a convoy making its way up the English Channel. Park already had one squadron in the air on patrol and immediately ordered five more of the nineteen available scrambled in Eleven Group. In the resulting melee, the RAF gave as good as they received in return, with the final tally at four Germans lost to three of the RAF. However, the tight formations used by the British pilots failed to go unobserved by the Luftwaffe pilots. This method of initiating battle, so stringently stressed at flight school, severely hampered the British pilots' ability to maneuver freely.

The next morning, another convoy was attacked. The British radar network picked up the Luftwaffe assembly and forwarded the information to Park's Group. Two squadrons were ordered airborne and although heavily outnumbered, the English pilots acquitted themselves well with the final tally two ME 109s and one Stuka for the loss of one Hurricane.

For the next few days activity was light as the weather closed and flying conditions were unsuitable.

For the next week, the Luftwaffe split their attention between Channel shipping, swift raids on key factories, and mining the Thames and Humber estuaries. Their morale was high, as the apparent weak opposition encountered so far led the German pilots into believing that the RAF was almost finished. However, the German pilots were virtually unanimous in praise of their adversaries, giving credit to the determination, skill, and bravery of the RAF airmen.

Machine for machine, both sides held some advantages. The Spitfires and Hurricanes of Fighter Command could not keep pace or hope to climb with the ME 109; but the English planes were more maneuverable. Then there were the Defiants; a lumbering two-seater that had no business in the battle. The Luftwaffe pilots were overjoyed to find these planes barring their way. On July 19, with little effort, a flight of Defiants was destroyed by the Germans with six British planes being destroyed and the remaining two seriously damaged.

On July 23, the Luftwaffe attacks on Channel shipping increased in intensity in an effort to draw the RAF into battle, and although the score still favored the RAF, Dowding and Park both knew that the Luftwaffe now controlled the skies over the Channel. Still, they refused to be lured into destruction by committing their entire force.

On July 25, five ships were sunk, and two days later, two destroyers suffered the same fate. But the constant attacks on shipping had failed to lure the RAF into the sky for a decisive battle. Park was refusing to snatch at the bait.

During one of the week's battles, a South African pilot, Sailor Malan, later to become one of the RAF's top aces, clashed with the top German Ace, Werner Molders. The latter was wounded so severely that he was out of action for over a month.

As a result of Park's refusal to commit all his forces, Hitler ordered all Luftwaffe units in the west to prepare for phase two of the battle. This phase was called Adlertag (Eagle Day) by the Germans and designated the beginning of the Battle of Britain. On the other hand, the English were convinced that the battle had already begun, at the beginning of the month.

Goering's two air fleet commanders, Kesselring and Sperrle, informed their chief that it would take at least a week, and perhaps longer, to prepare their formations for an all-out effort. Meanwhile, the attacks in the English Channel continued.

During the first week in August, Goering confirmed Hitler's intentions and issued orders that henceforth, a new approach would be adopted. Fighter Command itself would now be the primary objective with sector stations and airfields the major targets. If the attack on shipping failed to lure the RAF into a decisive fight, then surely strikes at their very heart would accomplish this. How could they refuse to defend their own positions? (See Map 5)

Despite the anxiety of conducting the operations of Fighter Command during these crucial days, Dowding's exhausting daily routine remained constant. He would arrive at his office promptly at 9:00 A.M., familiarize himself with the events of the previous twenty-four-hour period, and begin his daily work. He always returned home for lunch and dinner but they were the only two breaks that he allowed himself. After dinner, he would return to his office and work late into the night. Before leaving for home, his final stop would be the operations and filter rooms to see what was happening. Frequently, during these long evenings, he would return home later than usual and his sister, who was in residence

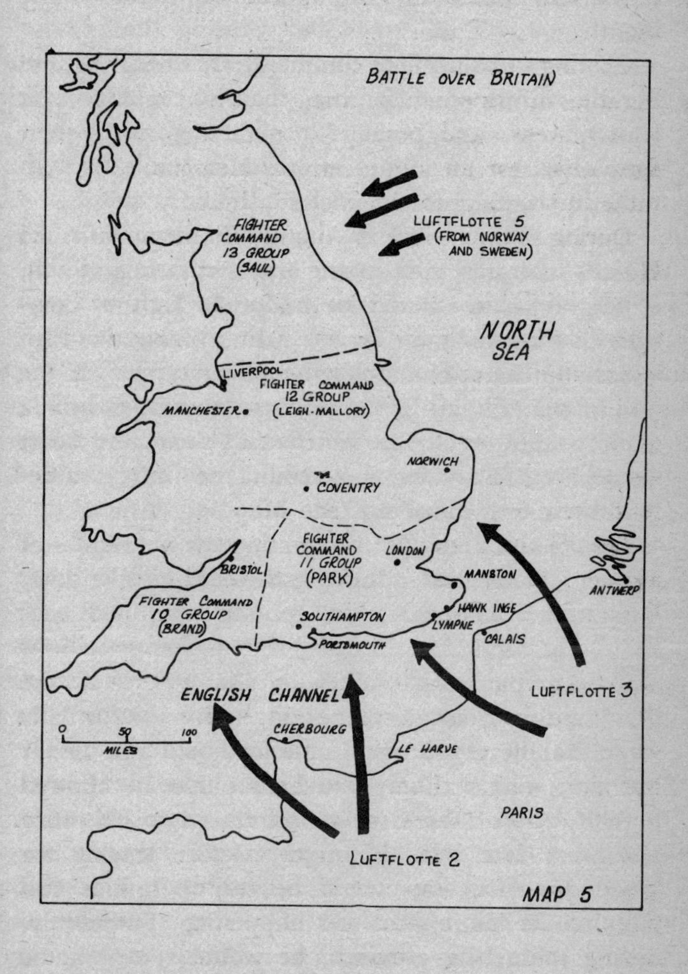
BATTLE OVER BRITAIN
FIGHTER COMMAND 13 GROUP (SAUL)
LUFTFLOTTE 5 (FROM NORWAY AND SWEDEN)
NORTH SEA
LIVERPOOL
FIGHTER COMMAND 12 GROUP (LEIGH-MALLORY)
MANCHESTER
NORWICH
COVENTRY
FIGHTER COMMAND 11 GROUP (PARK)
LONDON
BRISTOL
MANSTON
ANTWERP
HAWK INGE
LYMPNE
CALAIS
FIGHTER COMMAND 10 GROUP (BRAND)
SOUTHAMPTON
PORTSMOUTH
LUFTFLOTTE 3
ENGLISH CHANNEL
0 50 100
MILES
CHERBOURG
LE HARVE
PARIS
LUFTFLOTTE 2
MAP 5

and kept house for him, knew that he had been visiting some airfield whose units were engaged in night fighting. Aside from having to deal with the fierce Luftwaffe's onslaught of daytime, Fighter Command's responsibility included resisting the bomber raids mounted during the night by the enemy against manufacturing and shipping centers. These raids usually went unopposed for night fighting was a relatively new technique and was not mastered by either air force until much later in the war.

Dowding did, however, have one weapon in his arsenal with which to oppose the German raids. The English could not understand how the Luftwaffe was able to pinpoint their targets with any degree of accuracy during the nationwide blackouts. Eventually it was suspected that the Germans were using a series of radio beams directed at specific targets with uncanny accuracy. This system consisted of two parallel beams, one of dots and the other of dashes along which planes flew. If the pilot strayed too far off course, the receiver in his plane would emit stronger signals thus confirming that he was straying too far off course depending on which signal, dot or dash, his apparatus picked up. When he was over the target, the impulses from an intersecting beam informed the pilot that he could now release his bomb load. The Germans called this system Knickebein (Bent Leg). Verification of the German system came only after extensive interrogation of captured aircrews and discovery of the monitoring apparatus in a downed bomber. Thus forewarned, Dowding was able to devise countermeasures which included jamming the German signals; but as previously mentioned, because night fighting was then in its infancy, few bombers were lost to interceptors. Unless they had the proper optical equipment, it was virtually impossible for pilots to detect and intercept a target traveling at high speed through the black of night. Later, the Germans refined their methods somewhat and the best Dowding, always a keen advocate of the application of science to modern warfare, could hope for was that his jamming procedures would destroy the German accuracy. For the duration of his career Dowding wrestled with the problem of those nightly raids and the ordeal proved a tremendous burden and drain on his strength.

Even though the Luftwaffe was unprepared to launch the great attack, they did manage to continue the attacks on Channel shipping without stop. On August 8, E Boats operating from French ports sunk three ships from a convoy. Prior to this, these torpedo boats would not have dared sail in the English Channel unless they expected to encounter heavy opposition from the RAF. But now, with the Luftwaffe's domination of the skies, they found themselves able to operate with relative immunity. As the convey reached the Isle of Wight, the Stukas attacked with a fury. Seven squadrons were scrambled from Ten and Eleven Groups, and in the biggest clash of the battle to date, the Luftwaffe lost thirty-one planes to the RAF's nineteen. The German losses were primarily the slow lumbering Stukas which made easy targets. Unfortunately, six more ships of the convoy were lost.

On August 12, Newell again wrote to Dowding stating that the latter could now consider his appointment to be of an indefinite period of time or until the cessation of the battle. Although miffed at the air staff's continued lack of courtesy, Dowding concurred and felt a sense of relief for now he could get on with the battle without having the ever present threat of retirement hanging over his head.

Inclement weather postponed the beginning of Eagle Day beyond the week demanded by Kesselring and Sperrle. On August 12, however, Adlertag began in earnest with heavy attacks on the chain of radar stations along the southern coast of England. Time and again Park's controllers maneuvered their squadrons into the air to beat off waves of attacks. The radar stations took a severe pounding but only the one at Ventnor was put off the air. The forward airfields at Manston, Hawkhinge and Lympne also received a great deal of attention from the enemy and the former was put out of action for twenty-four hours. Incredibly, instead of maintaining the pressure, the follow-up raids by the Germans concentrated once more on shipping in the Channel.

The next day, Goering made another in a long series of major errors. Believing that one day's attacks was sufficient attention for the radar installations, he ordered further attacks on these targets to cease. Instead, his pilots were directed to concentrate on airfields, and in particular, those sector stations so crucial to Dowding's chain of communications. Had Goering concentrated on knocking out the eyes of Fighter Command via attacks on the radar stations, he would have dealt the RAF a serious and perhaps fatal blow.

That same day Goering's orders were put into effect. A flight of bombers attacked Eastchurch, a

Coastal Command airfield. 111 Squadron was ordered to intercept and knocked down five Dorniers. During the return flight, Hurricanes of 151 Squadron and Spitfires of South African Sailor Malan's 74 Squadron intercepted the Germans and blasted the survivors.

Another flight of Dorniers ran headlong into 43, 64, and 601 Squadrons from Tangmere and were turned back. But the day was not over. 601 Squadron assisted by two squadrons from Ten Group again intercepted a flight of German bombers, this time ME 110s. The Germans lost five bombers. In the afternoon, the Luftwaffe dispatched ninety bombers to various other targets. All of Park's squadrons were involved and he was forced to call once more on Ten Group for assistance. Brand dispatched 609 Squadron, one of his best. As a result of the day's fighting, the Luftwaffe lost forty-five planes to the RAF's thirteen.

Park's tactics were paying dividends. The warning system did not give sufficient time to allow Eleven Group's squadrons to gain great height. However, it was enough time to allow the RAF pilots to get above the bombers whose escort of fighters flew at a much higher altitude. Park and Dowding stressed the importance of not allowing the bombers through, which accounted for the higher rate of German casualties. The bombers proved vulnerable to the attacks of the Spitfires and Hurricanes. Unfortunately, this method also allowed the German fighters to swoop down on the RAF pilots and attack them at will. Consequently, Fighter Command suffered grievous losses of its own. Nevertheless, the British strategy was correct, for preventing the bombers from reaching their goals was the prime concern. Engaging in dogfights with the ME 109s was no way to prevent damage to strategic targets.

August 14 was relatively quiet as low clouds proved unsuitable for flying operations. But on August 15, the battle resumed with full intensity. This time Goering ordered all three Luftflotte into the air. This marked the beginning of an all-out, four-day effort to drive the RAF from the skies once and for all. A series of bluffs, feints and small attacks kept Eleven Group pilots constantly in the air or on alert. Meanwhile, shortly before noon, Stumpff, commander of Luftflotte Five, operating from Norway and northern Europe, sent two flights off with the mistaken impression that all available reserves from the north had by now been shifted southward. Instead, Dowding, who had seen so many pilots lost from exhaustion during World War I, constantly rotated squadrons to insure that fresh squadrons were always available and to allow worn out squadrons to rest. Thus, Luftflotte Five was in for a nasty surprise, as it was intercepted by not only fresh, but experienced pilots. Once more the early warning system aided the British and allowed them to intercept the enemy well in advance of the target. Saul's Thirteen Group scrambled three squadrons of Spitfires and one of Hurricanes which met one German flight far out to sea. This time the British did have the advantage of height and Seventy-two Squadron waded in. Within minutes, the Germans were in headlong retreat leaving fifteen downed planes behind. The cost to Fighter Command was zero.

Further south, fifty more JU 88s from fields in Denmark approached England. These were met head on by 616 and 73 Squadrons from Leigh-Mallory's Twelve group. Although some of the enemy managed to get through and drop their loads on a Bomber Command airfield, the flight lost eight planes to the guns of Leigh-Mallory's pilots. Luftflotte Five, thoroughly routed, made no more daylight raids during the Battle of Britain.

While Ten and Twelve Groups were experiencing success in the north, Eleven Group found that it had its hands full. At mid-morning, heavy attacks hit Lympne and Hawkhinge. The former was thoroughly smashed and out of action for two days. At the same time, a flight of ME 109s strafed Manston. (See Map 6)

Shortly after noon, Martlesham found itself the target of a flight of Stukas. A few hours later, eleven of Park's squadrons fought a pitched battle against 250 planes from Luftflotte Two.

After dinner, the Luftwaffe shifted their emphasis again and attacks were launched at Biggin Hill and Kenley. This attack was successfully broken up but West Malling was attacked again. At day's end, the score showed thirty-four RAF planes downed to seventy-five for the Luftwaffe, mostly bombers. Among the RAF pilots downed was Al Deere again, who managed to make his way back to base after safely parachuting from his burning plane.

Rest became a precious commodity and that night it was denied to all but a few. The Luftwaffe sent small flights of bombers to various scattered points in England and kept the defenders on the alert

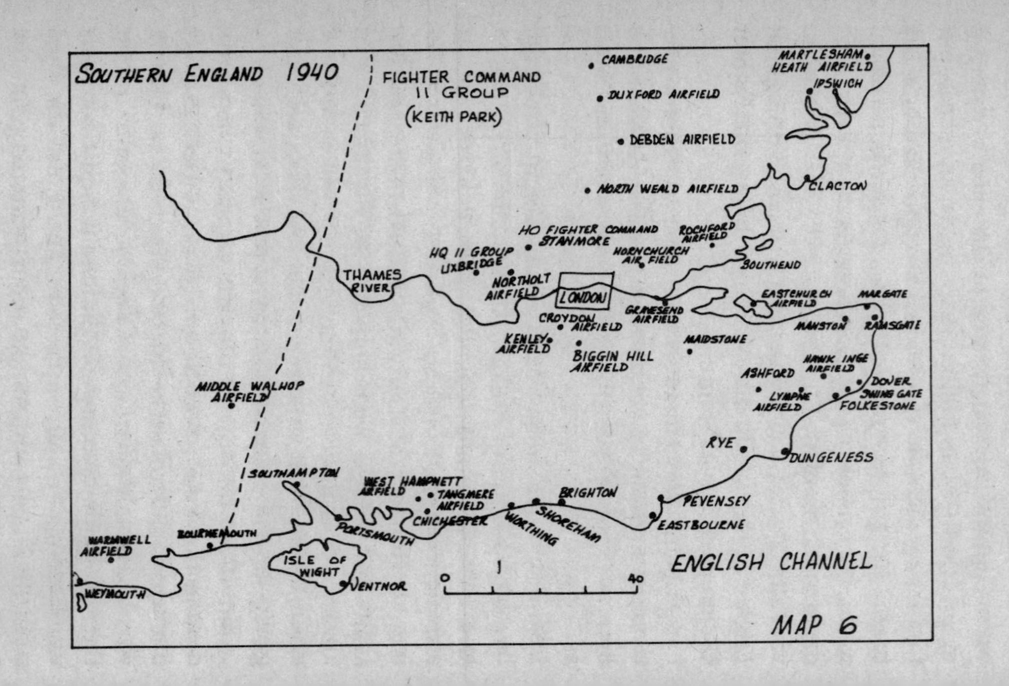
SOUTHERN ENGLAND 1940
FIGHTER COMMAND
11 GROUP
(KEITH PARK)
CAMBRIDGE
DUXFORD AIRFIELD
DEBDEN AIRFIELD
NORTH WEALD AIRFIELD
MARTLESHAM HEATH AIRFIELD
IPSWICH
CLACTON
HQ FIGHTER COMMAND STANMORE
ROCHFORD AIRFIELD
HORNCHURCH AIR FIELD
SOUTHEND
HQ 11 GROUP UXBRIDGE
THAMES RIVER
NORTHOLT AIRFIELD
LONDON
GRAVESEND AIRFIELD
EASTCHURCH AIRFIELD
MARGATE
RAMSGATE
MANSTON
CROYDON AIRFIELD
KENLEY AIRFIELD
BIGGIN HILL AIRFIELD
MAIDSTONE
HAWK INGE AIRFIELD
ASHFORD
DOVER
SWING GATE
FOLKESTONE
LYMPNE AIRFIELD
MIDDLE WALHOP AIRFIELD
RYE
DUNGENESS
SOUTHAMPTON
WEST HAMPNETT AIRFIELD
TANGMERE AIRFIELD
CHICHESTER
BRIGHTON
PEVENSEY
PORTSMOUTH
WORTHING
SHOREHAM
EASTBOURNE
WARMWELL AIRFIELD
BOURNEMOUTH
ISLE OF WIGHT
VENTNOR
WEYMOUTH
0
1
40
ENGLISH CHANNEL

MAP 6

throughout the night.

August sixteenth dawned bright and cheerful. Over seventeen hundred sorties were flown by the Luftwaffe that day as the pressure on Dowding's pilots was maintained. West Malling was again attacked, but fortunately this field was not one of Dowding's key bases. Tangmere, however, was, and it was assaulted while its squadrons were returning to refuel, with disastrous results. In this attack, an American volunteer pilot, Billy Fiske, was killed. Throughout England, the Luftwaffe continued to pound Fighter Command's airfields.

The next day gave a brief respite as weather conditions once more intervened to give the RAF a breather; but the following day was not so pleasant, as August 18 witnessed another all-out effort by the Luftwaffe. The crucial station at Biggin Hill was heavily attacked by a flight of bombers that came in low, under the radar. This was followed up by another raid at high altitude. Radar had given warning of the high altitude group, and when the low flight group arrived Biggin Hill's squadrons, circling above, waiting the arrival of the former, swooped down for the kill. Seven Dorniers from the low flight group and four from the later attack were lost.

Kenley was not so fortunate—six Hurricanes were destroyed on the ground and many buildings were damaged. The Luftwaffe left this field a blazing wreck. West Malling and Croydon also came in for their share of attention as the day was just warming up. Later, Croydon's turn came again and the field suffered heavily. It was an exhausting day for the RAF. All of Eleven Group's squadrons saw action and for the most part were constantly in the air.

Dowding meanwhile, found himself facing the dire need for replacement pilots. Thanks to Beaverbrook's efforts, replacement planes were readily available. Men to pilot them were not and the pilot shortage was beginning to tell. Therefore, Dowding besieged the Air Ministry with demands for replacements from Bomber Command and army Co-Op Command. After intense pressure from the head of Fighter Command, the Air Ministry gave way and fifty pilots were made available.

During the next week, the pressure subsided slightly. Adlertag, the great four-day offensive had failed to achieve the desired results. At his estate at Karinhall, Goering raged at his fighter pilots and blamed the failure of the effort and the heavy losses on them. He demanded a greater effort on their part. His two leading fighter pilots, Adolf Galland and Werner Molders, were thoroughly angered and when the Reichsmarshal asked the former for suggestions, Galland requested a squadron of Spitfires. This, of course, endeared him to Goering forever. Nevertheless, Goering did agree to withdraw the Stukas from the battle. These slow aircraft had proven to be merely cannon fodder for the British and had suffered dreadfully.

Unbeknown to Goering, Fighter Command was not in as good a shape as it appeared. In addition to the severe shortage of experienced pilots, by August 19 over three-quarters of its squadron commanders had either been withdrawn for rest, had been killed, or were languishing in hospitals recuperating from wounds.

Park, meanwhile, continued to revise his tactics to meet the current situation. He reemphasized his position to Eleven Group's flight controllers:

> We cannot afford to lose pilots . . . in the sea. Against these mass attacks dispatch a minimum of squadrons to engage enemy fighters. Our main objective is to engage the bombers.[17]

As squadron commander Peter Townsend so aptly put it, "Park had no intention of dancing to Goering's tune."

At Dowding's suggestion, Park ordered his controllers to ask Twelve Group to provide covering patrols for the fields at North Weald. Hornchurch, and Debden, when all of Eleven Group's squadrons were engaged.

The situation at Twelve Group was another can of worms that Dowding should not have had to be exposed to. As Eleven Group fought for its life, it appeared that Twelve Group was being forced to take a back seat. To Douglas Bader, the tenacious commander of 242 Squadron, this was intolerable. For days he had been raging at the lack of combat. Bader's zealousness and patriotism led him to question Park's and Dowding's tactics. He advocated that squadrons not be thrown into the fray in groups of one or two. Instead, Bader said, large formations or wings consisting of three or more squadrons should be hurled against the enemy, and those squadrons should come from Twelve Group. He proposed this tactic to his Group commander, Leigh-Mallory. History may show Bader in a bad light, but the worst that can be said for him is that he allowed his dedication, fighting spirit, and patriotism to stand in the way of good judgment. In all battles, there are conflicting ideas in strategy and tactics and Bader cannot be faulted for forwarding his own ideas. His bravery, ability as both pilot and commander, and courage were well known, but in his enthusiasm he was blinded and innocently allowed himself to be used by the devious Leigh-Mallory, whose feelings towards Dowding and Park were no secret. Schemers and intriguers are almost always clever and dangerous people and Leigh-Mallory was a master at the art of deviousness. However, in order for his schemes to succeed, he required the collaboration of someone higher in command with influence at the Air Ministry. Who that co-conspirator was will soon become evident.

On August 24, the battle resumed at the previous rate. Manston was hit by no fewer than four attacks. So severe was the resulting damage that the field was abandoned. In the interim, Kenley, Croydon, Biggin Hill, West Malling, Hornchurch, Rockford, Debden, Hawkhinge, and Lympne were all attacked heavily. Per Park's instructions, the controllers at Eleven Group asked Twelve Group to provide a patrol over North Weald. Twelve Group squadron never appeared and this field was left to its fate, suffering cruelly.

That night, a group of Luftwaffe bombers headed for the oil storage targets east of London, but lost their way and unloaded their bombs on the town of Cripplegate. Civilian casualties were high but their sacrifice may just have saved the country.

In retaliation, the next night Bomber Command dispatched a flight of eighty planes to attack Berlin.

The psychological effect on Hitler and Goering was out of proportion to the actual results achieved in way of physical damage.

On August 26, as the assault against Fighter Command's airfields continued, Eleven Group once again requested assistance from Leigh-Mallory's Group, this time to patrol the skies over Debden. Although a squadron was eventually dispatched from Duxford, only ten miles away, it arrived late and the unfortunate Debden airfield was hit by over one hundred bombs.

Dowding now found himself unable to rotate squadrons. So severe was the pressure applied by the Luftwaffe that the shortage of experienced pilots reached the critical stage. The pressure on Eleven Groups's fields continued without letup. On the thirtieth, Biggin Hill was again ravaged by low-level attacks that wrecked its installations, destroyed most of its structures, and caused heavy casualties among the support personnel. The beleaguered field was finally forced to briefly suspend operations.

Squadron Leader Peter Townsend in his magnificent chronicle, *Duel of Eagles*, describes August 30 as the fiercest day of the entire battle. Pilot Officer Tom Gleave of 253 Squadron accounted for four of the enemy himself in one sortie and one more in another before being shot down himself and badly wounded the next day. 56 Squadron alone flew no less than seven sorties on this day alone.

The next day, Biggin Hill was back in operation but it was only for a brief period of time. On the first day of September the field was again the target of heavy German attacks and for the seventh time in three days, bombs rained down on it. The attack destroyed the operations room, eliminating the field's effectiveness.

Biggin Hill was not alone in the ordeal. During the three day period Manston, Hawkhinge, and Lympne received their share of attention from the Luftwaffe and nearly suffered the same fate as Biggin Hill, coming close to total annihilation.

One can but imagine what the pilots of Eleven Group were going through during this time. As their fields were literally blasted out from underneath them, all squadrons were constantly in the air valiantly trying to hold off wave after wave of enemy attacks.

Day after day Luftwaffe formations gathered over France and were picked up by radar. After flying over these stations they were picked up in turn by ground observers as they split into smaller groups and continued the onslaught against the airfields. When it appeared that the forward fields were all but destroyed the Luftwaffe bombers roamed inland and subjected the rear fields to the horror of their fury. Flying from North Weald, 310 Squadron comprised of free Czechs broke one attack aimed at Duxford on September 3, but their success was the exception rather than the rule. The frequency and fury of the German attacks caused Park and Dowding to feel that a few more days of sustained attacks would be all that was needed to effectively eliminate Fighter Command. Then, with victory in sight, the German attacks against the airfields ceased abruptly. Goering and Hitler had committed a fatal blunder. As their adversary stood exhausted and all but defeated, the

Luftwaffe received orders to shift the emphasis of the attacks to London in retaliation for Bomber Command's earlier raid on Berlin on August 25.

Not only was Park's manpower and leadership severely depleted, he was now obliged to order those squadrons at North Weald, Debden, and Hornchurch to remain on patrol over their fields until units from Twelve Group arrived to relieve them. This order had its foundation in Leigh-Mallory's apparent reluctance to provide adequate and timely support. The besieged Park was now ready to pull out all stops and involve Twelve Group heavily. It was not a concession made out of the spirit of harmony but one of absolute necessity.

Reichsmarshal Hermann Goering himself arrived at Cape Gris Nez during the first week in September and gazed across at England as the Luftwaffe mounted a heavy attack. Wave after wave of bombers circled above their airfields awaiting the fighter escort. These formations were observed by the British radar stations and the information was passed along to Eleven Group whose controllers made preparations to defend Hawkhinge. As the German formations swept across the English Channel the plotters were amazed to find that the enemy was making for London. The first wave was relatively unmolested as they made their bomb runs over the city, but by the time their bomb bay doors were open, Fighter Command had recovered their wits. Enroute home, the Luftwaffe flight was severely mauled by 303 Polish Squadron. As the day progressed, the Luftwaffe continued to pound targets in and around London, but the RAF was waiting for those waves that followed the first. By the end of the day virtually all of Eleven Group's squadrons, as well as a handful from Twelve Group, had participated in the defense. Bader's big wing was also ordered into the air but was unable to assemble in time to intervene.

The next day was relatively quiet as the Londoners began to recover from the shock and ask what had gone wrong. Where were the defenders? Why had they been left to the mercy of the Hun? These questions were being asked throughout Fighter Command as well. The answer was relatively simple. Who had ever expected the Germans to shift their attention when victory was but a hairs breadth away. The air controllers, rightly anticipating yet another day of attacks against the airfields, simply directed the RAF squadrons to patrol the threatened areas in pairs. Only when the bombs began to fall on London did the controllers recognize their error. Subsequent German attacks were met head on but not until after London suffered dreadfully.

The next day the RAF was ready for the Luftwaffe. Park placed as many of his squadrons as was practical at the forward airfields. As a force of more than one hundred bombers swept over the coast no less than nine squadrons rose to accept the challenge. In the face of determined Fighter Command attacks, the bomber force broke formation, scattered their bombs over Canterbury, and lit out for home. A second heavily escorted attack also failed to reach its objective—the London docks. Before the fight reached its peak Ten and Twelve Groups were called upon for assistance. Leigh-Mallory authorized Bader's big wing to try again. This flight was requested to provide cover for the airfields at North Weald and Hornchurch. But the impetuous Bader, in what can only be construed as direct disobedience of orders, eager for action, left these fields unprotected and led his flight against the retreating bombers with a large measure of success. At day's end, the tally read twenty-eight German planes downed to nineteen for the RAF.

Back at his home field Bader continued to carry on with the tactics of Fighter Command. In a conversation with his commander, the impulsive squadron commander informed Leigh-Mallory that the big wing should be formed immediately upon receipt of information that the Luftwaffe was forming over France. It then could attack the bomber swarms while Eleven Group harassed the retreating Germans. An admirable idea indeed but where would the big wing intercept the incoming bombers? Only after the Germans crossed the coast was their final destination apparent. By then, it would be too late to intercept from the distant airfields at Twelve Group. Nevertheless, Leigh-Mallory continued to encourage Bader and informed him that the "right people" would be made aware of the latter's proposals and success.

On September 10, Hilter announced that he would wait another four days before making up his mind about Sea Lion, but his disenchantment with Goering's boasts was more and more in evidence. In turn, Goering promised results. He then turned on his fighter commanders and berated them for a lack of enthusiasm, informing them that responsibility for failure was entirely their's. The fighter pilots were quite naturally bitter at this turn of events for they felt that they had fought bravely against a determined and highly skilled foe. Once more they clamored for Goering to allow them more freedom of maneuver instead of tying their hands as nursemaids for the slow, ineffective bombers.

For the next four days London remained the focus of attention and the city was badly mauled. Despite an all-out effort of all three fighter groups, a large number of bombers still managed to get through and unload their bombs. Kesselring too was pulling out all stops and every available plane was hurled against England.

Sunday morning, September 15, dawned quiet and sunny, a typical warm, late summer English day. At mid-morning the air controllers at Eleven Group were astonished as Winston Churchill and his wife strolled into their domain at Uxbridge. Keith Park informed the Prime Minister that all was relatively serene at the moment and offered Churchill a tour of the installation. Shortly, however, the station began to hum with activity as a large assembly of enemy planes was reported over France. It took less than an hour for this assemblage to join up and cross the Channel. Acting under Park's personal direction, Eleven Group controllers ordered twelve squadrons up in groups of two, pairing Spitfire squadrons with each other and Hurricane squadrons likewise.

Meanwhile, five squadrons under Bader were forming in the skies above Twelve Group. The large wing resembled a veritable United Nations with Canadians, Poles, and Czechs teamed with a pair of English squadrons.

As the Luftwaffe entered the skies above England they were attacked by the RAF squadrons and harassed all the way to the target. The hard pressed Eleven Group called for help from its two neighbors and Ten Group dispatched three squadrons while Bader's "Duxford Wing" set flight for London. Thanks to Park's tactics, most of the attacks were broken up and many of the bombers failed to reach their target. But the best was yet to come. As the German attacks were scattered and the bombers turned for home, Bader's wing waded in sixty strong and chased the enemy out over the Channel. Because of difficulties in maintaining formation, the big wing attack failed to achieve the predicted spectacular results. The sight of this mass of planes attacking did though have a negative effect on the Luftwaffe pilots. If Fighter Command was truly on its last leg how could this many planes be available to intercept incoming attacks?

As the crescendo of battle reached its peak, Churchill, fascinated by the amount of lights lit on the control panels, asked Park where were the reserves. A glance at the board indicated that all squadrons were involved and Park's answer was that no reserves were available. Suitably alarmed and impressed, Churchill departed.

Although most of the attack had been beaten off, some bombers managed to get through and unload their deadly cargoes on the heart of London. One bomb actually fell in the grounds of Buckingham Palace. As morning turned to afternoon, the attacks continued and Park's squadrons, attacking in pairs, exacted a heavy toll on the enemy, but for the most part, the later German attacks lacked the determination of those earlier in the day. With the onset of darkness, however, the fires from the bombed out areas of London attracted yet another Luftwaffe attack that caused considerable casualties since the RAF was powerless to oppose the enemy at night. The spectre of the lack of night fighter tactics continued to haunt Dowding.

Though the damage to London had been heavy and Fighter Command was reeling from losses and exhaustion, September 15 marked the beginning of the end. Faced with the obvious fact that Fighter Command was still able to contest any German effort, Hitler called off Sea Lion and admitted that Goering and the Luftwaffe had failed. Faced with this, the Luftwaffe attacks continued but in a much watered down manner. The attacks on London continued around the clock marking the beginning of "the Blitz," but for all intents and purposes, the steam had gone out of the Luftwaffe.

Kesselring later tried the tactic of arming ME 109s with bombs and using them to attack RAF factories. But, although heavy damage resulted from some of these raids, the spirit of the English remained unbroken.

Another tactic attempted by the Luftwaffe was to have the bombers fly high, at altitudes that allowed them to bomb relatively unhindered. Eventually, however, the ratio of Luftwaffe losses to that of the RAF increased to a point that was totally unacceptable to the Germans and they reverted to strictly attacking at night. Overall, in three months, the vaunted Luftwaffe lost over twenty-five percent of its effective strength.

Dowding's critics were not silenced by the spectacular victory gained by Fighter Command. If anything, now that the crisis was past and more time was available, their criticism increased in tempo.

After pouring over the daily records of the fighting and thoroughly reviewing the entire battle, Dowding made up his mind by mid-October to get rid of Leigh-Mallory. Little did he realize what fate had in store for him.

On October 17, Dowding and Park were summoned to the Air Ministry to discuss tactics. Johnnie Johnson has called this meeting the "meeting of the bloody marshals." Present at the meeting besides Park and Dowding were Newell, Sir Charles Portal (Newell's designated successor) and Leigh-Mallory. The deputy chief of air staff, Sholto Douglas, presided over the gathering. Incredibly, at this meeting of senior air marshals, Douglas Bader was present with his chief. Just as incredible was the conspicuous absence of Saul and Brand, neither of whom had been invited. It was a setup.

Douglas began by praising both Leigh-Mallory and Park for their theories and elaborated on the good points of each. Dowding, on the other hand, was taken to task for his failure to promote better relationships between Eleven and Twelve Groups. Soon Bader was given the floor and allowed to expand on his theories of the big wing versus the tactics used by Park and encouraged by Dowding. The chief of Fighter Command was appalled that so junior an officer was allowed to attend the meeting and heap criticism on his commander in chief.

Park was so taken back by the affrontery of it all that he was shocked into silence. Only after the meeting adjourned did he comment that it appeared as if Douglas had acted as public prosecutor. Just as obvious was the fact that when Leigh-Mallory had kept repeating his promises to Bader about bringing affairs to the attention of someone in high places, this someone was Douglas, who acted as co-conspirator. In his memoirs, *Combat and Command*, Douglas vehemently denies the existence of any conspiracy, but at the time of their writing Leigh-Mallory was dead and unable to admit to anything.

The controversy over the big wing had now put Leigh-Mallory and his accomplice, Douglas, firmly in the driver's seat. As for Bader, his part was simply as a tool used by Leigh-Mallory to achieve his avowed goal of seeing Dowding destroyed. Douglas Bader cannot be faulted for championing his own theories, many men have done it throughout history. His only crime is that he played right into Leigh-Mallory's hands and allowed himself to be used.

The use of big wings was an excellent concept had circumstances favored their use. They would kill more of the enemy but the amount of time it took for them to make formation would have allowed the enemy to get through. Therefore, only after the attackers had unloaded their bombs over the target could they be successfully engaged while enroute home. Dowding's comment on the subject was:

> If big wings had been used at this time, many more bombers would have reached their target without opposition.[18]

Park simply stated:

> Had I tried to adopt Bader's theories of the big wing, I would have lost the Battle of Britain.[19]

What Dowding overlooked in his own defense was the fact that when Leigh-Mallory's Twelve Group area was attacked, squadrons were scrambled in individual groups, as there was not enough time to form a wing. This was precisely Park's dilemma. Douglas and Leigh-Mallory held that the fact that the enemy bombers were allowed to get through was immaterial, as the only thing that counted was the number of enemy planes destroyed. This, they advocated, was paramount to all other considerations. Obviously they were more interested in using statistics to further their own interests than they were in preventing casualties to the English populace. The citizens of London would have been gladdened by their stand.

Furthermore, had Park sent big wings aloft, he would have played right into Goering's hands from the outset. All along it was the German intent to lure the RAF into the air where it could be destroyed. Park simply refused to take the bait.

The reproof for not seeing to it that relationships between groups was better, Dowding admits:

> This is a point that must not be ignored. I might have been right or I might have been wrong in doing that but I did not want to control completely the tactical work of the Groups. That was mainly because I appreciated that different situations arose in different groups and I was

> most reluctant to give any of the Group Commanders daily orders about the tactics that were to be employed. I gave general directives, which I expected them to follow and in some ways, I suppose, it could be said that I gave them too much rope.[20]

Park's remarks were more damning to his neighbor.

> Thanks to the friendly cooperation afforded by Ten Group they are always prepared to detail two to four squadrons to engage from the west, mass attacks.
>
> up to date Twelve Group . . . have not shown the same desire to cooperate by dispatching their squadrons to the places requested . . . When Twelve Group offered assistance and were requested by us to patrol our aerodromes, their squadrons did not in fact patrol over our aerodromes.[21]

Yet Park failed to call this to the attention of Dowding so the latter was powerless to intervene.

As for Park's tactics, the fighter pilots of Eleven Group, for the most part, felt that perhaps bigger wings were called for. Bob Tuck and others have attested to this. But they unanimously agree that the size of the wings proposed by Bader was totally impractical. When developments allowed Park to alter his tactics, he adopted the two squadron wing which his pilots acclaimed.

Unperturbed by the controversy around him, Dowding went with the business of operating Fighter Command. Foremost among his concerns was the increased Luftwaffe activity at night and how to counter it. Then, on November 17, he received a call from the secretary of state for air ordering him to relinquish command immediately. When Dowding asked for clarification of the term immediately, he was told that it meant the very next day. He was relieved as head of Fighter Command and his services were rudely dispensed with early in the young war. Into his shoes at Fighter Command stepped none other than Sholto Douglas himself.

It was clear that Dowding's passing foretold that Park's days were numbered as well. Sure enough, shortly thereafter Douglas transferred the proud New Zealander to command a training group and replaced him with Leigh-Mallory who have coveted command of Eleven Group for so long.

Dowding's final message to his pilots was filled with admiration and devotion. It read:

> My Dear Fighter Boys:
>
> In sending you this last message I wish I could say all that is in my heart.
>
> I cannot hope to surpass the simple eloquence of the Prime Minister's words; 'Never before has so much been owed by so many to so few.' That debt remains and will increase. In saying goodbye to you I want you to know how continually you have been in my thoughts, and that, though our direct connection may be severed, I may yet be able to help you in your gallant fight.
>
> Goodbye to you and God Bless you all.[22]

To the day, these same pilots are stunned and bitter over the shabby treatment accorded their brilliant leader. The aces of Fighter Command have responded accordingly.

Ginger Lacy:

> We were tired, and frightened, and under strength, but we were never lacking in morale, and certainly not over the fact that we were not using big wings. Far from morale being affected by the lack of big wings, with the job we had to do in Eleven Group, we preferred to be without them.[23]

Al Deere:

> I hold that Bader's wing concept was wrong. I know that most wing leaders agree with me, and certainly those who had the benefit of later experience.[24]

But perhaps Johnnie Johnson summed it up best when he said that Dowding and Park won the Battle of Britain but lost the battle of words that followed.

Unlike other victorious English commanders, Dowding was not immediately rewarded with high office or recognition by a grateful royalty. Not until a few years later were his feats recognized by elevation to the peerage. The one and only goal he sought was denied him, the rank of marshal of the RAF, while his contemporaries and critics alike reached this plateau.

In short, for winning the most significant battle of the young conflict and perhaps of the entire war, he was treated very badly at best. Even Winston Churchill, who denied forehand knowledge of Dowding's sacking was duly impressed by the effort put forth by Fighter Command, Dowding's creation. His visit to Park's command on September 15 had visibly moved him and caused him shortly thereafter to compose his famous speech about the debt of so many to so few. The Prime Minister though, prided himself on keeping abreast of every situation and could not have been unaware of Dowding's fate. He simply elected to ignore it.

Dowding's retirement was postponed for another year as the Air Ministry requested his assistance in studying manpower problems; but he never again held active command. Finally, in 1942, he retired permanently. A year later, an apologetic Prime Minister and a grateful English public witnessed Dowding's elevation to the peerage with the title of Baron.

Of the leading personalities whose careers were entwined with Dowding's during the Battle of Britain, Douglas Bader was later shot down over France and after a series of unsuccessful escape attempts, confined in Colditz Castle for the duration of the war. Sholto Douglas later commanded the RAF in the Middle East and afterwards, Coastal Command. After the war he became an airline executive and died in 1969. Douglas attained the rank of marshal of the RAF and himself was elevated to the peerage as Lord Douglas of Kirtleside.

Keith Park later commanded the air forces at Malta (where he used the same small wing tactic to great success) and then in South East Asia before retiring to New Zealand in 1946 as air chief marshal.

As for Dowding's chief antagonist, Leigh-Mallory, he eventually achieved his cherished goal and was appointed head of Fighter Command. He was later put in charge of the air forces for the Normandy Invasion as air chief marshal but perished in a plane crash in France enroute to take command of the air forces in South East Asia. Ironically, this vacant position was then filled by Keith Park.

Dowding himself spent his retirement years pursuing hobbies of interest. He was a dedicated member of the Battle of Britain Fighter Association formed by his pilots and was elected that organization's first president. In 1970, at the age of 88, Lord Dowding passed away peacefully.

Throughout history, there had been few events to rival the dismissal of Dowding. And, since that time, there have been virtually no occasions when the author of so spectacular a victory has been so poorly rewarded. Indeed, Dowding's treatment seems without parallel in the annals of military history. His achievements and the treatment accorded him was best expressed by one of his pilots, Ginger Lacy:

> The treatment he received after the battle still baffles me. I cannot understand how the authorities were able to talk about the fate of civilisation hanging on the outcome of the Battle of Britain and yet discard the victor. Where would we have been if Stuffy had lost the battle?[25]

Field Marshal Sir Claude Auchinleck

Chapter 3

At the time of the writing of this chapter, the ninety-six-year-old warrior, Claude Auchinleck, ("the Auk"), still walks the face of the earth. Whether he will still be among us at the time of publication only God knows. One thing, however, will always be with us when the great commander passes on to his well-deserved reward—his reputation as one of England's greatest and most innovative commanders of the Second World War.

Claude John Eyre Auchinleck was born in Aldershot on June 21, 1884, the eldest child of Lt. Col. John Claude Alexander Auchinleck and Mary Eleanor Eyre. The Auchinlecks traced their roots back to thirteenth century Scotland. The military life was a family tradition. Thus Auchinleck's father entered the army where he saw action in the Indian Sepoy Mutiny of 1857 and the Second Afghan of 1878-80. When young Claude was a year old, Colonel Auchinleck moved his family from Aldershot to India where he commanded the Royal Horse Artillery batteries at Bangalore. Thus Claude John's first remembrances were of India and the military.

While campaigning in the jungles of Burma during the Third Burmese War, the elder Auchinleck developed anemia and became seriously ill necessitating his premature retirement from the army in 1890. The family returned to England where in December of 1892 he died when Claude John was only eight years old. His mother thus became the dominating influence in his life.

Claude attended the Dame school in Sothsea, but in 1894 switched to Crowthorne, which traditionally acted as a military preparatory school for future army officers. It boasted Wellington of Waterloo fame as its most prestigious graduate.

A military career was the only one Claude desired to pursue. "I never had any other career in mind," he once stated. In 1896 he entered Wellington for six years of schooling and training. Though above average in history, geography, English and theology, he struggled with mathematics and was known for his quiet demeanor. Yet he possessed a sense of humor. Early in life he gave the impression of a modest individual lacking any tendency towards arrogance or personal glory and renown, traits that remained with him.

While at Wellington he was faced with the decision whether to join the artillery, infantry, or cavalry; the British or Indian army. His poor aptitude in mathematics ruled against the artillery and so his choice fell on the infantry. His next step was to enter Sandhurst which he did in January, 1902, upon passing an examination aimed at a vacancy in the Indian Army's infantry. The course at Sandhurst lasted one year. While there he managed to keep pretty much to himself, not associating with fellow students who were destined for the prestigious regiments in the British army. The arrogant attitude of those destined for these regiments towards those in the Indian army was a perpetual problem of the British system of military training and one that would haunt Auchinleck for the balance of his military career. He graduated in the eighties out of a total of three hundred and sixty cadets.

In March, 1903, the bright eighteen-year-old newly commissioned lieutenant boarded the line Britannia and set sail for India where he was to join the Indian army and begin a forty-five-year relationship filled with devotion and love. Auchinleck quickly felt at home in the Indian regiment to which he was assigned. In Roger Parkinson's biography on "the Auk," he explains the close-knit relationship which was formed between a recruit and his regiment in the Indian army.

> Service in India inspired deep devotion on the part of both British officers and Indian troops . . . the individual regiment was considered to be home, with attitudes towards this unit resembling those directed at a close knit family. The Indian recruit gave whole-hearted and often almost blind obedience to the regiment: disloyalty was considered the worst of all possible offences; it became a matter of honour to be a good soldier.[1]

From its officers to its newest recruits, a deep camaraderie was developed among the men. Auchinleck has said, "I think with me and with most of us the feeling was especially in the Indian Army that you were responsible for these chaps, these men under you, and that you had to see they got the best that could be given them." With his mild, humane disposition Claude found himself right at home in this army. He proved to be highly concerned for his men, always mindful of their welfare, and heedful that he was dealing with human beings and not inanimate statistics.

Upon arrival in India, he was first assigned to a British regiment attached to the Indian army. Then, in April of 1904 he joined the Sixty-second Punjabis. Being British in the Indian army offered the young lieutenant many opportunities for advancement and leadership not readily available to those in British regiments. From 1904 to 1914 he served in many and varied places; the mountains of Tibet and Sikkim, the jungles of Assam, again in the idyllic land of Sikkim, and then in the holy city of Benares on the sacred Ganges River, where Auchinleck was exposed to the many rites and rituals associated with the Hindu faith. He remained in Benares until 1912.

During the years in India he developed those traits that were to remain with him for his whole life. He fostered loyalty. His troops trusted him and would go to great lengths for him. The feeling was mutual, for Auchinleck cared for and respected his men, forming many close and endearing relationships. Though his manner was not overpowering his stature was straight and his appearance commanded respect. But it was not his appearance alone that earned him the respect of his men, it was his personality. He was honest and open, perhaps too much so and never sought to advance himself for his own sake.

While serving in India and enjoying the experience thoroughly, war clouds hovered over Europe as ancient hatreds and entangling alliances burst forth in an orgy of hate. On August 3, 1914, Britain declared war on Germany after the German horde violated the neutrality of Belgium in its wide sweep towards France. Abruptly, Auchinleck's idyllic years came to an end. Capt. Claude Auchinleck braced himself for the coming fury as the Sixty-second Punjabis boarded ship in October and set sail for the war.

The original destination of the regiment was the freshly dug trenches of France, but in the interim, the war broadened as Turkey joined the Central Powers of Germany and Austria-Hungary in the war. Shortly after joining hostilities, Turkey bombarded the Russian ports of Odessa and Sevastapol on the Black Sea. This presented England with a grave threat to the Suez Canal, her lifeline to India. Because of these new developments, the Sixty-second Punjabis were spared the trenches of the western front and were diverted to the deserts of the Middle East.

Upon disembarking, Auchinleck found his assignment to be the protection of the Suez Canal. His first action came on February 3, 1915, as twenty-two thousand Turkish troops approached the canal from both the Sinai and the sea. The fighting was as brutal as anything Europe had to offer but Auchinleck and his men gave a credible showing in their first engagement. The British managed to hold the Turks despite persistent energetic attacks. Little did the Auk realize that in less than thirty years he would again find himself defending the very same canal.

In July, the Sixty-second Punjabis were transferred to Aden on the Arabian Peninsula. While there two major campaigns were attempted against the Turks, one at Gallipoli and another in Mesopotamia. Gallipoli proved to be a major disaster, while in Mesopotamia, Baghdad was nearly captured. Despite some initial success, the British found themselves in dire straits by December of 1915. At Kut, over ten thousand were besieged and were reduced to only a sixty-day food supply and inadequate medical facilities. The Sixty-second was among the relief forces dispatched to help relieve the trapped forces at Kut. They arrived from Aden during the closing days of December.

Sailing by paddle steamer, Auchinleck's regiment proceeded up the ancient Tigris River and on January 7 was sent into the attack. The terrain being contested was featureless and the tactic employed was the costly frontal attack against superior enemy defensive positions. Casualties were high as the British continued this costly type of attack. While casualties mounted among the relief forces, the situation in Kut deteriorated at an alarming rate.

The campaign to relieve the town became a long, drawn out, confused campaign lacking in proper direction from top authorities. Lack of leadership was not the only difficulty. The natural elements were horrendous, characterized by cold, mud, beetles, slugs, scorpions and lice. Finally, after months of exhausting, fruitless, and wasteful battles, the besieged forces at Kut negotiated a surrender. The capitulation took place on April 26, 1916. Thirty thousand casualties was the cost, twenty-three thousand among the relief forces alone. The Sixty-second Punjabis had lost five hundred and sixty men but Auchinleck had learned what not to do, a lesson he would never forget.

By December, the British and Indian troops, after months of rest and replenishment, were ready to move again against the Turks. The Sixty-second moved into combat towards the end of January, 1917. In February Auchinleck was named temporary regimental commander. As its new leader he led his forces forward on its final thrust in the renewed offensive against the enemy holding Kut. The method of attack was again the wasteful frontal attack. Auchinleck had no choice but to attack in that manner but he modified the advance. He ordered his men to attack in section single file; five men, one behind the other, with wide gaps in between the groups of five. The usual method of attack was a long extended line of waves of men. As the rapid firing machine guns tore into the ranks of the attacking regiments, the Sixty-second Punjabis suffered fewer casualties while still accomplishing its assigned task. Regiments to its right and left suffered fifty percent casualties or more; not so the Sixty-second.

By March 11, Kut had fallen and Auchinleck relinquished temporary command two days later. That summer Auchinleck became brigade major to the Fifty-second Brigade, the group with which he would remain until the end of the war. On November 2, 1918, Turkey sued for an armistice and the Auk's war career ended, while his unit was actively engaging the enemy in the Kurdustan Mountains.

Auchinleck learned many valuable lessons during the First World War from the mistakes of his commanders, who foolishly wasted lives in useless offensives such as Kut. He also observed that clear cut orders and a strong command were prerequisites for success. When these were lacking, confusion in the higher ranks of command usually resulted, bringing with it wasted efforts and total disorder. He was also upset with the wretched conditions fought under and was convinced that a commander must care for his men if the morale and fighting pitch of the ranks were to remain sharp.

> From that time forward Auchinleck would therefore cling to two strong principles . . . a commander in the field . . . has got to think of the men under him and avoid if possible unnecessary casualties to them without an adequate result . . . Secondly, subordinate commanders should not be pestered from above.[2]

Auchinleck became a firm believer in the doctrine that if you give a man a job to do, then let him do it. Do not interfere. In later years he clung tenaciously to this method of command. Thus Auchinleck moved into peacetime soldiering, but the lessons of war became an integral part of his makeup.

With war's end, Auchinleck, now a major, remained in the Middle East as a general staff officer for a year. In August of 1919, he was promoted to lieutenant colonel.

Newly promoted, Auchinleck sailed to India where he was offered a vacancy at the Staff College at Quetta, the equivalent of the Camberly Staff College in England. Auchinleck claimed that what he learned at Quetta was as much and just as good as at Camberly. However, those in the British army looked down their noses at those who went to Quetta. The British versus Indian army problem again.

While on leave in France late in 1920, the thirty-six-year-old Auchinleck married. Though deeply in love, the years of strain and long absences during the Second World War eventually brought the marriage to a sad divorce.

Upon returning to India he established his household in Simla and spent four years as deputy assistant quartermaster general. The Auchinlecks went home on leave in 1926 and while there the officer was notified that he was to attend the Imperial Defense College for a one year course in advanced war studies. This was indeed a very high honor but not once did Auchinleck boast about it. At the Imperial Defense College he came into contact and formed a great friendship with the chief instructor, John Dill, later to become chief of the Imperial General Staff during the dark days of 1940. Also attending the course was Alan Brooke, Dill's eventual successor.

In 1928, Auchinleck found himself back in India where he rejoined his regiment and by the end of year was appointed its commander.

Early in 1930 he returned to Quetta where he became chief instructor of the junior division with the rank of full colonel. He left there late in the same year, and following a brief home leave, was given command of a brigade in Peshawar. Under his command, the brigade saw limited action against the Mohmand tribesmen. For his role in this brief campaign he was named Companion of the Bath.

In 1935, a more serious uprising broke out and Auchinleck was chosen to lead his brigade into the mountains to counteract the rebels. During this campaign he worked in close association with another brigade, the Nowshera, under the able command of Harold Alexander. The two quickly became close friends.

In joint action, Alexander and Auchinleck defeated the insurgent tribesmen, and two commanders received the coveted Commander of the Star of India decoration. Both were also promoted to the rank of major general but Alexander left India while Auchinleck, after another brief home leave, returned there as deputy chief of the General Staff. At this time he met yet another officer who would remain his lifelong friend, Col. Eric Dorman-Smith, who was serving as director of military training. Dorman-Smith later served Auchinleck during World War II only to fall, along with his chief, in the August purge of the Middle East Command.

While deputy chief of the General Staff, Auchinleck became concerned with the growing tension in Europe and its potential effect upon India and the Indian army. He realized the need to expand and modernize the army to meet any possible demands that a future war could place on the Empire. As Hitler ranted and raged, the needs of the Empire consumed the Auk. In 1939, he returned to England to participate in a higher command course. Late in the spring he and his wife traveled to England and then on to America. When he returned to Scotland in August, the dark shadow of war hovered over Britain. In late August he received orders to report to Edinburgh on September 3. Meanwhile the German blitzkreig was unleashed against Poland with German panzers cutting through the Polish ranks as easily as knife cuts through butter. Auchinleck arrived in Edinburgh and to his surprise found the hotel crammed with Indian army officers. All were being recalled to their regiments. On the morning of September 3, they boarded the Canadian Pacific liner, *Duchess of Bedford*, when the fateful words of Neville Chamberlain were heard over the radio announcing Britain's declaration of war.

When he reached Bombay at the beginning of October, Auchinleck began preparing the Third Indian Division for war. Destiny, however, called Auchinleck for another assignment. Within three months of his return to India he was ordered back to England.

By the time he could complete the return passage in January, 1940, the quick German conquest of Poland was already history, the Finns and the Soviets were locked in a devastating Winter War, and the British and French forces had settled in on the quiet western front. He was ordered to raise, train, and take command of the British IV Corps. Auchinleck immediately faced two major problems, time and background. He was told to have the Corps ready to move to France by June, a short amount of time to train a completely green corps. The second problem proved to be his Indian army background. His total experience had been with this army but he now found himself in command of a purely British corps. Prejudice runs deep and the snobbery of British army divisions towards their counterparts in the Indian army was a live issue. Nevertheless, Auchinleck went to work ingratiating himself with the divisions in his corps.

IV Corps was comprised of territorial troops rather

than regular soldiers and Auchinleck soon found that they were woefully unprepared for war. He immediately initiated urgent programs to wield his forces into fighting shape in short order. Lack of training facilities however, proved a severe handicap.

While the western front remained quiescent, events in the far north afforded the British an opportunity of striking a blow at the all-important German iron ore supply. Sweden was a major producer of this ore and Germany was the prime beneficiary. The iron ore was sent from Sweden via the Norwegian port of Narvik. "Strike while the iron is hot," declared Winston Churchill, the bellicose first Lord of the Admiralty. Using the pretext of sending aid to the Finns in their uneven struggle against the Soviets, Narvik, he argued, could be seized thus cutting off Germany's supply of iron ore and drastically reducing its armament output. Two birds could be killed with one stonc. Unfortunately for the British and French, Finland capitulated on March 12, one day before the Allies were ready to move. Therefore the pretext for occupying Narvik was gone.

In the interim, the Germans hatched their own plans. The previous December, Admiral Raeder, commander in chief of the German navy introduced Vidkun Quisling, head of the Nazi Party in Norway, to Adolf Hitler. Quisling told the Fuhrer that he could deliver Norway to Germany. Hitler was attentive but brushed off Quisling's offer. However, in February, the British violated Norwegian neutrality when the destroyer HMS *Cossack* under Capt. Philip Vian seized the German ship *Altmark* in Norwegian territorial waters. The ship had been carrying merchant seaman prisoners captured by the German Pocket Battleship, *Adm. Graf Spee.* Hitler was quickly alerted to the danger from the north and realized that he had to do something about it. Thus, he ordered plans drawn up for the invasion of Norway and Denmark as well.

With the surrender of Finland, Chamberlain hesitated about sending forces to Narvik. Instead, he ordered the mining of Norwegian waters. This operation commenced on April 8. The very next day the Germans struck at Denmark and Norway. By evening, Copenhagen, Oslo, Bergen, Trondheim and Narvik were occupied, Denmark had capitulated, and Norwegian forces were scattered.

The War Cabinet in London ordered immediate intervention. Those troops originally earmarked for Finland were therefore dispatched to Norway. From the beginning, the campaign was a muddled affair, lacking in organization and essential equipment. The forces found themselves deficient in aircraft, antiaircraft guns, antitank guns, tanks, transport; and most important, training.

Meanwhile, Auchinleck was still preparing his corps for its initiation into combat. He flew to France to inspect the area his command was to occupy in June. While there, he met with his old friends, John Dill, Alan Brooke, and Lord Gort. When he returned to England, he found that Dill had also returned to assume the position of vice chief of the Imperial General Staff. With Dill in such a lofty position, Auchinleck could expect to find his career moving upward.

On Sunday, April 28, during a high level meeting

of the War Cabinet, a decision was made to send Auchinleck to Norway to command all the troops in northern Norway. Late that same night he was called to the room of the chief of the Imperial General Staff, General William Ironside who proceeded to inform him that he would depart with part of his IV Corps posthaste.

Auchinleck immediately plunged himself into the study of the country. As maps were unavailable, he was reduced to using tourist guides. While Auchinleck readied himself, the Allied forces in Norway were suffering one reverse after another as the Germans consolidated their hold on more and more Norwegian soil.

Narvik was the main British objective. Although Auchinleck felt that a port further south should be the objective, the British chiefs were adamant that British prestige be restored, and so Narvik was to be wrested from the Germans.

On May 6, Auchinleck and his staff traveled to Scotland and early the next morning set sail for Norway. While on the high seas, word was received that the Phoney War had abruptly ended with German mechanized forces crashing through the Low Countries. Word was also forthcoming that Neville Chamberlain had resigned as Prime Minister and that the first sea lord, Winston Churchill, had been named in his place.

Auchinleck realized that his situation was now made doubly difficult. Thanks to the German attack threatening France, he could not reasonably expect reserves for the forces in Norway. On the morning of May 11, Auchinleck reached Harstad, Norway, and reported to General Mackesey's headquarters. The general informed the Auk about the difficulties of waging war in Norway. Next, he made contact with Admiral Lord Cork where he was appraised of the naval preparations.

Assuming command in the midst of an already existing crisis is not the easiest task for any commander. Auchinleck approached the job with all the determination and expertise he possessed. The task was hectic, frustrating, and dangerous, but he attempted to consolidate the existing position around Narvik. The difficulties were enormous. The Germans dominated the sky, the British antiaircraft defense was inadequate, and German ground troops were pressing hard from the south. Auchinleck knew that reinforcements from England were necessary if he was to fulfill his basic assignment of defending northern Norway. Instead, because of the crisis in France, his strength was eroded. It was truly a baffling situation. A stiff message was sent to Churchill detailing the plight of the forces in Norway and their ability to defend it.

The Defence Committee of the War Cabinet received a message from Churchill on May 21 regarding the possibility of withdrawing all forces from Norway. The committee considered the proposal and, on May 24, informed Lord Cork that, in view of the developments on the western front, the evacuation of Norway would commence as soon as possible. Auchinleck received the word on May 25. The message stated that the whole of northern Norway was to be evacuated since the men and material were urgently required for the defense of the United Kingdom.

However, they left Cork and Auchinleck free to decide whether Narvik should be taken before evacuating the forces. It was agreed to proceed with the planned assault. Auchinleck explained why:

> We simply had to make a plan to get the troops out without letting the Germans know that we were doing it to begin with. So we went ahead and captured Narvik.[3]

He realized the danger involved in the evacuation. If the Germans could be convinced that the British were there to stay, perhaps they would not take notice of the preparations for total evacuation.

The attack on Narvik commenced in the late evening of May 27. By 4:00 A.M. the next day, the first wave of troops were moving toward the town. Fierce fighting ensued and by late evening the Narvik peninsula had been cleared. The shame of it all was that the whole attack was but a diversion. As such, it was successful. Even the Norwegians themselves, who cheered the liberation of Narvik, were convinced that the British were there to stay. The cheers turned bitter shortly afterward. When the Norwegian government and High Command learned the truth, they showed their obvious disappointment but loyally continued to cooperate.

The evacuation began on June 3 and continued smoothly. The Narvik deception had paid huge dividends and the Germans were caught off guard.

Auchinleck waited until the last unit boarded ship before he embarked on the four-day passage to Scotland. Some tense moments occurred as the convoy accidentally came dangerously near two German battle cruisers, *Gneisenau* and *Scharnhorst*, which were heading for Narvik to take part in operations against the Allied forces still believed to be in possession of that port city. Anxious moments occurred as the British lost a number of ships, among them two destroyers, the *Aden* and *Acasta* and the aircraft carrier, *Glorious*. The only positive result was the damaging of the two German battle cruisers which laid them up for many months.

Auchinleck's ship, the light cruiser *Southampton*, docked safely at Greenock on June 12. From there he took a train to Glasgow, then on to London where he presented his report in person to the War Office. One very important point he emphasized in this report was the performance of the British troops involved in the Norwegian operation. They lacked proper training, he stressed, and this was one deficiency he was determined to change.

On June 14, Auchinleck was informed that his new command was to be V Corps in Southern Command. His job was to train and prepare for an anticipated German invasion. It was expected that France would soon capitulate, leaving England alone to feel the main weight of the German horde.

The divisions allotted to Auchinleck were totally inadequate for the coastal area they were supposed to defend. He and Brooke, the head of Southern Command, both argued for more troop allotments for V Corps. As June turned into July, the struggle over shortages continued to plague the British commanders. A doctrinal struggle ensued over the best method of repelling the invasion. Should the invaders be met at the beaches or should strategic mobile reserves be formed in the interior which could be readily sent to the endangered areas whenever and wherever the Germans struck? A similiar debate would be reenacted four years later, among the German commanders, regarding the best strategy to be used against a cross-Channel invasion.

On July 19, Brooke was promoted to command Britain's home forces and Auchinleck succeeded him as G.O.C. of Southern Command, an unusually high position for a man brought up in the Indian army. The promotion spoke well for the high regard his superiors held of him. General B. L. Montgomery succeeded to the command of V Corps.

Auchinleck had a personality which bred warmth and friendship. During his long and successful military career he made few, if any, enemies, but he now found one. He could not be remotely blamed for it either. From the very beginning, Montgomery disliked Auchinleck and this hostility grew with the passing years. In Auchinleck's defense, it must be remembered that, with the exception of Brooke, Montgomery showed absolutely no respect for any superior officer. Even Alexander was not immune to his wrath.

What could have caused this dislike? Perhaps jealousy on the part of Montgomery. Auchinleck was popular and well-liked. On the other hand, Montgomery had to go out of his way to do that which came naturally to Auchinleck. The Auk was of the Indian army and was spoken of quite highly by his superiors. Montgomery might have felt a keen dislike for having to serve under a former Indian army officer. In his memoirs, Montgomery very tersely states:

> In the V Corps I first served under Auchinleck, who had Southern Command; I cannot recall that we ever agreed on anything.[4]

A clash between them was inevitable.

As G.O.C. of Southern Command, Auchinleck was kept busy inspecting, organizing, and inspecting. Meanwhile, the Battle of Britain increased in intensity and by early September, the home forces felt prepared to meet an invasion. The air war was extremely bitter as the Luftwaffe attempted to destroy the Royal Air Force as a prerequisite for the invasion. By September 15, an all-out air offensive by the Luftwaffe had failed and the critical stage had passed. Invasion scares would continue but tension began to ease somewhat among the defenders as the focus switched to the cities. Night terror bombing raids became the last-ditch attempt by Germany of bringing Britain to her knees.

On October 11, Auchinleck received word from War Secretary Anthony Eden that he was to be appointed commander in chief, India. He was reluctant to leave at first, but the feeling was quickly overcome. In fact, the reluctance was replaced by a feeling of relief. The threat of invasion was gone and Montgomery was proving a royal pain in the side, so, he felt rather happy with the prospect of leaving Montgomery behind to harass some other commander. In fact, Montgomery had proven to be Auchinleck's greatest headache. Whenever he wanted his own way, he thought nothing of going over his commander's head. At times he even publicly mocked Auchinleck's orders. For example; Auchinleck issued an order for soldiers not to be separated from their personal weapon at the height of the invasion threat, and Montgomery, like a wisecracking schoolboy, responded, "What happens when a soldier goes to bathe in the sea or when he is with his girl friend in the dark in the back of cinema?" This type of sophomoric attitude was totally unbecoming to the dignified Auchinleck.

Auchinleck's new appointment was made official on November 21, 1940, and his successor at Southern Command was Gen. Harold Alexander, a wise choice indeed.

Enroute to India, Auchinleck stopped off in Cairo to discuss operations with Sir Archibald Wavell, commander in chief of the Middle East. He was present to personally experience the elation at British headquarters over the recent victories of Gen. Richard O'Connor over the feeble Italian forces.

Auchinleck finally reached New Delhi during the second week of January, 1941. Upon assuming command he found one of his basic tasks to be the maintenance of the military manpower of the Indian army. The army was the prime feeder of forces for the Middle East and the Auk was responsible for maintaining the flow of manpower to that active theatre. In addition, he was responsible for the security of India itself.

The industrious Auchinleck plunged into his work with vigor, traveling around his extensive command visiting subordinate headquarters, troops in the field, training establishments, and recruiting areas.

Meanwhile, the situation in the Middle East rapidly

deteriorated. Wavell was prodded by Churchill to send troops to Greece to bolster the Greek army in its struggle against Italy. At first, Greece declined the aid which enabled Wavell to continue pushing the Italians halfway across Libya. Then, however, the situation changed drastically and Greece sought the aid. Wavell was then forced to send his crack desert forces to Greece, leaving behind a weak defensive screen to cover El Agheila from possible counter-attack.

Meanwhile, back in India, Auchinleck was pushing for an operation against the pro-Axis government of Iraq. From his World War I experience, he realized the strategic importance of Iraq to India's defense and security. Churchill was impressed with Auchinleck's determination regarding Iraq. So much so in fact that he wanted to dispatch him quickly to Cairo to work with Wavell as second in command. Though that command structure never became a reality, what possibilities it held. A Wavell-Auchinleck team would have been a formidable combination.

The situation in the Middle East continued to go from bad to worse. In February, 1941, Gen. Erwin Rommel arrived in Tripoli in order to bolster the Italian position. Following on his heels came German panzer forces and by late March Rommel was ready to use them against the weak British position at El Agheila. The major forces of the British were still engaged in Greece. As Rommel struck in the Western Desert, German mechanized forces also crashed into Greece. General O'Connor, who was resting in Cairo, was immediately dispatched to bolster the faltering and inexperienced General Neame in the Western Desert. Both were captured leaving the desert forces temporarily without a commander. Wavell tried to fill this position himself; however he was pressed by other serious problems, Greece being one of them. By late April the British had to be evacuated from Greece, while in the desert they were spilling over the Egyptian border with Rommel in hot pursuit. The elation of January was turned into abysmal despair by May.

Sir John Dill, who was originally in favor of Auchinleck becoming Wavell's second in command, now nixed that idea. Auchinleck's presence was needed in India. Besides, Dill felt, Wavell might feel superseded by Auchinleck's presence and might look upon it as Churchill's way of moving him out. Dill convinced Churchill not to bring Auchinleck in, except as Wavell's replacement should the Prime Minister ever lose faith in Wavell's ability to command.

As the situation continued to deteriorate in the Middle East, the Iraqi situation boiled over. Rashid Ali, the Iraqi leader, signed a secret treaty with the enemy, cementing his country firmly to the Axis cause. Auchinleck, recognizing the dangers that this could lead to, dispatched troops to meet the mounting crisis. Churchill was suitably impressed with Auchinleck's fine handling of the Iraqi situation.

While Auchinleck was rising in Churchill's esteem, Wavell was traveling the opposite path. Churchill believed that Wavell lacked suitable aggressive policies as evidenced by the recent reversal in fortune. In reality, Wavell was beset by a multitude of problems in a theatre command that demanded more than he could give. From Greece and Crete, Iraq and Syria, to the Western Desert with Rommel approaching the Egyptian border, Wavell's responsibilities far outweighed the means at hand to cope with all danger spots equally. Churchill demanded action and felt that Wavell could not provide it. On the other hand, the Prime Minister saw Auchinleck aggressively pursuing a dynamic policy in India against Iraq. This impressed him and he decided that a change in command was just the thing needed to breathe new life into the Mideast.

On May 24, Auchinleck and Wavell met at Basra for an important conference designed to clarify the complex Mideast situation. There was so much high level discussion on the proposed Wavell-Auchinleck switch that it caused a certain amount of confusion, even between the two commanders themselves. The discussions took place in a cordial atmosphere. Each explained their different viewpoints on Iraq. For Auchinleck, Iraq played a decisive part in the defense of India, while for Wavell, Iraq was not nearly as important as his other threatened areas, especially Egypt. The talks ended with Wavell returning to Cairo and Auchinleck still in India.

Iraq as a threat had to be eliminated. British troops advanced on Baghdad on May 27 and within forty-eight hours the government of Rashid Ali collapsed, with Ali fleeing to Persia. The mayor of Baghdad quickly sued for an armistice which was signed on May 31.

Wavell, meanwhile, still retained Middle East Command but did not know for how much longer.

The critical situation argued against an immediate change, one that might cause too much confusion, for Wavell was in critical maneuvers. First was the evacuation of Crete which began on May 28 and continued for three days. Second was a planned offensive in Syria scheduled to begin on June 8. The last was a major desert operation due to commence on June 15, codenamed Operation Battleaxe and designed to drive the Axis powers from the Egyptian border and relieve the Australian forces who had managed to hold on to the Libyan port of Tobruk during the British exodus in April.

Churchill held high hopes for Battleaxe and reinforced the desert forces in anticipation of a decisive offensive. Two days after its beginning, the operation failed dismally and with it fell Wavell's command. Churchill sent a letter immediately to Wavell:

> I have come to the conclusion that public interest will best be served by appointment of General Auchinleck to relieve you in command of the Armies of the Middle East. I have greatly admired your command and conduct of these armies both in success and adversity . . . I feel however that after the long strain you have borne, a new eye and a new hand are required in this most seriously threatened theatre.[5]

Auchinleck sincerely liked Wavell and was truly sorry to have to take command under the prevailing circumstances. Besides, he was happy with his current position in India. But the Middle East was a fighting command which offered unlimited possibilities to utilize his talents.

Dill, the chief of the Imperial Staff, was not as enthusiastic about the choice as one might think, since Dill and the Auk went a long way back in their friendship. Perhaps Dill felt that Churchill and Auchinleck would clash over how the command should be run. The Prime Minister could be an overbearing, overpowering influence. Wavell was totally exasperated with Churchill's incessant interference and was concerned that the same fate awaited his friend Auchinleck. The possibility existed that Churchill might prod Auchinleck into premature action. The command, Dill probably reasoned, might be just as injurious to his friend's career as it could be beneficial.

Auchinleck arrived in Cairo on June 30 and found Wavell very cordial and cooperative. He took the Auk around headquarters, introducing him to the senior officers and staff. Wavell tried to make the transition as smooth and as painless as possible. With that feat accomplished, he left Cairo on July 7 and headed eastward, first to Palestine, then on to his final destination, India. He and Auchinleck had swapped commands.

In his defense it must be said that Sir Archibald Wavell was one of the finest soldiers produced by the British Army. His relief from the Middle East Command should not in any way reflect negatively on his abilities. The theatre he managed was simply too broad and his forces inadequate. High praise should be given instead for the superb job Wavell did manage to do under the awesome prevailing circumstances. On top of all the handicaps he operated under, none was as damaging to him as the impetuous interference of the Prime Minister.

Auchinleck found himself responsible for an enormous theatre. The Western Desert was the most active and one that demanded most of his attention. From El Agheila in Libya the Western Desert stretched to Alexandria in Egypt. It was a monotonous desert of hard gravel, firm dry sands, and rocky plains, with a few areas of soft sand and occasional shrubs. There was a coastal escarpment several hundred feet high and some low hills in the interior, but other than that the keynote was barrenness. The desert, however, presented a variety of discomforts. The heat, the early morning cold, the dry barren wastelands, not to mention the incessant desert flies. One historian has written of the flies:

> The foul and dismaying thing about the flies was their oneness. None was separate from its fellows any more than the wave is separate from the ocean, the tentacle from the octopus. As one fly, one dark and horrible force guided by one mind, ubiquitous and immensely powerful, they addressed themselves to the one task, which was to destroy us body and soul. It was useless to kill them, for they despised death and made no attempt to avoid it. They existed only in the common will, and to weaken that we should have to destroy countless millions of them. None the less, we killed them unceasingly. We killed them singly and in detachments with fly swats and the dead lay so thick in our lorries that we had to sweep them out several times a day . . . We slew them in mounds with our bare hands until the crunch of minute frames and the squash of microscopic viscera, felt rather than heard . . .

> when you shut your eyes, flies tried to open them, mad for the delectable fluid. We couldn't always be killing them but we had to keep brushing them away, otherwise even breathing would have been difficult. Our arms ached from the exercise, but still they fastened on our food and accompanied it into our mouths and down our throats, scorning death when there was an advantage to be gained. They drowned themselves in our tea and soup.[6]

The only consolation for the British was that the conditions were equally discomforting to the enemy.

Before he could make any decisions Auchinleck had to become acquainted with his staff and associates and be apprised of the current situation. To make the transition smoother, he retained Wavell's chief of staff, Gen. Sir Eric Dorman-Smith. He also formed a close relationship with the chief airman in the theatre, Arthur Tedder. This friendship later blossomed into one of the most successful partnerships of the Second World War and resulted in the army and the RAF working together in total harmony and unison. He also formed a close relationship with Adm. Sir Alan Cunningham, the naval commander in chief of the Mediterranean. Thus Auchinleck, Tedder, and Cunningham formed the command triumvirate in the Middle East; but the greatest responsibility was borne by the army.

Auchinleck realized that the consolidation of his position and the regrouping of his forces was required before he made any offensive moves. The big question soon to be encountered was would Churchill allow him the time or would he prod him into attacking prematurely? Dill sent an informal letter advising him not to be prodded by Churchill. The former became Auchinleck's greatest pillar of support during the coming months. His unswerving support in many ways damaged his own relationship with Churchill and might even have led to the deterioration of his own health.

By July 1, Auchinleck had already received a signal from Churchill stressing the importance of striking the Germans quickly in light of their recent involvement in the Soviet Union. The Prime Minister also emphasized the situation in Tobruk and the importance of relieving that besieged city.

Auchinleck responded that "No further offensive in the Western Desert should be contemplated until base is secure." He stressed that threats in other parts of the theatre would have to be eliminated before any offensive could be initiated. He further stated the need for more armour and air superiority. Unfortunately, he was at variance with the Prime Minister, who wanted Auchinleck to strike immediately, not during September as the Auk had proposed as a possible date for the offensive. Churchill responded that:

> It is difficult to see how your situation is going to be better after the middle of September than it is now and it may well be worsened. I have no doubt you will maturely and swiftly consider the whole question.[7]

For the following few months the exchanges continued unceasingly. Meanwhile, Auchinleck started to initiate changes. Foremost among these was the location of General Headquarters. He firmly believed that senior officers should not enjoy undue luxuries denied to the lower ranks. Cairo offered too many comforts; country clubs, cafes, parties, etc.; thus creating a wide gulf in the life-styles between General Headquarters staff and the soldier in the field. Auchinleck refused to accept this inequity. He presented a plan for moving his headquarters out into the desert with the staff living and working in tents. The proposed plan, however, proved too impractical so he presented a modified version whereby the staff would live in the desert and would each day commute to headquarters in Cairo. In time, transport became a problem and the entire scheme was shelved. Undaunted, Auchinleck refused to have himself pampered and so kept his residence in a tent in the desert at Mena. He believed wholeheartedly in the principle of the closest possible relationship between an officer and his men and was not a person to ask someone else to do something that he was not willing to do himself.

Hostilities in Syria finally ended on July 11, thus securing that part of his command. Once more Churchill pressured Auchinleck to launch an offensive as soon as possible aimed at the relief of Tobruk. Auchinleck and his colleagues were in total unison in their opinion that an offensive was not feasible until the number of forces available were adequate and that these forces be properly trained for offensive action. In a reply to the chief of staff, the Auk and his staff stated most emphatically that the earliest an offensive could be launched would be sometime in November. It might be argued that Auchinleck was too cautious since in light of Ultra, he knew the state of the Axis forces. In his book *Ultra Goes To War*, Ronald Lewin states that during the period before Britain's "Operation Crusader," Ultra intelligence was not operating too well. Bletchley had problems receiving German intelligence. In fact, it was not until November, just before the British offensive was nearing its launching that Auchinleck began to receive precise data from that source. And yet, Churchill continued to prod.

A cable reached the Auk on July 24, inviting him to London for face-to-face talks with the Prime Minister and the War Cabinet. He was about to face his most difficult trial thus far. Auchinleck left Cairo for London determined not to be intimidated by Churchill's rhetoric. In reality, he thought rather highly of the Prime Minister. It was the latter's incessant interference which he detested.

On July 31, Auchinleck presented his position to the War Cabinet at a meeting at 10 Downing Street. He was acutely aware that he was speaking to an unsympathetic group who along with Churchill, were clamoring for an immediate offensive. He attempted to explain to them that he did not possess enough armoured strength as yet to attack and stated that Tobruk could hold out, but it was necessary to shore up the rest of the theatre before making any major commitment for an offensive. He did however, concede that consolidation was proceeding according to schedule.

The next day, Churchill and the War Cabinet presented their side and put Auchinleck through a grueling session. Churchill said:

> The next three months seemed to present a great

> chance in the Western Desert. The Germans were fully occupied in Russia.[8]

Now was the time to strike, Churchill emphasized. Eden, always the diplomat, stressed the importance of striking swiftly so that the Russians could see that the British were doing their part to destroy the Axis. The first lord of the admiralty stressed the fact that massive naval losses were being incurred in an attempt to maintain Tobruk. Churchill intermittently shot back with more arguments.

After a break for lunch during which Auchinleck retired to Buckingham Palace to dine in the pleasant company of King George, the meeting reconvened at 3:00 P.M. Seated again after the delightful repast, the Auk was bombarded with Churchillian rhetoric. Auchinleck readily replied that the last offensive had failed because it had been launched prematurely. As for himself, he stressed, he would not jeopardize his tank forces and Egypt. Again, Churchill and his colleagues shot back, but Auchinleck remained adamant. Churchill snapped, war could not be waged on the basis of waiting until everything was ready. And so the arguments continued.

The interminable meeting dragged on till seven o'clock when the Prime Minister finally concluded the session. Churchill had lost. Auchinleck would not budge. Churchill said:

> I was myself unconvinced. But General Auchinleck's unquestioned abilities, his powers of exposition, his high, dignified and commanding personality, gave me the feeling that he might after all be right, and that even if wrong

he was still the best man. I therefore yielded to the November date for the offensive and turned my energies to making it a success.[9]

Auchinleck was invited to remain with Churchill at Chequers for the weekend. On August 10, he started back to Cairo via Gibraltar and Malta, reaching Egypt two days later. Though the conference had been a grueling affair, most participants admired him for his firm resolve. Tedder, who had accompanied him to London, later commented on how impressed he was with Auchinleck's adamance.

The major issue confronting Auchinleck on his return to the desert was the selection of a commander for the Western Desert Force. Churchill had suggested General Maitland ("Jumbo") Wilson but Auchinleck did not feel comfortable with Wilson. Instead, he leaned towards Gen. Alan Cunningham, the victor over the Italian Abyssinian forces in East Africa. Churchill disagreed with the choice and Montgomery in his memoirs concluded that Auchinleck "was a poor picker of men."[10] That criticism is partially correct but not as regards the choice of Cunningham. Coming from the Indian army, Auchinleck was handicapped by not personally knowing that many officers in the British army, nor was he aware of the comparative reputations of its rising men. Cunningham, however, seemed a good choice. In just eight weeks' time he had marched virtually halfway across Africa and his speed and dash delighted the British public. His performance completely impressed Auchinleck.

I asked for Cunningham as I was impressed by

> his rapid and vigorous command in Abyssinia and his obvious leaning towards swift mobile action. I wanted to get away from the idea, which seemed to be prevalent, of clinging to the coastal strip.[11]

O'Connor, of course, would have been the best selection, but he was a prisoner of war. From Auchinleck's perspective then, Cunningham appeared to be the only remaining intelligent choice.

The appointment of Cunningham meant that preparations for the offensive could proceed in earnest. The Western Desert Force which Cunningham now commanded was a unique formation, made up of soldiers from India, South Africa, Australia, New Zealand, and Britain. Auchinleck was familiar with the Indians, but was painfully aware that each contingent had direct access to its own governments.

> One had to think of this the whole time . . . I felt that the Governments were watching you and they did watch you, there's no doubt about it.[12]

One obvious example of this interference and concern of the Commonwealth Governments was in regard to Tobruk. The garrison of this besieged town was made up of Australian troops. The new Prime Minister of Australia, A. W. Fadden, clamored for the relief of the garrison and immediately began to apply pressure on Churchill to expedite it. Auchinleck feared that to do so would jeopardize the overall chance of success of the projected offensive. The Australian leader, however, was adamant. Fadden's administration fell in early October providing a ray of hope, but his successor, John Curtin, refused to reverse the decision. The relief was accomplished with the loss of three ships and severe damage to four more. Because Tobruk was much too valuable a position to abandon, all that was accomplished was the replacement of the Australians with other forces. Auchinleck was of course furious with the whole episode and protested at the political interference with a commander in the field.

Amongst these difficulties, Auchinleck prepared to take the offensive. He was confident that a full scale attack could be launched by November. Originally, he had intended to launch only a limited offensive but he now felt sure that a full scale attack could be launched with a reasonable chance of success in November, rather than waiting for winter to set in. In preparation for the offensive, Auchinleck stressed that success would depend upon British ability to destroy the enemy armoured forces and exploit that success.

On September 2, Auchinleck issued his first directive to General Cunningham indicating that the autumn offensive would be aimed at driving the enemy out of North Africa completely. That goal would be achieved, he went on, in two stages. First would be the capture of Cyrenaica (eastern Libya) to be followed by the conquest of Tripolitania (western Libya).

Meanwhile, in mid-September, Rommel dispatched the Twenty-first Panzer Division towards Sidi Barrani in Egypt. The division was aimed at an area in which it was believed that the British had a fuel dump. The British defenders fell back rapidly, convincing Rommel that they were in no way prepared for an offensive. This misconception from "Midsummer Night's Dream," as the German operation was codenamed, implanted a number of misconceptions in Rommel's mind that stayed with him until the British struck in November. In *The Life and Death of the Afrika Corps*, Ronald Lewin states:

> There is no doubt that as the date for his cherished attack on Tobruk approached, Rommel sealed his mind against any suggestion that it might be anticipated by a British offensive.[13]

As Rommel's probe petered out, Auchinleck ordered troops and a fuel dump constructed around Sidi Barrani. Rommel, convinced that the British lacked offensive plans, turned his attention towards Tobruk and away from the border.

On September 26, Western Desert Force officially received its new title: Eighth Army. Three days later, the Eighth Army commander formally submitted his plans for the offensive. Cunningham had not had long to adapt himself to his new station. He had only two months to acquaint himself to the vastness of his responsibilities. "He was rather like a successful owner of a village shop suddenly put in charge of a London department store,"[14] said Corelli Barnett. The size and complexity of the command were new to him. Here he was, in charge of an entire army when the largest force he had ever previously commanded was four brigades of infantry. He also knew little about the use of armour and had never commanded it, and he only had two months to learn.

Cunningham was influenced by the opinion that

tanks could, and would, win battles by themselves. Indeed, his entire organization reflected this view. He split Eighth Army into two corps: an infantry corps (XIII) and an armoured corps (XXX). The primary armoured force was the Seventh Armoured Division which itself was divided into three armoured brigades and a support group of guns and mobile infantry. Armour and infantry were kept completely segregated. The infantry corps did possess tanks, but these were the obsolete "I" tanks designed only for cooperation with the infantry and lacking the requisite speed for a battle of maneuvers.

Auchinleck presented Cunningham with two plans for Crusader. One was aimed through Jalo and the other involved a direct blow along the coast. Cunningham liked neither. He proposed instead that the main line of attack be launched across the Egyptian-Libyan frontier between Sidi Omar and Fort Maddalena, with the bulk of the armour striking northwest to occupy the area around Gabr Saleh. This maneuver was designed to entice Rommel to send his two panzer divisions there to compete in an all-out tank battle. Once the armour was engaged, the Tobruk garrison could then push out of its defenses. Meanwhile, Cunningham went on, while this armoured Armageddon was taking place, XIII Corps would contain and envelop the Axis frontier positions before thrusting through Bardia toward Tobruk. (See Map 7)

As XIII and XXX Corps would be separated, Cunningham felt it necessary to place one of his armoured brigades, the Fourth, in reserve to flank XIII Corps in the event Rommel shot the gap between the

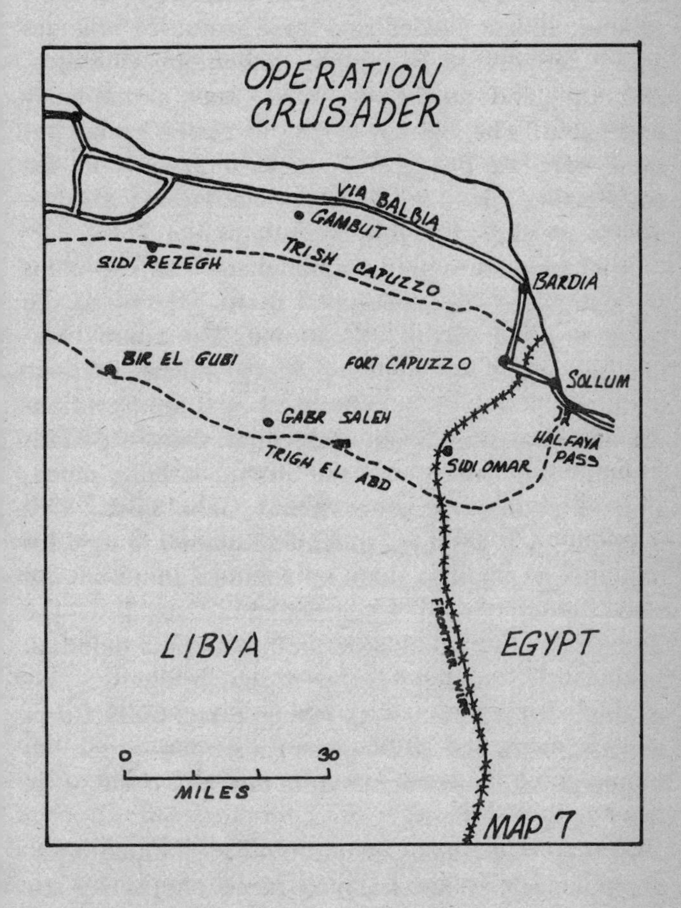
OPERATION
CRUSADER
VIA BALBIA
GAMBUT
TRISH CAPUZZO
SIDI REZEGH
BARDIA
BIR EL GUBI
FORT CAPUZZO
SOLLUM
GABR SALEH
HALFAYA
PASS
SIDI OMAR
TRIGH EL ABD
FRONTIER WIRE
LIBYA
EGYPT
0
30
MILES
MAP 7

two corps. Once however, it became obvious that Rommel had taken the bait at Gabr Saleh, then the Fourth Armoured Brigade would be free to join its parent unit in the all-out tank battle.

General Norrie, commander of XXX Corps, was critical of Cunningham's propositions. He felt that to use the Fourth Armoured Brigade as flank cover was a dangerous dispersal of effort. He also felt that Gabr Saleh was not the proper objective with which to entice Rommel, for it had no proper military significance for the Germans. Norrie claimed that there was no reason at all to suppose that occupation of that position would force the decisive action. What if Rommel failed to react to it at all? Instead, Norrie proposed that the British armour strike directly for Tobruk and force Rommel to fight. On the other hand, General Godwin-Austin of XIII Corps insisted on flank cover for his corps and was also a firm believer that tanks could only fight tanks.

In the final plan, Cunningham retained the Fourth Armoured Brigade as flank cover to XIII Corps, but planned to leave it there only until Rommel's tank forces were engaged. He refused to change the directive as Norrie had suggested. Gabr Saleh would remain the focal point for the decisive battle. The Eighth Army commander was firmly convinced that British armoured presence in this central position would force Rommel to concentrate in order to defend either his siege of Tobruk or the frontier defenses. The ideal tactic would be for Rommel himself to split his forces. Though approving the aforementioned plan, Cunningham did have reservations. With his faith shaken, he plunged ahead, determined to stick to his plan.

Meanwhile, Churchill and Auchinleck were again bantering over the starting date of the offensive. Churchill insisted that it should begin in early November but Auchinleck pressed more for the middle or latter part of the month. Furious letters were forwarded to Auchinleck from the Prime Minister querying him as to why he was procrastinating. The Auk stated that his reasons were multiple. They included his concerns in the rest of his enormous theatre, and the number and preparation of his tanks. Time was needed to accumulate and ready the tanks for the offensive. The Prime Minister was exasperated but conceded. After all, what could he do? The date was finally fixed for November 18, 1941.

Just prior to the launching of Crusader, a change took place in London that would profoundly affect Auchinleck. Sir John Dill was replaced as chief of the Imperial General Staff by Gen. Alan Brooke. It was probably the strained relationship between Churchill and Dill that precipitated the change, for Dill was a close friend and champion of Auchinleck. Alan Brooke, however, was also considered by Auchinleck to be a friend. It remained to be seen just what the future would bring.

Cunningham spent the rain-swept night of November 17 full of anxiety. The burden weighed heavily on him.

> On the eve of Crusader he seems to have reached that stage of mental and physical fatigue when even ordinary tasks and decisions loom immense and daunting to a man.[15]

The early morning hours of November 18 witnessed the beginning of the long awaited Operation Crusader. Cunningham accompanied the XXX Corps commander, Norrie. All day they moved into Rommel's rear without causing any noticeable reaction on his part. There was no hardening resistance—no local counterattacks. By evening, XXX Corps was in its battle position near Gabr Saleh, but Rommel failed to react just as Norrie had cautioned. The German commander, who had only just returned to the desert the previous day, thought that this was merely a British reconnaissance in force and paid it only passing attention. Besides, he was preoccupied with preparations for an offensive of his own against Tobruk.

Cunningham, amazed at the lack of Axis response, divided XXX Corps on the night of the eighteenth, sending Twenty-second Armoured Brigade to attack the Italians at Bir el Gubi. This was his first mistake, dissipating his tank strength. In retrospect, he should have kept his forces intact and advanced in force towards Sidi Rezegh. Meanwhile, Auchinleck sent an optimistic message to Churchill stating that the Axis had been caught by surprise.

On the morning of the nineteenth, advance tanks of the Twenty-second Armoured Brigade encountered Italian tanks near Bir el Gubi. They were units of the Ariete Division, one of Italy's finest. As the battle flared, General Gott, commander of the Seventh Armoured Division, committed the whole of the Twenty-second Armoured Brigade into the battle. This was the beginning of the process of disintegration of the British forces. Not until evening did Norrie and Cunningham even hear of the battle at Bir el

Gubi. While the Twenty-second Brigade was occupied, Seventh Armoured Brigade was advancing northward toward the armoured encounter that Cunningham believed to be the pivot of his plan. But now, instead of proceeding there in total strength, he was reduced to but a third of his armour. The Seventh Brigade soon occupied the Sidi Rezegh area.

Evening found the Twenty-second Brigade beaten back by the dug in Italians, Seventh Armoured Brigade lying dangerously exposed at Sidi Rezegh, and the Fourth Armoured which was providing flank cover for XIII Corps, moved instead to the old battle position at Gabr Saleh. The whole integrity of Cunningham's original plan was destroyed.

Ironically, General Cruewell, commander of the Afrika Korps, managed to convince Rommel that the British forces represented a threat and should be attacked. After an indecisive action, the Afrika Korps withdrew eastward followed by the Fourth Armoured Brigade. Cunningham was groping in the dark for some direction.

A wireless breakdown on the night of the nineteenth caused even more confusion for Cunningham. Fortunately, Cruewell was suffering from the same malady.

On the afternoon of the twentieth, Cruewell advanced towards Gabr Saleh with the Fifteenth Panzer Division. Cunningham immediately ordered Norrie to send the Twenty-second Armoured Brigade from Bir el Gubi eastward to Gabr Saleh. Finally, the major tank battle seemed to be in the offing. A savage battle ensued, but with only the Fourth Armoured Brigade at Gabr Saleh involved, where Cruewell inflicted heavy losses on the British. Finally the Twenty-second Armoured arrived on the scene and was ordered to drive into the right flank of the Germans. However, by that time, Fourth Armoured had been driven to the south. As night fell, the battle ebbed and died away.

That night, Cunningham felt confident. He believed that since his forces had not been destroyed and that the Axis formations had suffered heavy losses, he must have won the decisive tank action. His orders for November 21 reflected that optimism.

Cunningham ordered the Fourth and Twenty-second Armoured Brigades to attack the German armour as soon as possible and pursue it. He also decided that this was the best time for the Tobruk garrison to break out through El Duda and make a junction with the Seventh Armoured Brigade at Sidi Rezegh with the Fifth South African Brigade enroute for support.

Cruewell suggested to Rommel that the Twenty-first Panzer Division link up with the Fifteenth and strike the Seventh Armoured Brigade in its rear flank. By morning of the twenty-first, the Germans were moving on Sidi Rezegh with the British brigades in close pursuit under the impression that the Germans were in full retreat. Cunningham was ecstatic. He called General Godwin-Austin of XIII Corps and informed him that he could now advance towards Tobruk. Godwin-Austin ordered the New Zealand Division to advance along the Trigh Capuzzo towards Sidi Rezegh and Tobruk. Thus, the whole of Eighth Army was on the move against what they considered to be a beaten enemy.

A complicated situation then developed. According to the official British history:

> A complicated situation which if suggested for the setting of a training exercise, must have been rejected for the reason that in real life things simply could not happen.[16]

Visualize how complicated it was. In the north was the British Seventieth Division pushing out of Tobruk. Opposing it were German and Italian troops. South of these was the Seventh Support Group which included part of the Seventh Armoured Brigade. Next came the rest of the Seventh Armoured Brigade facing south in the vicinity of the Sidi Rezegh airfield, awaiting the approach of the Fifteenth and Twenty-first Panzer Divisions. Following the Germans were the British Fourth and Twenty-second Armoured Brigades. One element was layered upon the other. "Rarely had the fog of war been so thick."[17]

The battle around Sidi Rezegh raged far into the next morning with the British suffering heavily. Cunningham was exasperated and seemed to have lost the handle on the battle. Worse yet, it appeared that his nerve was faltering. Auchinleck too was unsure of the situation. He had been fed inaccurate information, most of it stating that the battle was progressing rather nicely.

Then dawned Sunday, November 23. Another major tank battle took place near Sidi Rezegh and by nightfall, the Fifth South African Brigade had virtually ceased to exist. Pessimism changed place with optimism at British headquarters. Thirtieth Corps had lost over two-thirds of its armour, and worse yet, with the original Crusader plans dashed to pieces, belief in a retreat permeated the ranks of the Eighth Army. Cunningham quickly dashed off a message to the commander in chief in Cairo.

Up until this point, Auchinleck had not interfered with the conduct of the battle. He was a firm believer that the commander in the field should not suffer interference in the conduct of a battle unless absolutely necessary. Arriving at Eighth Army headquarters at Maddalena late that Sunday evening, Auchinleck took Cunningham aside and immediately judged that Cunningham had indeed lost his nerve. The Eighth Army commander muttered that the battle was lost and retreat was inevitable. The corps commanders was horrified at the prospect of calling the offensive off. Therefore the Auk was faced with a heavy decision.

It was raining that Sunday evening, adding to the gloom hovering over Eighth Army headquarters. Auchinleck was weighed down by the burden of this decision. However, he quickly recognized the seriousness of the situation and made a decision, one diametrically opposed to what Cunningham advocated. Auchinleck ordered the army to attack, believing that the enemy too had suffered heavy tank losses. Now, he insisted, was the time to apply pressure on Rommel. It was a dynamic decision made by a dynamic man. On this decision rested the entire fate of Crusader.

Precisely at this time, Rommel too estimated that the enemy was spent and decided to deal it a decisive blow. Against the advice of Cruewell, Rommel ordered his famous dash to the frontier wire with the objective of cutting off the retreat of XXX Corps and supporting the frontier garrisons against the XIII Corps. This operation was very risky but Rommel was confident that the psychological factor of his presence in the British rear would panic the enemy into collapse. It might have worked were it not for Auchinleck's brilliant mastery of a critical situation.

By mid-morning of the twenty-fourth, German panzers were heading to the frontier with Rommel, as usual, leading the advance in person. The German advance spread panic but Auchinleck worked in spite of the fear around him. He issued a detailed directive confirming the attack order, stating that the attack would continue with the main objective being the destruction of the enemy tank forces. The ultimate objective was still the conquest of Cyrenaica and the destruction of the Axis hold on North Africa.

Cunningham doubted the feasibility of Auchinleck's orders. He was at Norrie's XXX Corps' headquarters when word of Rommel's approach reached him and spread panic at the headquarters. He quickly fled. Meanwhile, Auchinleck saw that firm possession of the Rezegh-Duda ridge by XIII Corps and the Tobruk garrison was the key to the battle. As far as Rommel's dash to the frontier:

> He is making a desperate effort, but he will not get very far. That column of tanks simply cannot get supplies. I am sure of this.[18]

How right he was. Rommel had shot his bolt and his formations were forced to forage for supplies.

Auchinleck was now faced with the difficult decision of what to do with Cunningham. He knew that the Eighth Army commander was finished, but he also knew that his own presence was needed back in Cairo. In addition, he was aware that his continued presence at Eighth Army headquarters would only serve to discredit Cunningham in the eyes of his subordinates. The only solution was to find a replacement for the commander of the Eighth Army. Auchinleck knew all the difficulties entailed in changing command, especially in the midst of battle. Who could succeed Cunningham? Norrie? Perhaps Godwin-Austin. No. They were engaged in combat and it would be too confusing to wrench them from their corps. Auchinleck instead chose Lt. Gen. Neil Ritchie, his deputy chief of staff at Cairo. This decision would cause an uproar and much criticism, but the Auk stated that it was only temporary. A permanent commander could be found later.

Now came the difficult task of informing Cunningham. Auchinleck wrote him a letter:

> It's no use, I am afraid my telling you how I hate to have had to do this thing, but I must act according to my belief and I have done so. It is most painful to me because I like and respect you a very great deal, and I have never thought that I should have to act in this way towards you. I can only assure you that I do so because I honestly feel that it is necessary to ensure the total defeat of the enemy in the shortest possible time.[19]

Ritchie, who had not held a field command since the First World War, assumed command of Eighth Army on November 26. His first step was to continue the consolidation of the scattered forces of XXX Corps. Meanwhile, the New Zealanders under General Freyberg had passed Sidi Rezegh, captured Belhammed, and joined hands with the Tobruk garrison which had broken out over the Ed Duda escarpment. Though badly mauled, the brave New Zealanders rejoiced at their triumph. Unfortunately, their joy was short lived.

Rommel had already returned from his fateful dash to the wire and realized now that he faced a very grave situation. While he was hitting the frontier, the British were consolidating that ground which he had taken from them before the frontier dash. Rommel did some consolidating of his own on November 28 and the following day struck at Sidi Rezegh. After a two day battle he secured the ground again and once more isolated Tobruk.

Auchinleck returned to the battlefront on December 1 where he remained for the next ten days. He guided, encouraged, and gave heart to Ritchie in his first major command. The issue would now be won by the force having the greater reserves. Fortunately for the British, their supplies were abundant. On the other side, Rommel faced acute shortages of supplies and he was curtly informed not to expect any significant change in the situation until the end of the month. Rommel recognized the inevitable.

On December 5, Auchinleck admitted that the situation was finally in hand. On December 7, Rommel told Cruewell:

> If the enemy was not beaten today we should have to abandon the Tobruk front and go back to the Gazala position.[20]

On December 8, Tobruk was finally relieved after a siege of 242 days. The following day Rommel wrote to his wife:

> Dearest Lu,
> You will no doubt have seen how we're doing from the Wehrmacht communiques. I've had to break off the action outside Tobruk on account of the Italian formations and also the badly exhausted German troops. I'm hoping we'll succeed in escaping enemy encirclement and holding on to Cyrenaica. I'm keeping well. You can imagine what I'm going through and what anxieties I have.[21]

The Crusader battle was over. Eighth Army emerged victorious. In reality, it had muddled its way to victory even though Rommel had lost one-third of his command. Curiously enough, Montgomery would later destroy the same number at the celebrated victory of El Alamein in November of the following year. Crusader, however, had been won by a weaker Eighth Army, both in numbers and in equipment, against a Rommel who was stronger than he would be in 1942. Though it was indeed a muddled victory, Auchinleck's intervention definitely had saved the day. Without his presence on November 23, the Eighth Army would have retreated and Crusader would have gone the way of Battleaxe in June.

What was Auchinleck like at the front? He lived a spartan life there and normally shunned creature comforts. This went double for the battlefield. Most nights he slept in the open despite the cold and wet. He refused to eat special foods not served to the fighting men. He was setting an example; "I was trying to avoid the appearance of overluxury and overcomfort among the staff and commanders." He was human, warmhearted, generous, easy to warm up to, and very solicitous of his men.

What was Ultra's role in the battle? According to Lewin, Auchinleck certainly received a sequence of Ultra signals during the battle, but these primarily reflected Rommel's anxiety about fuel and air cover. This intelligence contributed to the sustaining of Auchinleck's confidence in final victory. However, he received no hard tactical intelligence. There was no open window into the Axis camp during Crusader.

Was Auchinleck an infallible commander? Obviously the answer to this question is no. Though he was a remarkable person, his poor judgment in choosing subordinates must reflect upon his overall performance. With Cunningham he could be excused. The choice of Ritchie could be understood as a temporary measure in light of the urgency of the situation at the time, but retention of the latter in command can only be considered a gross error. When he chose Ritchie, he appointed a man to a position far beyond the scope of his experience. Ritchie had never even so much as commanded a division or a corps in the field and suddenly found himself in command of an entire army. Though he justified the choice during Crusader, it was questionable to retain him in command once that the battle was over. Two reasons for Auchinleck's actions appear evident. The first was the successful conclusion of Crusader. The second was that Ritchie was hailed in the newspapers as the successful commander of Eighth Army. How would it look if Auchinleck now replaced him after leading his forces to victory? How bewildering it would be to replace commanders again after so short a time. "After all, if there is any need for assistance," Auchinleck said, "I can always go forward." Therefore, he retained Ritchie in command.

On December 11, the Auk flew back to Cairo leaving Ritchie alone to pursue Rommel. Arriving at Cairo, he found himself faced with an entire new set of circumstances. On December 7, the Japanese had bombed Pearl Harbor, plunging the United States and Great Britain into a war with Japan. Although Britain now possessed a strong ally, before America's power could be brought to bear, the Empire would have to be defended by an already overstretched army. Auchinleck now faced the prospect of losing forces just when he needed them the most. Ironically, Wavell and O'Connor had faced a reduction of their forces in the previous year just after achieving victory and now again the same thing was being repeated. In Wavell's case, the forces were dispatched to Greece, for Auchinleck, it was the Far East.

Ritchie meanwhile, was pursuing the retreating Rommel. By December 12, the latter had reached Gazala but was soon obliged to retreat further west. At year's end, Cyrenaica was in British hands. Success! But the cost was high. The Eighth Army had suffered the loss of over 17 thousand men, 3 hundred tanks, and 278 aircraft. If the British were to continue the pursuit, they needed to be reinforced quickly. The spectre of the Far East now began to plague the desert forces.

Singapore, Burma, and India desperately required

men and materials. Australia was clamoring for the return of her troops. On the other hand, the Axis forces were receiving valuable reinforcements daily now that their supply line was reduced. Earlier in the month, Field Marshal Albert Kesselring was brought into the theatre and quickly recognized the significance of destroying the British naval and air bases on the island of Malta. Even though the British could read the German code, without interference from Malta's air bases, Axis convoys would reach their destination unhindered, and so they did. Armour was again flowing into Rommel's waiting arms. The tanks he received were the superior Mark V which could outshoot and outfight any tank then possessed by the British. This situation had all the earmarks of a nasty turn of events, particularly since the British were dealing with an individual who had justifiably earned a reputation as "The Desert Fox."

The situation was frustrating for Middle East Command. The Axis forces lodged themselves at El Agheila and when the Eighth Army arrived there, it simply lacked sufficient strength to stop Rommel from regrouping his formations. In addition, British tanks were suffering from mechanical problems and faced serious fuel shortages because the supply line was nearly five hundred miles long from the nearest railhead. Time was needed for a buildup of supplies in the forward areas before any further western movement could be contemplated. It was reasonably estimated that the offensive could be resumed by February 10. Meanwhile, Kesselring made his presence known as Axis air activity markedly increased throughout January.

As the situation in the Far East deteriorated, the Middle East Command was forced to mark time in frustration. On January 19, Auchinleck issued a perceptive operational instruction to Ritchie. He told the Eighth Army commander that the offensive was to continue with the objective of seizing Tripoli; but he also mentioned a contingency plan for a withdrawal should the latter become necessary. Included in the message was a sentence which later caused much confusion. It stated that if the Eighth Army were required to retreat, Tobruk was not to be held permanently. The same applied to any locality west of the Egyptian border. Auchinleck did not desire a repetition of the previous year. Furthermore, he prophetically noted that work would continue on a defensive position in the El Alamein vicinity.

Forty-eight hours after issuing this directive, Rommel, the wily fox, struck. The morning of January 21 saw the Ninetieth Light and Twenty-first Panzer Divisions reeling down the coastal road while the rest of the Afrika Korps bolted forward in the interior. Eighth Army, outnumbered and scattered, retreated immediately. Rommel had achieved complete surprise.

To Ritchie, Rommel's advance presented itself as a reconnaissance in force that would be followed the next day by retirement. Unfortunately for Ritchie, Rommel did not retreat. The British First Armoured Division was routed and fled eastward. Ritchie was dumbfounded. He was obviously no match for the Desert Fox.

Auchinleck was on his way to Palestine when the first reports reached him of Rommel's moves. When he returned to Cairo on January 23, he was confident that Ritchie had the situation well in hand. He was not, however, informed of the confusion reigning at Eighth Army headquarters. Ritchie was hampered by the lack of reconnaissance due to bad flying weather locally and the local commanders were confused by the dual enemy advance. Contradictory orders were being sent which only added to the confusion. Ritchie was in a muddle and now his lack of experience began to show. The situation deteriorated rapidly. So much so, in fact, that Auchinleck saw fit to go to the front on January 25 in order to obtain a clearer picture of the situation. He felt that Rommel could be stopped because he would soon overreach himself. Meanwhile, Churchill was hearing rumors of possible retreats by units of the Eighth Army. Auchinleck tried to reassure the Prime Minister by telling him that the initiative would soon be regained and that he had full confidence in General Ritchie.

It was Rommel, however, who retained the initiative. Excellent wireless interception informed him of the confused state of the Eighth Army. The Afrika Korps continued eastward. Rommel was now at Msus where he threatened both Mechili to the northeast and Benghazi to the northwest. Which way would he go? Godwin-Austin advised a general withdrawal from the Benghazi area. At first Ritchie agreed but then changed his mind. He would fight for Benghazi. Rommel now lived up to his reputation fooling Ritchie completely (which was not hard) and even outfoxed the Auk. He made a feint towards Mechili causing Auchinleck and Ritchie to move their armour to the east thereby exposing Benghazi and the Fourth

Indian Division stationed there. Then Rommel lunged towards the coast, cutting off the hapless Indians, who only with much difficulty, managed to free themselves. But Benghazi fell to the enemy on the twenty-ninth with a huge quantity of fuel and food. Thirteen Corps retreated to Gazala. Western Cyrenaica was again under Axis control.

In a contrite signal to Churchill, Auchinleck explained the reasons for the British failure. Dispersal of effort was at the top of the list. He then went on to state that the British two-pounder guns were inferior to the German ones and that the Cruiser tanks were mechanically unreliable.

Churchill's confidence in Auchinleck began to erode. Auchinleck himself accepted ultimate blame for the setback. In a sense it truly was his fault for he was responsible for placing Ritchie in command and that officer was plainly not the man for the job. General Godwin-Austin of XIII was unhappy with Ritchie's handling of the army and resigned his own command in protest. He was succeeded by General Gott.

By the first week in February, the Eighth Army was firmly established in its position on a line running from Gazala south to Bir Hacheim. A lull now settled over the battlefield as each side rearmed themselves for a further push.

Auchinleck now faced the task of restoring Eighth Army's confidence and efficiency. He also knew that he had to restore the Prime Minister's confidence in him. Events in the Far East influenced Auchinleck's preparations for future operations. The fall of Singapore on February 15, 1942, and the dire threat to Burma necessitated the immediate dispatch of additional reinforcements for that theatre. At the end of the month, Auchinleck sent Churchill a seventeen-page appreciation of his intentions. In it he stated that he intended to continue to build up an armoured striking force in the Eighth Army as quickly as possible. Meanwhile, the Gazala, Tobruk, Sollum, and Maddalena positions would be made as strong as possible. Finally he stated that forward reserves of supplies were to be built up in anticipation of renewing the offensive. However, he indicated that no offensive would be possible prior to June 1, and to attempt one prior to that date would be too dangerous. Once more Auchinleck faced an irate Prime Minister who demanded immediate action.

Churchill was furious over Auchinleck's assessment and insisted that the attack take place much sooner, but the Auk firmly stood his ground just as he had done the previous summer and fall. Churchill was in complete disagreement. Malta was undergoing an enormous pounding from the Luftwaffe and the Prime Minister reasoned that an offensive in Cyrenaica would serve to relieve the pressure on that besieged island, as a destroyed Axis army would have no further need of supplies. Without that need for supplies, the necessity of besieging Malta would cease to exist. Auchinleck did not see it quite that way. He was of the opinion that Egypt could survive without Malta, but the Middle East and even India could not survive if the Axis was given the opportunity to destroy an Eighth Army committed to a premature offensive.

To Churchill and the War Cabinet Auchinleck's attitude appeared to be too defensive and it caused a rift between the Auk and London, particularly with Brooke, the chief of the Imperial General Staff. As an example, a misunderstanding ensued between the London and Egyptian commands over the number of tanks available. London saw in the books that 1,315 tanks were available to Middle East Command. Therefore, why should Auchinleck procrastinate since it was obvious that he had numerical superiority in armour? In truth, of the tanks listed in the ledger, only 591 were actually in use; the rest were under repair. These facts were simply ignored in London but they served to contribute to the decline of Auchinleck's reputation.

Churchill sent a signal to Auchinleck on March 7, inviting him to London for another high level discussion. The Auk responded negatively, stating that his presence in the Middle East at that time was urgently required. The Prime Minister was furious and considered replacing Auchinleck. Once more Auchinleck was requested to travel to London but he suggested that instead, Brooke himself come to the Middle East so that he could see things firsthand for himself. Instead of sending Brooke, an enraged Churchill sent Lord Privy Seal Sir Stafford Cripps and Vice Chief of the Imperial General Staff, Gen. Robert Nye. Actually, Cripps was enroute to India to inquire into internal Indian affairs when he was detoured to Egypt.

During the subsequent talks, Auchinleck calmly presented his position and Cripps, in a cordial manner, absorbed all that was presented. Nye asked some pertinent questions but Auchinleck and Tedder answered every one of them satisfactorily. Cripps went away satisfied with what he had heard and sent off a letter to Churchill commenting on the talks. Churchill was not content and said as much in a letter to General Nye.

> I have heard from the Lord Privy Seal. I do not wonder everything was so pleasant, considering you seem to have accepted everything they said, and all we have got to accept is the probable loss of Malta and the Army standing idle, while the Russians are resisting the German counter-stroke desperately, and while the enemy is reinforcing himself in Libya faster than we are.[22]

Nye refused to be swayed from agreeing with Auchinleck and concluded that no offensive operations would be justified before May 15.

Overwhelmed by Cripps' and Nye's positions, Churchill privately vented his anger to Brooke, but the climax had been reached. Auchinleck was allowed to stay, but his relationship with Churchill deteriorated to a point from which it would never recover. Had Auchinleck gone to London for a face-to-face conference with Churchill and his advisors just as he had done the previous summer, much of the misunderstanding might have been dispelled. Churchill probably would have regained some of his lost confidence in Auchinleck.

Still the debate did not subside. Auchinleck felt that the date for the offensive should be changed from May 15 to June 15 or ideally, even later. He again pointed to the threat of exposing Egypt and India should the Eighth Army be destroyed. Churchill was unmoved; he emphasized the threat to Malta.

As the bantering continued, Ritchie began developing the Gazala position both as the springboard for an offensive and as a defensive area for the protection of Tobruk and eastern Cyrenaica. He found himself caught in a difficult position, preparing for both an offensive and defensive action.

As for the preparations themselves, Auchinleck was not happy with the British practice of using large armoured formations unsupported by infantry. He therefore broke down the armoured division into self-contained brigade groups with their own artillery and engineers. In the armoured divisions, he replaced the two armoured brigades and a support group with a single armoured brigade group and two mobile infantry brigade groups, thus giving each division equal fighting power similiar to a German panzer division. The infantry would be motorized so that they could keep pace with the armour. Unfortunately, the Germans struck before the preparations were complete. (See Map 8)

Ultra's amazing information accurately forecast the date when Rommel would attack. Although forewarned, Auchinleck did not receive any hard information concerning the route that Rommel would take. When Ritchie (who was not informed of the Ultra system) heard that Rommel was preparing an offensive, he assembled a linear fixed defense from Gazala to Bir Hacheim, forty miles to the south, which he manned with infantry and artillery while his armour was held in reserve in the rear. Between Gazala and Bir Hacheim were boxes (independent strongholds of guns and infantry). This type of

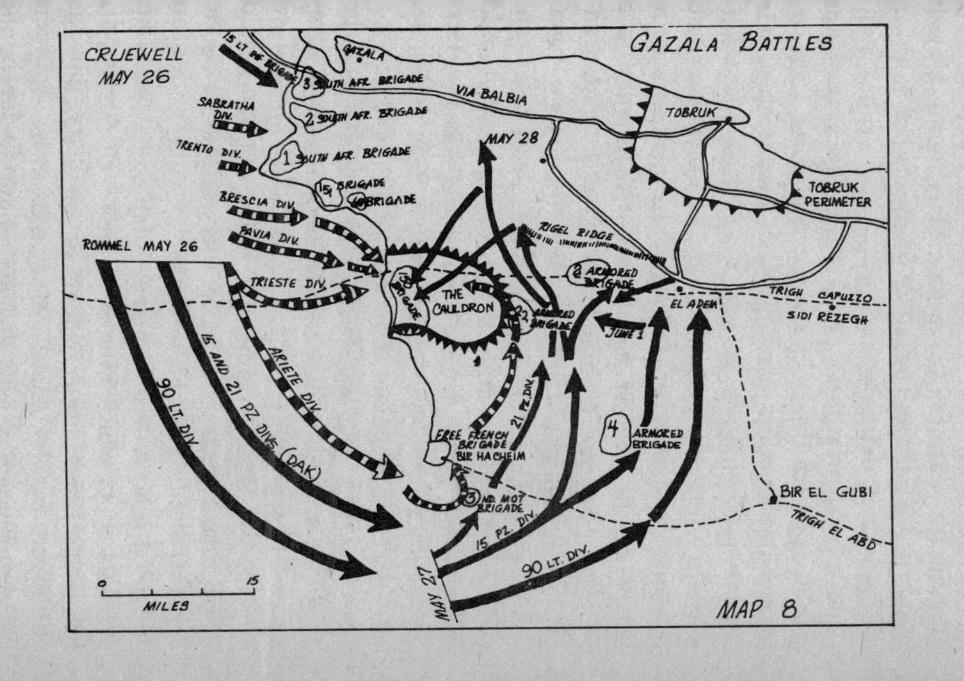
GAZALA BATTLES
CRUEWELL
MAY 26
15 LT INF BRIGADE
GAZALA
3 SOUTH AFR. BRIGADE
2 SOUTH AFR. BRIGADE
1 SOUTH AFR. BRIGADE
SABRATHA DIV.
TRENTO DIV.
BRESCIA DIV.
PAVIA DIV.
TRIESTE DIV.
VIA BALBIA
TOBRUK
TOBRUK PERIMETER
MAY 28
RIGEL RIDGE
2 ARMORED BRIGADE
22 ARMORED BRIGADE
THE CAULDRON
150 BRIGADE
TRIGH CAPUZZO
EL ADEM
SIDI REZEGH
JUNE 1
ROMMEL MAY 26
ARIETE DIV.
15 AND 21 PZ DIVS. (DAK)
90 LT. DIV.
FREE FRENCH BRIGADE
BIR HACHEIM
21 PZ. DIV.
4 ARMORED BRIGADE
3 IND. MOT BRIGADE
15 PZ. DIV.
90 LT. DIV.
MAY 27
BIR EL GUBI
TRIGH EL ABD
0
15
MILES
MAP 8

defense merely proved how little Ritchie understood the nature of mobile and mechanized desert warfare. Nowhere was this more evident than in his deployment of the army in forward positions rather than keeping them back and mobile. With the southern flank (Bir Hacheim) left exposed, Ritchie invited encirclement. Furthermore, his armour lay stretched all over the desert, the lessons of Crusader were abandoned. A swift advance by German armour could conceivably plough through each scattered brigade.

In Cairo, Auchinleck recognized the danger and advised Ritchie to place both his armoured divisions, the First and Seventh, well concentrated and to the north, astride the Trigh Capuzzo. He further emphasized that the armour must not be committed piecemeal. Unfortunately, that very thing happened.

The obstacles facing Panzerarmee Afrika were formidable. The forty mile long defensive line with its series of fortified infantry boxes could have been a major obstacle except for one major flaw. Not only was the Bir Hacheim box immobile, it was also isolated at the southern end of the line and unsupported by any other force. A wide flanking movement around this position could, if successful, present an unprecedented opportunity for rolling up the entire British rear. Characteristically, this was just the route Rommel selected for his advance.

On the other side of the line, Ritchie was totally in the dark as to which avenue of approach the Desert Fox would select; north, center, or south. Auchinleck envisioned the combination of an Axis thrust through the center coupled with a drive around the flank at Bir Hacheim. As already stated, he advised that the main armoured concentration be in the north so that it could cope in strength with either or both of these possible threats. Ritchie ignored the advice and left the armour scattered, condemning it to fight piecemeal.

Rommel fed on Ritchie's uncertainty. Using large fans mounted on camouflaged vehicles, the Germans drove round the front and center of the British positions, stirring up clouds of dust and leaving the impression that large formations of armour were on the move in these areas. Ritchie was completely taken in by the ruse.

On May 26, Rommel's attack began in the north during daylight hours. However, this attack was merely a feint, for the Afrika Korps already had begun the sweep around Bir Hacheim as the Italian Trieste and Ariete Divisions pushed into the gap north of this position.

Rommel experienced stiffer opposition than expected as his units drove into the interior of the Eighth Army position. The fighting on the next day was confused with neither side holding the advantage at nightfall. General Cruewell butted against strong defenses in the north and Bir Hacheim stood firm at the other end of the line causing Rommel a great deal of concern. But the Eighth Army counterattacked piecemeal allowing the Fifteenth and Twenty-first Panzer Divisions to advance to the Trigh Capuzzo tract. Rommel commented:

> Ritchie had thrown his armour into the battle piecemeal and had thus given us the chance of engaging them on each separate occasion with

just about enough of our own tanks. This dispersal of the British armoured brigades was incomprehensible.[23]

The Axis advance proved slow and costly with the Germans suffering heavy casualties. The Ninetieth Light was then dispatched northeast towards the British positions at El Adem in order to lay siege to Tobruk and prevent the garrison there from intervening in the battle, while the rest of the Afrika Korps began hitting the British armoured brigades that were flung piecemeal against them. To Rommel's great surprise and dismay, the British had introduced the new American Grant tank. The Grant proved superior to the German Mark III which constituted the bulk of the German armour. Only the relatively few Mark IV tanks proved a match for the Grants. Accordingly, Rommel suffered heavily.

On the twenty-eighth, Auchinleck held an important conference in Cairo. Present at this conference were "Freddie" du Guingand and an old friend of the Auk who had arrived only ten days previously to assume the position of deputy chief of staff, Col. Eric Dorman-Smith. As they studied the latest reports from Ritchie, they concluded that thus far the battle had proceeded satisfactorily. However, they did agree that now was the time to concentrate the armour against that of the enemy before Rommel had time to establish a defensive position. Once Rommel could be contained and destroyed, they reasoned, the Eighth Army could proceed with its own offensive. Indeed, Auchinleck was so optimistic that he even wrote to Ritchie mentioning the possibility of switching over to the offensive. Dorman-Smith went forward to Ritchie's headquarters on the twenty-ninth and hand-delivered Auchinleck's letter. He found the prevailing atmosphere to be very optimistic.

Meanwhile, despite suffering heavy losses, Rommel ordered his forces to concentrate, and miraculously they were able to do so. The area of concentration came to be known as The Cauldron. There Rommel managed to establish his defensive flanks, the very thing Auchinleck had cautioned against. The battle of The Cauldron continued into early June with each successive British assault sent in individually. These attacks were repulsed and destroyed in detail. Surely, the lack of concentration was taking its toll among the British formations. Would they never learn?

Auchinleck continued to receive optimistic reports from Ritchie, but the situation was not developing as optimistically as these reports indicated. Once more Auchinleck found himself in the unenviable position of having doubts as to the outcome of the battle and in the ability of his commander. He was still reluctant to interfere, not wanting to risk undermining the confidence of the commander of the Eighth Army.

On June 10, Bir Hacheim fell to the Germans after a two week battle against the gallant and brave free French forces defending the position. It was truly an epic struggle, one that filled all free Frenchmen with great pride. With the fall of Bir Hacheim, Rommel's supply line was now completely secure. In addition, those troops who were involved in the long siege of Bir Hacheim were now free to head north. On June 11, the Axis formations burst out of The Cauldron and by evening, Rommel had established his headquarters in the El Adem area.

Auchinleck was very apprehensive and went himself to the front just as he had during the Crusader battles. He arrived at Eighth Army headquarters on June 12. Although he refrained from interfering, he carefully apprised himself of the situation. Unfortunately, the battle was so fluid and events moved so fast that much of the information was outdated by the time it was received.

That same day, Rommel continued to move forward and by evening he was able to boast of the destruction of the British Second and Fourth Armoured Brigades. The survivors of the brutal fighting regrouped to the south of Acroma in the defensive box known as Knightsbridge. Rommel had succeeded in smashing through the main Eighth Army defenses.

Unrealistically, Auchinleck returned to Cairo on the thirteenth confident that the Eighth Army would hold Rommel. Ritchie had reiterated his strong determination to fight. Was it but wishful thinking on his part or did he really think that he would be able to contain Rommel? Most historians agree that it was at this point that Auchinleck should have taken direct control of Eighth Army. He was simply unable to perceive that Ritchie had lost his nerve, believing instead that the latter still had the situation under control. This was a tragic error of judgment.

Churchill himself accepted Auchinleck's assessment that Ritchie had the situation well in hand. The disaster continued to build. On the night that Auchinleck returned to Cairo, the Knightsbridge box fell and the next day, Eighth Army began its eastward withdrawal. This was the very opposite assessment previously put forth by Ritchie.

The spectre of Tobruk now loomed large on the horizon. It must be remembered that previously, on January 19, Auchinleck had stated in an operational instruction that it was not his intention to hold Tobruk permanently. What was Ritchie's intention?

At 10:30 on the morning of June 14, Ritchie sent a signal to Middle East Command outlining his new plans. He proposed to evacuate the Gazala defenses while a new mobile force of armour and infantry formed further west. He did not tell Auchinleck that XIII Corps already was heading for the frontier. In the meantime, he established a defensive line—Tobruk-El Adem-Belhammed.

Auchinleck quickly reacted to Ritchie's signal. He told Ritchie to hold a line west of Tobruk emphasizing that the enemy must not invest the port. This marked the Auk's first direct interference in the conduct of the battle. Ritchie felt that the line specified by his commander would be difficult to hold and he offered no guarantees. Auchinleck's desire to hold west of Tobruk could be traced back to his January directive. He did not want to go through another situation reminiscent of the previous year. Therefore, the Axis must be stopped west of Tobruk; not at the city itself. He would not sanction another siege. "Our forces will not be invested in Tobruk!"

Ritchie had already issued a contradictory command, specifying that the Eighth Army's plan was to withdraw to the Egyptian frontier and occupy defensive positions there. Tobruk was to be held as long as possible. Unfortunately, this made Tobruk the focus of action, exactly the opposite objective specified by Auchinleck.

As the situation in North Africa continued to worsen, Churchill was preparing to leave for Washington for a high level conference with President Roosevelt. He demanded to be kept in very close touch with the situation in the Middle East. The Prime Minister emphatically informed the Auk that Tobruk must not be lost under any circumstances. Auchinleck responded affirmatively stating that he had no intention of giving up the city and had no intention of leaving Eighth Army to be besieged within. He then sent Ritchie two orders. The first told him to deny the enemy the general line Acroma-El Adem-Bir el Gubi and the second ordered the Eighth Army commander not to allow his forces to be invested in Tobruk. Churchill responded:

> We are not satisfied with the orders to General Ritchie, which did not positively require him to defend Tobruk. To make sure I sent the following telegram. We are glad to have your assurance that you have no intention of giving up Tobruk. War Cabinet interpret your telegram to mean that, if the need arises, General Ritchie would leave as many troops in Tobruk as are necessary to hold the place for certain.[24]

Defend and hold were interpreted in different ways. For Auchinleck, defending Tobruk meant holding a defensive line west of the town. Meanwhile, the very thing Auchinleck desired least was about to happen. Troops were moving into Tobruk. Although he was forced to accept this situation, he did so only as a temporary expedient until such time as a counterstroke could be organized.

Never had so much confusion existed. Churchill believed that Tobruk would be held to the very end with all the resources available and set off for Washington holding firmly onto that belief. Ritchie was diverting forces to the port in anticipation of a withdrawal to the frontier. Auchinleck continued to insist that the defense of Tobruk be west of the city.

El Adem fell on the sixteenth with the Fourth Armoured Brigade withdrawing in panic towards the frontier. Rommel immediately wheeled to the north for Gambut, east of Tobruk. Auchinleck quickly flew to Ritchie's headquarters at Sollum two days later. He listened to Ritchie's overoptimistic and inaccurate reports and left confident that the latter recognized the need for an immediate counterattack against the enemy. He was supremely confident that Tobruk would hold and that Ritchie would soon counterattack. Ritchie even told the Tobruk garrison under the South African general, Klopper, that when Rommel attacked, a strong force from Eighth Army would smash into Rommel's rear. The problem, however, was that Rommel struck before Ritchie could do anything about it.

No sooner had Auchinleck informed London of Ritchie's plan when the Desert Fox struck. On June 21, Rommel's forces attacked in full strength, and in an unbelievable turn of events, Tobruk fell rapidly. Churchill was in Washington when word of the disaster was passed to him by Roosevelt. Thirty-three thousand troops fell into Rommel's bag along with tons of equipment. The British suffered one of their greatest humiliations. As for Rommel, it was his greatest triumph. Elusive Tobruk was finally his and Hitler rewarded Rommel with a field marshal's baton.

Ritchie was now in headlong retreat to the Egyptian border and beyond. Panic and fear spread through the ranks of the Eighth Army remnants. Rommel had become somewhat of a bogeyman. Auchinleck flew to the front on the twenty-second and witnessed for himself the fear, panic, and confusion and realized that he had to do something to offset the magical effect of the Rommel name. That name alone seemed to hold a bewitching effect. Therefore he issued the following message:

> There exists a real danger that our friend Rommel is becoming a kind of magician or bogeyman to our troops, who are talking far too much about him. He is by no means a superman, although he is undoubtedly very energetic and able. Even if he were a superman, it would still be highly undesirable that our men should credit him with supernatural powers. I wish you to dispel by all possible means the idea that Rommel represents something more than an ordinary German general. The important thing now is to see that we do not always talk of Rommel when we mean the enemy in Libya. We must refer to 'the Germans' or 'the Axis Powers,' or 'the enemy' and not always keep harping on Rommel. Please be sure that this order is put into immediate effect, and impress upon all commanders that from a psychological point of view, it is a matter of highest importance.[25]

Auchinleck now faced the dilemma of what to do with Ritchie. Even though the possibility was being debated in higher circles, he hesitated to dismiss the Eighth Army commander. For the second time in less than a year Auchinleck was confronted with having to make a drastic decision regarding the fate of his army's commander. He finally decided to wait before making a change, for it was felt that to do so now would create even more confusion: so the Auk stuck with Ritchie.

Since the evacuation of the Gazala line, Ritchie had been reorganizing his army in defenses along the Egyptian frontier. These were similar to the ones at Gazala and were just as vulnerable in that they presented an open flank thirty miles to the south. As the British no longer possessed an armoured force to speak of, he agreed that the frontier position should be abandoned and that the forces should withdraw to the Mersa Matruh area. With that decision made, Auchinleck returned to Cairo.

At Mersa Matruh Ritchie was determined to fight the final battle for Egypt. After a review of the situation, Auchinleck came to the conclusion that the same conditions prevailed at Mersa Matruh as had at Gazala. (See Map 9)

Meanwhile, Rommel was rapidly pursuing the retreating British formations. On June 23 he crossed the frontier and swept towards Sidi Barrani, covering one hundred miles in 24 hours. By nightfall of the following evening, he was in front of Mersa Matruh.

Ritchie's deployment at Mersa Matruh was doomed to failure from the outset. The defenses were simply too widely separated. One wing of the defense was

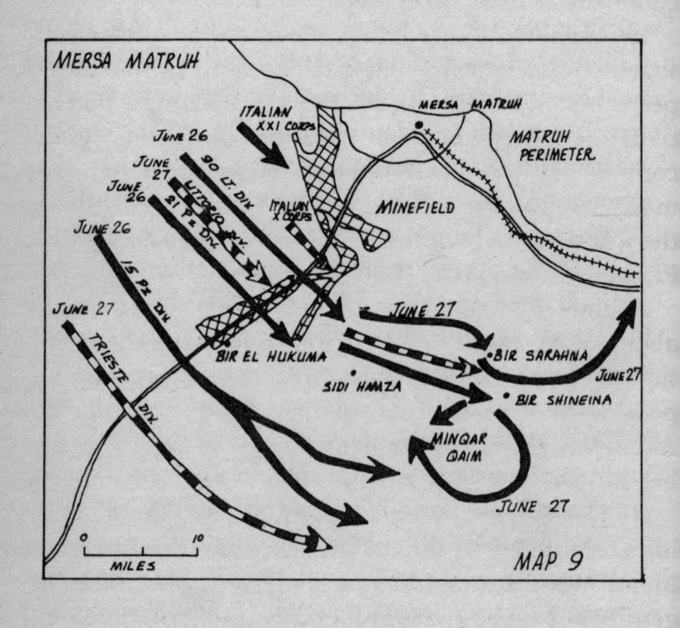
MERSA MATRUH
ITALIAN
XXI CORPS
MERSA MATRUH
MATRUH
PERIMETER
JUNE 26
90 LT. DIV
JUNE
27
LITTORIO DIV.
JUNE
26
21 PZ DIV.
ITALIAN
X CORPS
MINEFIELD
JUNE 26
15 PZ DIV
JUNE 27
TRIESTE
DIV.
JUNE 27
BIR EL HUKUMA
BIR SARAHNA
JUNE 27
SIDI HAMZA
BIR SHINEINA
MINQAR
QAIM
JUNE 27
0
10
MILES
MAP 9

manned by X Corps and that lay in the north with its back to the sea. Nine miles south of it, along an east-west escarpment, lay XIII Corps. Further west and a little south lay the Twenty-ninth Indian Brigade on the Sidi Hanza box and the New Zealanders manned Minquar Qaim. There Ritchie waited for Rommel with the fate of Egypt resting on his dispositions. Finally, the Auk relieved him and assumed personal command on the twenty-fifth.

In Ritchie's defense it must be said that Auchinleck shares the blame for placing a man far too inexperienced in command of the army. Though potentially a good commander, his inexperience in higher command most assuredly took a heavy toll on the man. Ritchie, by the way, resumed his career later in the war as a corps commander under Montgomery in France and conducted himself credibly.

Auchinleck took control just as the battle was about to commence. He had already made the decision to pull his forces back from Matruh as soon as possible and fall back to another position around El Alamein. He was determined not to let Eighth Army be trapped at Mersa Matruh.

At El Alamein, defensive positions were hastily being constructed. It became necessary for the forces at Mersa Matruh to hold out as long as possible without getting themselves trapped in order to buy time. In the official British history, Auchinleck's aims are clearly spelled out. (See Map 10)

> To keep all troops fluid and mobile, and strike at the enemy from all sides. Armour not to be committed unless very favourable opportunity

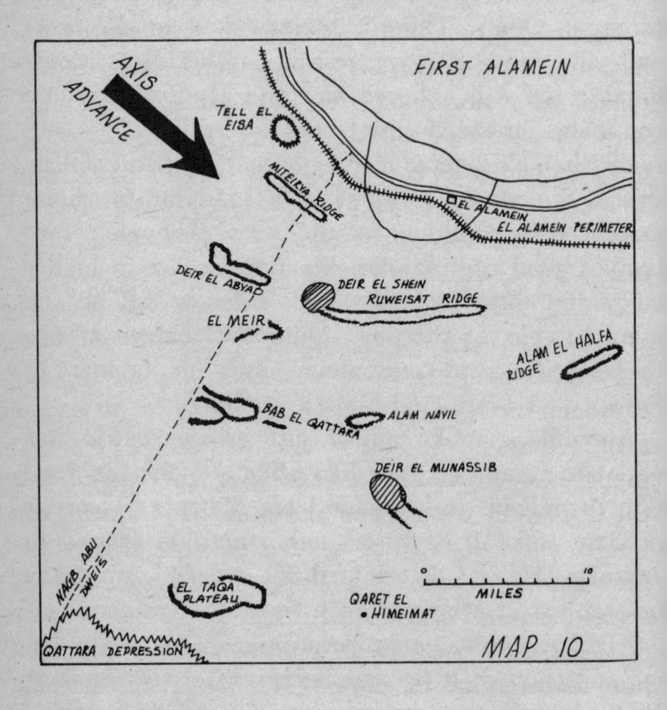
AXIS
ADVANCE
FIRST ALAMEIN
TELL EL
EISA
MITEIRYA RIDGE
EL ALAMEIN
EL ALAMEIN PERIMETER
DEIR EL ABYAD
DEIR EL SHEIN
RUWEISAT RIDGE
EL MEIR
ALAM EL HALFA
RIDGE
BAB EL QATTARA
ALAM NAYIL
DEIR EL MUNASSIB
NAGB ABU
DWEIS
0
10
MILES
EL TAQA
PLATEAU
QARET EL
HIMEIMAT
QATTARA DEPRESSION
MAP 10

> presents itself. At all costs and even if ground has to be given up, I intend to keep Eighth Army in being and to give no hostage to fortune in shape of immobile troops holding localities which can easily be isolated.[26]

Rommel struck hard at Matruh and victory appeared certain as the British conducted themselves in typical confusion reminiscent of Gazala and Tobruk. The casualties were heavy as the Eighth Army attempted to extradite itself and make for El Alamein. The battlefield itself was one confused mass of combatants, as enemy and friendly forces alike intermingled indiscriminately with each other. The fog of war was "indescribable."[27]

Auchinleck himself faced an incredibly difficult task. Although the strain was enormous, his strong character prevailed as he prepared to meet the enemy at El Alamein. In the event of failure there, he prepared another defense at the Suez Canal itself, but the Auk was determined that the El Alamein line would not fall. Critics of Auchinleck, particularly Montgomery, point to these plans of further withdrawal and brand Auchinleck a defeatist because of them. The truth of the matter was that the Auk had no intention of allowing El Alamein to become another Tobruk or even a Kut of his World War I days. Eighth Army must not be destroyed. If Rommel destroyed the Alamein position, the Eighth Army must get away to fight another day. In other words, Auchinleck never viewed the El Alamein "line" as a fight to the last man. Alamein must be held, he said, but Eighth Army must not be eliminated. Each man must fight to his ultimate but without annihilation. As Auchinleck ultimately saw it, El Alamein could be lost but the Eighth Army was all there was left to defend Egypt and the Suez Canal.

However, the British held some advantages at El Alamein. The so called "line" stretched forty miles into the interior abruptly ending in an impenetrable sea of sand called the Qattara Depression. The existence of this depression effectively prohibited the Axis from turning the left flank of the British position. In addition, along the line there were numerous high points which gave Alamein certain defensive characteristics.

As Rommel continued to advance, panic ensued in Cairo. The Germans were heady with victorious enthusiasm. Mussolini even crossed the sea with his beautiful white charger in anticipation of a triumphant ride through the streets of Cairo. Auchinleck and the Eighth Army were all that could prevent Rommel and Mussolini from their triumphant day.

Meanwhile, in Parliament, Churchill faced a no confidence vote. His political career was in the balance just as Auchinleck's military career was.

In the midst of a swirling, whirling sandstorm on the night of June 30, the tanks of the Afrika Korps approached the Alamein line. As terror-filled office personnel were preparing to burn confidential papers in Cairo, enemy artillery opened up with a heavy barrage. The battle of First Alamein was on.

Auchinleck's battle plan envisaged part of the Eighth Army (newly reinforced by troops from other parts of Middle East Command) to hold defensive positions while the remainder struck the enemy flan and rear as they moved into the gaps formed by the British static defenses. There were three main defensive positions. From north to south they were: Alamein itself; Bab el Qattara fifteen miles further south, situated below the Ruweisat Ridge; and one at Nagb Abu Dweis near the Qattara Depression. The work on these defensive positions was not yet complete by the time the Axis struck. In addition to the unfinished defenses, Eighth Army's infantry and armoured forces were severely depleted. More than ever, reliance on the RAF was necessary.

Norrie's XXX Corps was responsible for the front north of Ruweisat Ridge and Gott's XIII Corps defended a little further south. Auchinleck moved his headquarters to a position slightly north of the Alam el Halfa Ridge in the sector defended by XXX Corps.

Rommel concluded that the Alamein defenses were stronger than they actually were. Perhaps he was duped by British propaganda which made the Alamein line appear as formidable as the Maginot line. Therefore, he delayed the attack for twenty-four hours in order to prepare himself. He also believed that the southern section of the line was the area most weakly held and so he chose that avenue of advance. The Ninetieth Light and the Afrika Korps he ordered to thrust through the British defenses on both sides of the Miteirya Ridge; the Ninetieth Light to the north and the Afrika Korps to the south. Once through, Ninetieth Light was then to swing northward to the coast and isolate Alamein while the Afrika Korps armour blasted the defenses from behind. Speed was essential, Rommel emphasized.

Auchinleck was about to achieve his greatest victory. He knew the inherent danger of static defenses and so he thinned them out, leaving only that which was necessary, while the others he sent behind the line where they were formed into battle groups of mobile forces of fighting men. At Dorman-Smith's suggestion, Auchinleck now also placed all the regrouped artillery under his own command. This would allow the Eighth Army to defend and attack under the cover of massed gunfire. He also created an armoured brigade, the Fourth Light, composed entirely of armoured cars and which was intended to exploit breakthroughs at rapid speeds, much faster than tracked vehicles.

Attrition and a long supply line were affecting Rommel, but as already seen, his plan was to repeat his great victory at Matruh. Would the gods of war continue to shine favorably upon him? Unfortunately for Rommel, they did not. Inhibited by sandstorms, harassed by the RAF, and feeling the effects of attrition, Rommel launched his assault on the night of June 30.

By morning, the Axis spearhead was blunted. Rommel had underestimated the British defenses in his attack area between Miteirya and the Ruweisat ridges. The superb delaying tactics of the Eighteenth Indian Brigade at Deir el Shein proved invaluable for the defense of the entire line. Though suffering from lack of sufficient reinforcements and fuel, the Indians staunchly held on to their positions despite a severe pasting by the Afrika Korps. By late afternoon, the Indian position had fallen, but their brave and stubborn defense had delayed the Axis advance and took a heavy toll on their armour, giving the British the necessary time to enhance their defenses. Now the Twenty-second Armoured Brigade struck, pushing the Afrika Korps westward of Deir el Shein. The Ninetieth Light also found itself beset by immense problems, chief of which was the fight of the South African forces who battered the Ninetieth Light so fiercely that a situation of near panic almost developed in the German ranks.

Rommel admitted that, under the tremendous weight of British fire, his objectives for the first day were unfulfilled. Auchinleck could feel satisfied. July 1 marked the Auk's day of victory. He had achieved the near impossible—taking the shattered, scattered, and confused remnants of Eighth Army and creating a cohesive fighting force which was able to halt a victory-filled Axis force. Rommel soon realized that he was finally up against a talented and determined opponent.

By first light of July 2, Rommel readied his forces for yet another attempt, but Auchinleck too issued orders for the Eighth Army to go over to the offensive. Ironically, Rommel's attack and Auchinleck's counteroffensive began almost simultaneously. Rommel ordered the Ninetieth Light to swing north to cut the coastal road. The Afrika Korps was to join in the envelopment of the El Alamein box. The First South African Brigade was ready and waiting. Furiously bombed by the RAF, Ninetieth Light was halted in its tracks. South, below the Ruweisat Ridge, the Afrika Korps and the British First Armoured clashed. The bloody, thundering battle continued till dark but the Eighth Army forces held the field. Auchinleck had reversed the Rommel tactic of letting the armour attack and luring it into artillery traps. Rommel had used this tactic with devastating results in the past but he now found himself the recipient of this most unwelcome surprise. The Axis forces suffered heavily. Though the results of this day's fighting were not conclusive, the tide had unquestionably turned.

Back in London, the no confidence vote against Churchill had failed, but more than ever he realized that his political future and reputation depended on the military situation. So, preoccupied with his political problems, he failed to grasp the significance of just what Auchinleck had accomplished at El Alamein. Brooke had all he could do to calm Churchill down from attacking Auchinleck.

> I had an uphill-task defending him and pointing out the difficulties of his present situation. Also the fact that any rash move on his part at the present time would very quickly lose us Egypt.[28]

On July 3, it was obvious that Rommel had been halted. Auchinleck had outgeneraled him. The Auk hit Rommel at one point, then suddenly he would switch and strike at another. First in the north, then further south, attempting to keep the enemy off balance. Axis strength eroded even further. Rommel found himself in desperate straits. His tank strength and his supply line stretching back to Benghazi and Tripoli was constantly being harassed by the RAF. A battle of attrition would be suicide for him, but that was just the type of battle that was developing.

Rommel struck once more on July 3. The Panzer army fought their way eastward along both sides of the Ruweisat Ridge and by nightfall managed a small penetration. But the cost had been prohibitive. Rommel was highly impressed by the manner with which Auchinleck was conducting the battle.

> General Auchinleck . . . was handling his forces with very considerable skill and tactically better than Ritchie had done. He seemed to view the situation with decided coolness, for he was not allowing himself to be rushed into accepting a 'second best' solution by any moves we made.[29]

At least Rommel appreciated Auchinleck's talents even if Churchill did not.

Auchinleck hoped now to turn the tables on the Axis by having XXX Corps strike in the north as the XIII Corps wheeled from south to north against the Axis line of communication. Unfortunately, exhaustion was also evident on the British side. Auchinleck continued to prod his commanders. Finally, on the fourth, Churchill sent his first encouraging word to him as he began to finally realize what had been accomplished.

Throughout the fifth, XIII Corps attempted to consolidate for the renewed offensive but found itself progressing slowly. Auchinleck realized that his corps commanders were exhausted. Norrie of XXX Corps was replaced by General Ramsden. Gott, however, remained with XIII Corps even though the man was obviously at the end of his tether.

By July 7, Auchinleck reached the conclusion, albeit reluctantly, that he lacked sufficient strength to carry out his plan of swinging round the Axis from the southwest; but he still planned to continue in the north, which he did. This resulted in the recapture of

Tel el Eisa by the recently arrived Ninth Australian Division. Despite Rommel's dispatch of aid to the northern sector, Auchinleck's forces held firm. Meanwhile, Auchinleck moved his headquarters to the Ruweisat Ridge, a mere half-mile from that of XXX Corps. As the Auk said:

> In the conditions prevailing and the desperate nature of the situation, it seemed to me essential that the Commander should be as close behind the line as he could without risking dislocation by capture or bombardment. Ruweisat Ridge was in my opinion the key to the whole position.[30]

Rommel continued to attack, probing for that elusive victory. Mussolini had long since returned home to Italy, horse and all. Rommel launched yet another attack on the Alamein box on the afternoon of July 13, but in vain, as the South Africans refused to yield. Auchinleck continued to counterattack. He adopted a policy of hitting the Axis where they were weakest, in the areas held by the Italian forces. Rommel was forced to continually divert the German forces to bolster his faltering ally. The Desert Fox himself was at the end of his tether and his health began to fail.

Contrast now, Rommel and the Auk. Auchinleck was exhilarated and full of enthusiasm, for he had stopped the enemy and saved Egypt; while Rommel was depressed and physically failing. He was reduced to wondering not how to achieve victory, but how to prevent retreat.

Auchinleck had saved the Middle East but he could

not rest for there was danger in the Caucasus. The Germans had opened their major offensive in the Soviet Union designed to capture the major oil fields of Russia. A successful German breakthrough would threaten Persia. Troops were desperately needed for dispatch to that potentially dangerous area. Where would those troops come from? Eighth Army? Yes, but not until Rommel was destroyed. The added burden of worrying again about his flank forced Auchinleck into a premature all-out offensive. He knew he had to strike at Rommel quickly.

Auchinleck's forces did strike. But it was like hitting a stone wall. In reality, the Eighth Army was exhausted. They suffered heavy casualties and were feeling the effects of lack of armoured support and inadequate reserves. Finally, after six bloody, exhausting days, Auchinleck called off the abortive offensive on July 27. He had no other choice but to go over to the defensive. The Eighth Army could do no more for the present.

On the very day that Auchinleck ordered his forces on the defensive, Churchill signaled him stating that the Eighth Army must retain the initiative. Auchinleck and his chief of staff, Dorman-Smith, however, agreed that the best policy would be a defense combined with offensive gestures. Dorman-Smith went one better and said that the enemy should be induced to strike, and when it did, destroyed. He thus foretold the future German attack at Alam el Halfa. In fact, he was so precise that he even predicted the approximate date correctly. Dorman-Smith laid down the plan for the future British offensive. Ironically, it was the plan that Montgomery would later use, taking all the credit for himself.

On July 30, Auchinleck called his corps commanders together and issued his directives for the forthcoming campaign. First, he said that there were to be no further British attacks for the time being. Secondly, he stated that it would be mid-September before the next British offensive would take place and that this offensive would entail a set piece battle. Finally, he laid down special plans. He went on to note that the previous battles had shown that the cooperation of tanks, infantry, and artillery was far below the accepted standard. He emphasized that the distinction between armoured and infantry divisions must be abolished in favor of an all-mobile Eighth Army made up of divisions, each with its ratio of tanks, guns, and lorried infantry. This would allow each division an equal fighting force and give each divisional commander the necessary tools to do the job. Thus, as July turned to August, the Auk set in motion the necessary wheels for preparing for the next offensive with a new model army.

When Churchill received Auchinleck's telegram about going over to the defensive, he flew into a rage. He was now convinced that he would have to go to Cairo in person to deal with the depressing situation. In the early morning hours of August 2, Churchill and Brooke left for the Middle East.

Auchinleck was so close to victory but Churchill failed to see it that way. In fact, it was the Germans who appreciated what the Auk did more than his own Prime Minister. Gen. Fritz Bayerlein, Rommel's chief of staff, stated:

> All of Auchinleck's counter-attacks were tremen-

dously successful. If Rommel had not been beaten then, he would have advanced deep into Egypt. When Rommel lost Tel el Eisa and Ruweisat, he and all of us knew we were lost. It is a pity that no one in Britain recognized the marvellous, though smaller, battles Auchinleck won.[31]

Before continuing the narrative of Churchill's visit to the Middle East, let us try to digest just what Auchinleck had achieved and what the German commanders could so plainly see but his own political leaders refused to acknowledge.

First of all, Auchinleck prepared the way for total victory, a victory which he would not be allowed to share. Rather, an egotistical individual would usurp the honor and glory and retain it to this very day; Montgomery, Viscount of Alamein. Auchinleck, however, truly paved the path that Montgomery would later walk. He had infused an offensive spirit into an army which had suffered tremendous defeats at Gazala, Tobruk, and Mersa Matruh and dispelled the belief that the retreat would never end. It must also be pointed out that he introduced improved tactics, particularly that of letting the Axis armour batter itself against the implaced artillery rather than allowing his own armour to fall for that very same tactic. Futhermore, his strategy of selecting the weaker Italians as his principal target caused the German strength to be dissipated and was a stroke of genius. His reform of the basic British division went a long way towards making the division an all-around improved fighting unit. Lastly, it was the Auk who destroyed the Rommel myth, even if Churchill did not realize it and Montgomery never acknowledged it.

Even though Auchinleck had accomplished this, his esteem was still low in Churchill's eyes. The Prime Minister could not see that a great victory had been achieved. Unfortunately, politics severely hurt Auchinleck. Through Ultra, Churchill must have known what had been accomplished, but because of the secrecy of this weapon, Churchill could not reveal to the world what Ultra had revealed to him. Instead, what the world was presented with was a badly demoralized Eighth Army that required a shaking up from top to bottom. Churchill's need for a total victory to insure his political future would have to have an ultimate sacrifice—the Auk. Like Hugh Dowding after the Battle of Britain, political pressure won out.

Churchill and Brooke arrived in Cairo on August 3. Discussions immediately commenced at General Headquarters. Present at the talks along with the Prime Minister and Brooke were Corbett, Chief of General Staff in Cairo and Smuts, the South African leader. Auchinleck arrived in the afternoon.

That evening he and Churchill met cordially, but later, Brooke had to calm down the irate Prime Minister who angrily kept saying that the Auk would not resume the offensive until mid-September. In private, the two discussed who should get command of Eighth Army, the thought of replacing the commander in chief was not yet deliberated. Brooke and Churchill disagreed over who should get Eighth Army. Brooke wanted Montgomery while Churchill wanted Gott of XIII Corps. The debate continued.

On August 5, Churchill and Brooke visited Auchinleck's spartan headquarters on the Ruweisat

Ridge. There, the relentless Prime Minister prodded Auchinleck and Dorman-Smith to resume the offensive. Both stood their ground. Mid-September at the earliest, they said. Churchill left curtly and proceeded to RAF headquarters where he was treated to a lavish display of hospitality by Air Vice Marshal Coiningham. It was a great contrast compared to Auchinleck's headquarters. Upon returning to Cairo, he sent off a telegram to Clement Atlee, Deputy Prime Minister. He wrote:

> Just returned from a long but invigorating day with Eighth Army . . . Troops were very cheerful, and all seem confident and proud of themselves, but bewildered at having been baulked of victory on repeated occasions. I propose to visit all the formations, both forward and rear, while pondering on the recommendations I shall have to make to the Cabinet . . . Wherever the fault may lie for the serious situation which exists, it is certainly not with the troops, and only to a minor extent with their equipment.[32]

If it was not the troops or their equipment, then Churchill must have already concluded that the fault lay in one place: the command.

On August 6, the energetic Prime Minister burst into Brooke's bedroom overflowing with enthusiasm over a new idea. He recommended that the Middle East Command be split in half forming a new Near East Command and a Middle East Command which would cover Palestine, Syria, Persia, and Iraq. The Near East Command would be responsible for the western desert and Egypt. The Prime Minister went on to say that Auchinleck would be given the Middle East Command. At this point, he offered Brooke the Near East Command with Montgomery as the Eighth Army commander. Brooke declined the command but did not stand up for Auchinleck. Later in the day, Churchill recommended Alexander for overall command with Gott as Eighth Army commander. The die was cast. Not only would the Auk go, but so would Ramsden of XXX Corps, Corbett, and of course the scholarly Dorman-Smith. A clean sweep of the Middle East Command was in the wind.

All the while, Auchinleck was at his headquarters unaware of these developments. The War Cabinet discussed Churchill's proposals, and though in disagreement on some points, agreed after the Prime Minister applied some pressure. On August 8, Col. Ian Jacob was given the dirty task of delivering the letter to Auchinleck. "It was like killing a magnificent stag," Churchill told Alexander a few days later.

Auchinleck read the letter a few times in silence, trying to digest the contents. To Jacob, he seemed outwardly calm. What else could he do but accept the inevitable. He refused, however, to accept the new role Churchill offered him. He considered it an insult.

Auchinleck arrived in Cairo on the ninth and went first to see Brooke who was at the time briefing Alexander. He then met alone with Churchill for an hour. On the following day, the Auk discussed matters with Alexander and two days later, the "Savior," Montgomery arrived. Gott, who was to get the Eighth Army was killed a few days before. Montgomery does not write favorably about Auchinleck in his memoirs saying that he would not have been happy to serve under him and that he was a poor picker of men. Then again, Montgomery does not speak favorably of anyone unless his name just happened to be Bernard Montgomery. The new Eighth Army commander also got the impression and states so in his memoirs that

> If Rommel attacked in strength, as was expected soon, the Eighth Army would fall back on the Delta; if Cairo and the Delta could not be held, the army would retreat southward up the Nile, and another possibility was a withdrawal to Palestine. Plans were being made to move the Eighth Army headquarters back up the Nile.[33]

Montgomery completely misunderstood Auchinleck or else deliberately distorted the facts. Yes, the Auk considered the preservation of Eighth Army important, but retreat to the Nile and beyond was only a remote possibility. By the time Montgomery came on the scene, retreat was unspoken in Eighth Army, for the tide had already turned against the Axis. These false allegations presented by Montgomery have gone a long way towards obscuring Auchinleck's great achievements. When Montgomery's memoirs were published in 1958, enough had already been known for him to retract these false statements, but no, instead he continued the deceit stating that when he first arrived at Eighth Army headquarters, it was suffering from defeatism, confusion, low morale, and a severe lack of faith in the command. How very false were these statements. In fact, Churchill's wire to Atlee on August 5th refute these very statements. Yes, the troops were tired, or to be more specific, exhausted, but whatever else was wrong with the command structure, Auchinleck had recognized and was in the process of correcting. In fact, the state of Eighth Army was better than it had been in the past two months and that was due to the superb leadership of the Auk. Auchinleck left Cairo on August 15.

Two questions come to mind about the sacking of the Auk. One can be answered in the positive, the other in the negative. Was Churchill justified in replacing him? Yes. He was the Prime Minister and if he lost confidence in one of his commanders then he was fully justified in removing him. The second question is, was this lack of confidence justified? In this case, definitely not. Blinded by his political problems and anxious to restore complete confidence in his own abilities, Churchill did not fully appreciate Auchinleck's contribution. A clean sweep, Churchill felt, would be just the thing. New blood pumping in new ideas. John Strawson, in *The Battle For North Africa*, quotes General Bayerlein again:

> If Auchinleck had not been the man he was and by that I mean the best Allied General in North Africa during the war, Rommel would have finished the Eighth Army off.[34]

Leaving Cairo, the Auk flew to India where he rejoined his wife.

In the desert, Eighth Army repulsed another attack by Rommel in late August (just as Dorman-Smith had predicted) at the Battle of Alam el Halfa. In October the Second Battle of El Alamein took place resulting in a breakthrough by Montgomery on November 4. Churchill praised Montgomery but nowhere was

Auchinleck given credit for laying the foundation for victory. In fact, Montgomery continued to play up the supposed demoralized state of the Eighth Army prior to his arrival. As a result, even more doubts were cast on the Auk.

At the Casablanca Conference in January of 1943, Auchinleck's name came up for a position. Since the previous August he had been unemployed after having declined the Persia-Iraq command. Churchill, however, was having even more and more doubts about Auchinleck after witnessing Montgomery and having access to the latter's papers. Needless to say, Montgomery was anything but kind to his predecessor. Auchinleck had no idea that his reputation was being dragged through the mud.

> Auchinleck had no power of reply, and was in fact totally unaware of the charges against him, yet Montgomery's attack meant the end of his career as a field commander, despite his multitude of skills in this respect.[35]

The charges leveled against him were the lack of morale in Eighth Army at the time of Montgomery's assumption of command, disorganization, and lack of offensive plans. Auchinleck had completely lost Churchill's confidence as a field commander thanks to Montgomery. If he was going to be employed at all, it would be in a nonmilitary capacity.

Much debate and discussion continued about what to do with Auchinleck. Thanks to friends in high places and his thorough knowledge of the Indian army, he was subsequently offered the position of commander in chief of India, replacing Wavell who had been appointed viceroy.

Officially Auchinleck was still denied a field command. The lack of confidence on Churchill's part remained. The post of commander in chief of India was basically an administrative one, consisting of preparing plans and providing stores for the campaigns. A supreme commander for Southeast Asia was responsible for conducting the military operations. Adm. Lord Louis Mountbatten was named to that position, but before he could assume command, the Auk was required to stand in temporarily.

It did not take long for Auchinleck to once more clash with the Prime Minister, this time over operations in Burma. Again Auchinleck found himself in a theatre lacking enough resources to accomplish the job expected. Churchill demanded action, Auchinleck advised restraint until sufficient forces were accumulated. They also crossed swords over the suitable use of the Chindit forces under Gen. Orde Wingate. Churchill labored under the impression that this jungle-trained, long-range penetration group was capable of bringing victory to the theatre on its own. He pointed out that this force could fight the Japanese from behind their own lines. Auchinleck was much more conservative in his assessment of what Wingate's troops could achieve. Too much undue faith in the Chindits, he cautioned, could weaken the total forces being readied for the major operations scheduled for 1944–45. In addition, Wingate had made some unsavory comments about the Indian army and that had angered Auchinleck.

At the Quadrant Conference of August, 1943, the position of commander in chief of India officially was completely divorced from any military involvement. Auchinleck's responsibility was therefore restricted to the administration of India as a base for the forces in Southeast Asia. The active fighting would be directed by a supreme Allied commander.

Mountbatten arrived on October 7, 1943, Wavell became viceroy on the twentieth, and the Southeast Asia Command was officially activated on November 15. Mountbatten established his headquarters next to Auchinleck's in Delhi and both worked efficiently and harmoniously for the balance of the war.

Throughout the remaining months of the war, the Auk continued to raise and train the forces needed for the campaigns. He also continued to coordinate the dispatch of supplies to a war-ravaged China. In his book *Defeat Into Victory*, Field Marshal Slim has this to say of the Auk:

> It was a good day for us when he took command of India, our main base, recruiting area and training ground. The Fourteenth Army from its birth to its final victory, owed much to his unselfish support and never-failing understanding. Without him and what he and the Army did for us we could not have existed, let alone conquered.[36]

The Indian Army soldiers serving in Burma, on garrison duty in Italy, Iraq, or Persia, carried with them the mark of the Auk's personality. His hard work and unselfish devotion to his job however, led to a tragic divorce from his wife. The years of separation had led her to the arms of another man.

On May 31, 1945, Auchinleck was promoted to the

rank of field marshal. Soon after, the war cataclysmically ended with the atom bomb attacks on Hiroshima and Nagasaki. The official surrender was signed on September 2.

With the war's end, Auchinleck became occupied with the preparations of India for the forthcoming independence. This finally came about in August, 1948. The problems were monumental, especially since as the supreme commander for the division of forces, he was handed the sad task of separating the forces, Moslem from Hindu. Since most Indian divisions were comprised of equal quantities of each religion, this directive effectively ended the Indian Army as Auchinleck knew it.

Soon after the partition, Auchinleck was replaced as commander in chief of Indian forces because of his immense prestige. Whose forces could he command, Pakistani or Indian? In order to preserve the peace, the Auk was replaced.

Leaving India, he traveled via Italy to London where he absorbed himself in youth work. He was offered a peerage but politely declined. In 1968, he settled in Morocco because he felt that he could live more cheaply there and the Atlas Mountains reminded him of India's northwest frontier, an area he was particularly fond of.

His life is now occupied by painting, reading, and walking in the mountains. At the age of ninety-six he can boast of having lived a full life.

"Before Alamein we never had a victory. After Alamein we never had a defeat." With those words Winston Churchill characterized the importance of the victory at Alamein. That statement, however, is quite untrue and accounts for much of the under-evaluation of Auchinleck's achievements. Twice he took command in the midst of battle and brought about a victory; Operation Crusader and First Alamein. And what of those victories? The man operated under many handicaps. His theatre was much too broad. If he had been allowed to concentrate on the one job of defeating Rommel as his successors had been able to do, his great victories would have been more significant. Another great handicap that he labored under was his relations with and the uncalled for interference of his own political boss. The latter eventually led to his dismissal. Auchinleck's major errors were in his selection of Cunningham and Ritchie. Cunningham, however, did seem like a good choice at the time. Ritchie was an unquestionably a mistake.

All in all, Auchinleck was every bit the soldier and one of the finest to serve His Royal Majesty, King George VI.

Field Marshal Sir Harold Alexander

Chapter 4

> Men followed Alexander because they found in him all the qualities which they most admired. He projected the Army's idealised image of itself. He was brave, gallant, charming, modest and professional.[1]

With these words Nigel Nicolson sums up Field Marshal Alexander, Earl of Tunis.

When examining a picture of Field Marshal Alexander, one envisions a man possessed of great charm and moral integrity, whose appearance is one of a quiet, self-effacing man; two qualities highly unusual in great military commanders. He carried the bearing of a gentleman and throughout the war never lost that characteristic. Liddell-Hart has said of him, "He was a born leader . . . but he might have been a greater commander if he had not been so nice a man and so deeply a gentleman." Though this great historian gives Alexander a backhanded compliment, the fact that he was recognized as a gentleman is a point to be emphasized.

Of all the commanders of the Second World War, Sir Harold Alexander was the only one with whom nobody could quarrel. The reason for this was his habit of never forcing a course of action upon an unwilling commander. He was instead, open minded and willing to listen to arguments and learn from his subordinates. He firmly believed that if a commander forced an action upon an unwilling subordinate, then that subordinate would not have his heart in it and in the event of failure of the demanded action, that same subordinate would lose confidence in the leader's ability to command. This brand of leadership would cause many problems as portrayed within these pages.

Alex, as he was fondly known to his close associates, was also a very sensitive person, deeply conscious of the feelings of others but selfless to his own reputation. His sensitivity enabled him to identify with his men, making it easier for others to serve under him. This quality was particularly helpful when dealing with people of various cultural backgrounds, something he was destined to do throughout his tenure of command.

As a soldier he perpetually behaved in a professional manner and both believed in and demanded the highest standards. His sense of duty as a soldier was his greatest trait. As a leader, he believed that he must lead by example and was magnificent; but as a strategist he was uninspired. His campaigns were primarily planned from ideas produced by his staff and a good staff was an item that Alexander desperately required.

His contribution was thus to the art of command, not to the art of war, and it is this quality that the authors wish to highlight as we thread our way through the long, but eminently successful career of Field Marshal Sir Harold Alexander, Earl of Tunis.

Harold Rupert Leofric George Alexander was born on December 10, 1891. He was the third son of the fourth Earl of Caledon who died when Alexander was only six. As a child growing up on the huge estate in Ulster, Alexander developed courage, loyalty, self-reliance and a genuine love for living. He seldom read and could hardly be thought of as an intellectual. However, he truly enjoyed sports and painting. His fondest pastime was wandering along the green Irish countryside in pursuit of scenic views in which to practice his artistic talent.

He subsequently entered Harrow, one of England's most exclusive private schools that claimed as some of its illustrious alumni the poet Lord Byron and Winston Churchill. At Harrow he was considered well-balanced and level-headed, a young lad who excelled at games and made friends quite easily. Academically he was only average but stood out in sports, both at Harrow and later at Sandhurst, the prestigious British military academy.

Upon graduating from Sandhurst, he was commissioned a second lieutenant in the Irish Guards, a division which was raised in 1900 by Queen Victoria for the recognition of the gallantry of her Irish soldiers who had perished during the Boer War.

Alexander adapted himself to military life readily and found that it suited him aptly. Within two years of his commissioning, Lieutenant Alexander found himself embarking with Number One Company, First Battalion, Irish Guards for France as part of John French's British Expeditionary Force. On August 12, 1914, this organization was dispatched to stop the rapidly surging German horde rampaging through neutral Holland and Belgium.

The Irish Guards reached Le Havre early in the morning of August 13 and were immediately sent by rail to Wassigny, forty miles south of Mons, arriving on the evening of August 15. From there they were required to march to the brigade concentration area at Vadencourt where for the first time they went into French lodgings. There they remained for three days.

On August 20, the BEF* advanced on Mons, where on the evening of August 22, they heard for the first time the din of artillery fire far to the east. Alexander could not help but feel his heart thump as the rumble of guns and the flashing of shell bursts lit up the scarred landscape.

The next two months were characterized by defensive fighting followed by withdrawal, advance, and attack again. The retreat in the face of the German steamroller left permanent impressions on the young officer; valuable lessons that would be remembered in the future when he once more was faced with the necessity to conduct a withdrawal.

The Irish Guards were not involved again seriously with German advance units until September when they encountered the enemy in the wooded countryside around Villers-Cotterets. Again they were forced to retreat, this time across the Marne River which they reached and crossed on September 3.

The direction of the German right wing was aimed at driving the French and British forces away from Paris and ultimate destruction against the Alps. Thanks to a bad decision by the German General, von Kluck, who turned toward Paris earlier than he

*British Expeditionary Force

should have, the French commander, Joffre, was allowed to build up a strong French force around the capital which managed to successfully protect the city and doomed the Germans to a long bitter war rather than the rapid victory promised by the von Schlieffen plan. This successful French action became known as the "Miracle of the Marne."

By the end of September, the Irish Guards had established all the early elements of trench warfare. They did, however, participate in one last offensive before settling down to the stagnation of the trenches. This was the First Battle of Ypres. During this battle, Alexander was wounded in the thigh and hand, which necessitated his evacuation posthaste to England.

These first months of combat served as his apprenticeship to command. In his baptism of fire he acquired many valuable lessons and would apply them with great success in the grueling years of static trench warfare ahead. Not only had he learned how not to launch men into battle, but he also learned the basics of what not to do on the battlefield.

He returned to combat in the autumn of 1915, one year after receiving his wounds and was quickly introduced to combat at the bloody Battle of Loos. Here his reputation as a fine soldier, trusted by his men and bravely standing by them radiating confidence in the face of potential disaster, began to grow. His superiors soon recognized his ability and began to place more and more trust in him.

World War I was his best preparation for World War II. At the Battle of the Somme he learned lessons that he would never forget. The futility of the bloody Somme battles haunted him in later years when Churchill urged him to continue the Third Battle of Cassino. He recalled then how futile it was to fight in the mud in the face of superior defensive positions.

Alexander was once again wounded in the Battle of Passchendaele and was present at the Battle of Cambrai which was unique for the first use of massed tanks. In 1917-18 he moved up to command of a brigade. Thus, his total war experience was in the ranks, never once having to serve in a staff position. From company to brigade commander, Alexander experienced all levels of command. In 1923, in his history of the Irish Guards, Kipling wrote:

> It is undeniable that Colonel Alexander had the gift of handling the men on the lines to which they most readily responded . . . his subordinates loved him even when he fell upon them blisteringly for their shortcomings.[2]

With war's end, any soldier who had honed his talents to a fine cutting edge could not but help feel let down when it was all over. Feeling naturally elated that one's country had emerged victorious compensated somewhat but the unsurety of a military future faced the warriors when the world turned to the pursuit of peace after the madness of war. Alexander could not help his feelings of being letdown, that the struggle was over, and most assuredly he gave his future serious thought. The future as far as he saw it was without question to be the military career. He thrived on it and felt strong enough to place his future with it. Besides, the lessons learned in the war were too valuable to lay dormant. His talents could best be utilized in the British Army. The experience of the "war to end all wars" left indelible marks on him as he became a professional in all aspects of military life and now, with war's end, he sought a new challenge in order to utilize his talents.

This challenge was found in the struggle taking place in Latvia where he was appointed by the Allied Commission to command a brigade of German Balts called the Landeswehr, in a campaign to repulse the invading Bolshevik army. Alexander now found himself faced with totally unfamiliar challenges. First of all, he was now in command of foreign troops, ironically, many of them his former enemy, the Germans. The food supply was dangerously low, with clothing and other essentials required for campaigning in the harsh Baltic winter climate in pitifully short supply. Lastly, the tactics employed emphasized mobile warfare across the northern forests and frozen lakes, a type of warfare unfamiliar to one who had fought in the trenches for four long years.

In one month's fighting alone, Alexander's troops advanced one hundred miles under horrendous conditions, successfully engaging and dispersing no less than six Soviet regiments.

Finally, when peace came to Latvia, Alexander returned to England and his beloved Irish Guards. He was not destined to remain long there, however. The services of the Irish Guards were required in the Eastern Mediterranean to help keep the peace between Greece and Turkey. The Greeks desired to take Constantinople, the old capital of the Byzantine Empire, captured by the Turks in 1453, and return it to

Greek control. Alexander was sent to this city and his unit assigned picket duty in that historic place, with responsibility for keeping the Turks and Greeks apart. On May 15, 1922, at the age of thirty-one, he was promoted to the rank of lieutenant colonel. His career was widening on the horizon. By September, 1922, the crisis had subsided and Alexander accompanied his battalion on the return trip to England.

On the road to high command, it was necessary for an aspiring British officer to attend the Staff College. Alexander therefore attended this institution between 1926–28 and upon completion of the course of study went on to attend the Imperial Defense College before being given his first staff appointment at the Directorate of Military Training in the War Office. A year later, he was appointed general staff officer, first grade to Headquarters, Northern Command at York. During this period of his life, at forty years of age, he married Lady Margaret Bingham.

In 1935, Alexander was ordered to India where he was given command of the Nowshera Brigade on the turbulent Northwest Frontier. Here, for the first time, he commanded Indian troops and soon came to respect their fighting ability, while absorbing the tactics of mountain warfare, experiences that proved invaluable in his future campaigns. During his three years in command of the Nowshera Brigade, he fought two frontier campaigns, Loe Agra in early 1935 and the Mohmand later in the same year.

In recognition for his distinguished service in both campaigns he was appointed a commander in the Order of the Star of India. For him personally, the experience gained in the Northwest Frontier was priceless in sharpening his military abilities. In addition, during the course of these campaigns he came in close touch with another noteworthy British commander, Sir Claude Auchinleck.

In 1936, Alexander was appointed ADC to His Majesty, King George V and also was requested by the Second Punjabi Regiment to become their colonel, a very high honor for a man not brought up in the traditions of the Indian Army. This latter honor was a high tribute to his ability and popularity.

During his brief period of command in India he proved himself to be a master at organization, demonstrated by his ability to organize a force of soldiers into a harmonious fighting force and drawing the best out of the gunners, sappers, and logistic services. Alexander was now well prepared for the ordeals that lay ahead.

As events in Europe took a turn for the worse, with war clouds spreading ominously over the continent, Alexander left India for England where he was posted to command of the First Division. A fellow British officer, Bernard L. Montgomery was also promoted to divisional command, being assigned to the Third.

On September 1, 1939, the German blitzkrieg was unleashed on Poland. Two days later with the expiration of an ultimatum, Britian declared war on Germany for the second time in twenty-five years.

While Poland was being crushed by the German horde, the British Expeditionary Force under Lord Gort left for France; under-equipped in tanks, artillery, antiaircraft and antitank weapons and all the essentials of modern warfare. The BEF consisted of two corps, I Corps, under Sir John Dill containing the

First and Second Divisions and II Corps, under General Alan Brooke with the Third and Fourth Divisions.

During the period known as the Phoney War, the strength of the BEF grew with the addition of yet another corps, the III, under Gen. Sir Ronald Adam. Subsequently, Dill was recalled to the War Office where he became vice chief of the Imperial General Staff and Gen. Michael Barker replaced him as the new I Corps commander.

During the grim, bleak months of the Phoney War, Alexander sought to keep the fighting trim of his men from dulling and never once allowed them to deviate from the high professional standards expected of the fighting British soldier.

May 10, 1940, witnessed the unleashing of Hitler's blitzkrieg in the west, shattering the stagnation of the Phoney War. The Germans struck with two army groups, Army Group B, under Gen. Fedor von Bock in the north opposite Belgium and Holland, and Army Group A, under Gen. Gerd von Rundstedt which proceeded on an axis through the Ardennes forest.

According to Allied plans prepared months before and designated Plan B, when the Germans struck into Holland and Belgium, as expected, the French and British forces were to advance into Belgium to defend the Dyle line. As the cream of the French forces and the BEF engaged the Germans in Belgium, von Rundstedt's army group penetrated the Ardennes, reached the Meuse River at Sedan, and crossed in force spearheaded by Gen. Heinz Guderian's formidable panzer corps. Within a week, these panzer units reached the sea at Abbeville, trapping those forces which had advanced into Belgium. The pressure of Army Group B and the trapping movement of Army Group A resulted in the French and British forces finding themselves squeezed against the English Channel.

Alexander's First Division was defending at the Dyle and was forced to withdraw from that position and pushed back to the French border, where they were ordered to protect the southern flank against Rundstedt's panzer thrust. From there, they were to withdraw to Dunkirk and defend against von Bock's forces. Finally, at Dunkirk, under pressure from both German army Groups and the Lutfwaffe, they were placed aboard ships and evacuated from the continent.

It is important, however, to look deeper into this fateful campaign, focusing on the ability of Alexander and his faculty to function under adversity. When the First Division advanced to the Dyle along with the rest of the BEF at the beginning of hostilities in May, Alexander's division was instructed to deploy on the left hand sector of I Corps east of Brussels. Directly north of First Division was Montgomery's Third Division. During May 12 and 13, while Guderian's panzers were piercing the Ardennes, Alexander's division was primarily involved in preparing defensive positions in preparation for the anticipated battle ahead. On May 14, ominous reports were received. First, the Dutch army had capitulated to von Bock. Secondly, the Meuse was being successfully forded by Guderian's panzers. On May 15, German reconnaissance forces made contact with the Dyle line but only on Montgomery's section. Though not heavily engaged, the perplexed British were then ordered to withdraw. Shortly thereafter they were notified of the German breakout at Sedan and the potential threat to their southern flank.

Throughout the withdrawal, discipline in Alexander's Division was impeccable. On May 18, First Division was transferred to Brooke's II Corps and brought together for the first time the team of El Alamein, Brooke, Alexander and Montgomery. Brooke made this notation in his diary about the forty-eight-year-old major general.

> In taking over the First Division I was for the first time having the experience of having Alexander working under me. It was a great opportunity . . . to see what he was made of, and what an admirable commander he was in a tight place. It was intensely interesting watching him and Monty during those trying days, both of them completely imperturbable and efficiency itself. It was in those critical days that the appreciation I made of those two commanders remained rooted in my mind in the future selection of these two men to work together in the triumphal advance from Alamein to Tunis.[3]

The First Division held its position on the Escaut for the next four days, where on May 21, they were heavily attacked at the Pecq Bridge. As the British held the Franco-Belgian frontier, they waited for the promised French counterattack. When this finally came, the attack had little momentum and reflected the lack of substance in the French High Command. General Weygand, newly appointed commander in chief of French forces then called for an attack southward by two British and two French divisions. He hoped to accomplish a penetration of the exposed German flank which by now stretched from the Meuse to the channel at Abbeville. If this line could be severed, then it would be the Germans who would be trapped; not the Allies.

Alexander's First Division again reverted to I Corps. Meanwhile, while the French were preparing their so called "Weygand Counteroffensive," von Bock's army group hit the British and French forces hard near Courtoi. The effect of the renewed German offensive was decisive as far as the British were concerned. The Belgian army was near collapse and their capitulation would expose the northern flank of the BEF.

As the Germans closed in from all directions, Alexander's division was directed to fall back on Dunkirk. Unfortunately, the withdrawal of the division was stalled by cluttered debris of war along the road, endless rows of fleeing refugees, and two days of incessant rain. (See Map 11)

Operation Dynamo, the evacuation of the BEF, began immediately with the arrival of the troops at Dunkirk. The plan called first for the clearing out of as many specialists and administrative troops as possible before beginning the evacuation of the fighting troops. Then evacuation of those units would commence, III, II and I Corps respectively. The latter therefore was to act as the rear guard.

The chances of saving the entire BEF were considered to be slim at best. Churchill subsequently ordered Brooke and Gort to come home immediately for he felt that their services would be vital in the

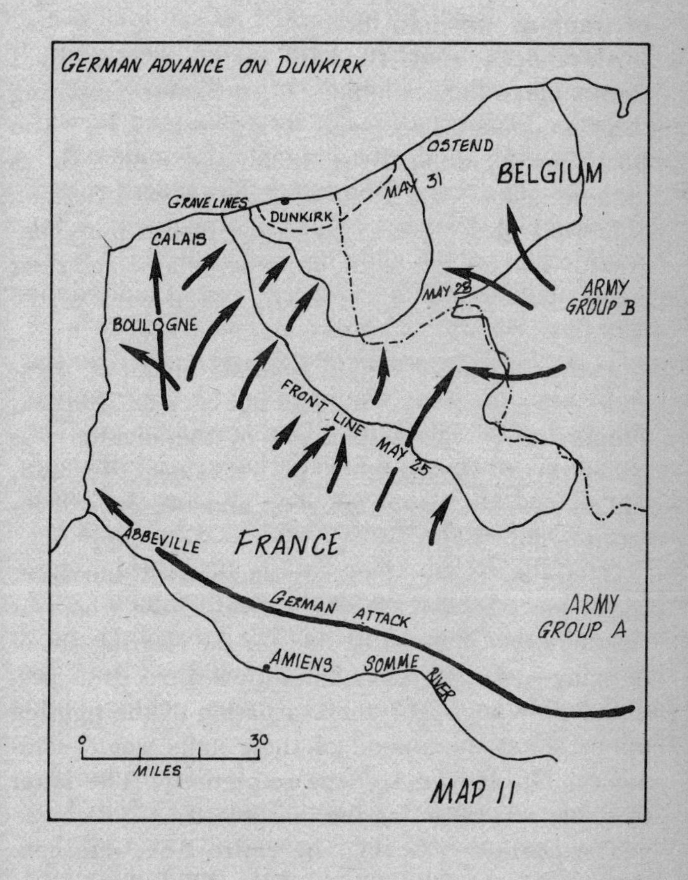
GERMAN ADVANCE ON DUNKIRK
OSTEND
BELGIUM
MAY 31
GRAVELINES
DUNKIRK
CALAIS
MAY 28
ARMY
GROUP B
BOULOGNE
FRONT LINE
MAY 25
ABBEVILLE
FRANCE
GERMAN ATTACK
ARMY
GROUP A
AMIENS
SOMME RIVER
0
30
MILES
MAP 11

training of a new army. Brooke nominated Montgomery as his successor and Gort appointed Alexander to command the rear guard.

In the early morning of June 3, Alexander toured the beaches and after satisfying himself that all British troops had left, he himself set sail for Dover. The French continued to fight for another twenty-four hours, which allowed for one more night's evacuation. Then, on June 5, forty thousand Frenchmen remaining within the perimeter surrendered.

A large controverys looms over Alexander's role in the evacuation. Was he justified in evacuating all the British forces while allowing thousands of French soldiers to march into captivity? Yes! If indeed he made this decision on his own recognizance, then he was very astute. In order for England to survive, she required troops, badly equipped as they were, to defend against a subsequent German invasion. The French were unable to motivate themselves sufficiently to defend their own country let alone be relied upon to defend the British Isles. Did he place the safety of the British troops above the Allied cause? No! He placed the safety of the British Empire itself above all other considerations. The French place the blame squarely on Alexander's shoulders. But, the problem stemmed from conflicting political and military directives.

While Alexander was busying himself with holding the Dunkirk perimeter, Churchill was in Paris making elaborate promises to the French and swearing that French and British troops were being evacuated equally, with the British providing the final rear guard. This message of Churchill's promise was given to Alexander by the French Admiral Abrial and General Fagalde, the French garrison commander. Alexander, however, did not view the situation in the same way. He saw the demoralized state of the French and realized that his primary objective was to get all British forces out of Dunkirk intact along with as many French as possible. To hold the perimeter beyond June 2 would invite disaster. Thus, Alexander chose to go.

His memoirs, however, shed light on the controversy surrounding events at Dunkirk. Alexander states that the Secretary of State for War, Anthony Eden, confirmed Churchill's demand for a 50-50 evacuation of the British and French troops surrounded at Dunkirk. Alexander readily agreed to this demand but events prohibited him from carrying out the order to the full extent of the letter. In Alexander's own words he explains:

> The French troops were given the same facilities as our own to go down to the mole at night and be taken off in Royal Navy vessels; but after a few nights the French quota fell far below our own, so I allocated one whole night for the evacuation of the French alone. But since no French soldiers turned up I realized I could do no more to help them, and we carried on evacuating the last of our own soldiers. I don't blame our French allies; as good Frenchmen they didn't want to leave France, but preferred to remain in their own country—even as prisoners of war.[4]

The French still feel that Alexander was the man who went back on Churchill's promise and maintain that a combined defense of Dunkirk would not have allowed the town to fall to the Germans. But the French were already by this time a defeated nation and simply refused to admit it. In their misery they were willing to see yet another country sacrificed to the wrath of the gods of war. Alexander was determined not to allow this futile gesture. A defeated England was of little value in the struggle against Nazi Germany.

It must be remembered, however, that during the total period of the evacuation, one hundred ten thousand French troops were successfully lifted safely from the beaches. France chooses to ignore this fact. To stay any longer at Dunkirk would have been an act of sheer stupidity rivaling the tragic errors of the Somme offensive during the Great War, which slaughtered hundreds of thousands to no avail. Alexander had learned his lessons well.

The British government did not blame Alexander at all. In fact, a week after landing at Dover, he was promoted to lieutenant general and given permanent command of I Corps with the task of refitting, retraining, and preparing for the anticipated German invasion of England. Alexander assembled I Corps headquarters and his units in northern England, where they were ordered to defend Lincolnshire and the East Riding of Yorkshire.

With the Luftwaffe's inability to destroy the RAF and gain air supremacy, the British High Command finally turned away from anti-invasion work and began planning for the future. On December 2, 1940, Alexander suddenly found himself appointed commander in chief of Southern Command, replacing Sir Claude Auchinleck who assumed the position of commander in chief of India.

Alexander was now truly in his element as he trained the British army for the severe test that lay ahead. Along with Brigadier J. F. Utterson-Kelso, he introduced the Battle School system of training. This system simulated actual combat conditions for the troops and provided the best training for those future experiences of the new recruit. Though the concept was Utterson-Kelso's, it was Alexander who implemented it and saw it through to success. The future performance of the British army owed a great debt of gratitude to this rigorous training. For over a year Alexander was not only involved in organizing and training, but also high level strategical talks with Churchill and the Imperial General Staff. Then came December 7, 1941.

The Japanese attack on Pearl Harbor not only brought the United States into the war but it also thrust upon the British Empire many new and dangerous concerns, chief of which was the protection of their Asian colonies.

The swift Japanese victories culminating with the humiliating and tragic defeat of Singapore in February of 1942, radically altered the direction of Alexander's career. The demoralizing situation in the Far East required a stabilizing influence. With Malaya and Singapore gone, Burma was obviously next in line. Loss of that country would then expose India to further Japanese aggression. In *The Hinge of Fate*, Churchill sums up the reason for his selection of Alexander. (see Map 12)

No troops in our control could reach Rangoon

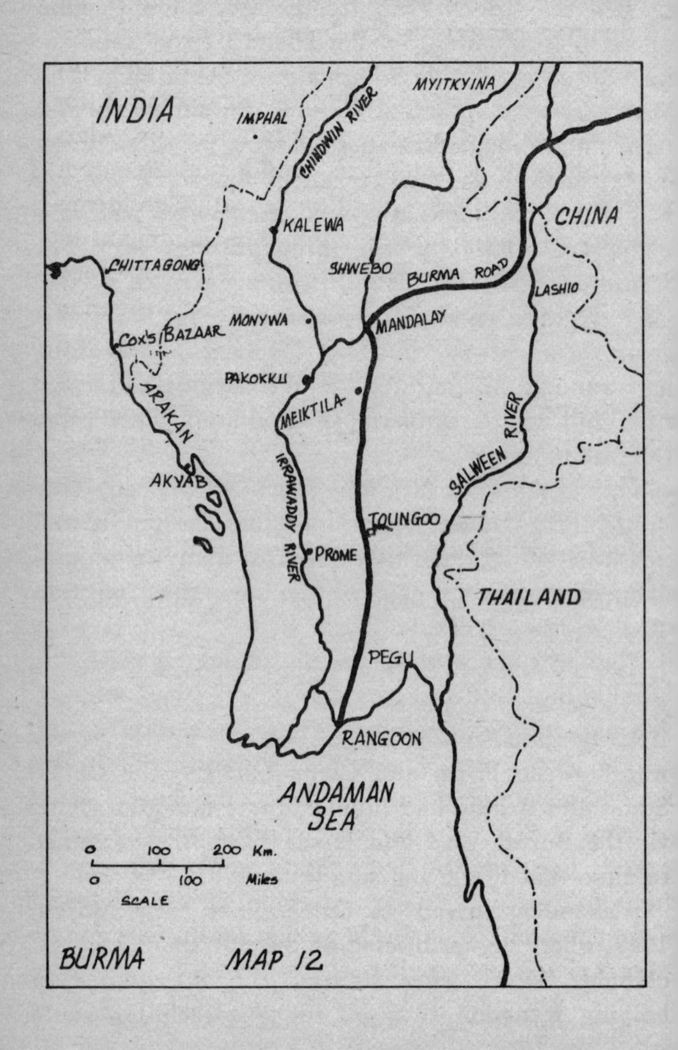
INDIA
IMPHAL
CHINDWIN RIVER
MYITKYINA
CHINA
KALEWA
CHITTAGONG
SHWEBO
BURMA ROAD
LASHIO
MONYWA
MANDALAY
COX'S BAZAAR
PAKOKKU
ARAKAN
MEIKTILA
SALWEEN RIVER
AKYAB
IRRAWADDY RIVER
TOUNGOO
PROME
THAILAND
PEGU
RANGOON
ANDAMAN SEA
0 100 200 Km.
0 100 Miles
SCALE
BURMA
MAP 12

> in time to save it. But if we could not send an army, we could at any rate send a man. It was resolved to send General Alexander by air to the doomed capital. A few hours before his departure, he dined at the Annex with me and my wife. Never have I taken the responsibility for sending a general on a more forlorn hope. Alexander, was, as usual, calm and good-humoured. He said he was delighted to go. Confidence spread around him, whether as a lieutenant or in supreme command. Nothing ever disturbed or rattled him, and duty was a full satisfaction in itself, especially if it seemed perilous and hard. But all this was combined with so gay and easy a manner that the pleasure and honour of his friendship was prized by all those who enjoyed it, among whom I could count myself. For this reason I must admit that at our dinner I found it difficult to emulate his composure.[5]

Burma was far down the list of Britain's priorities and dreadfully unprepared for the ordeal. The Japanese desired Burma because possession of it would serve to totally seal off China, its bitter enemy, from the outside. From the beginning of the lengthy war between Japan and China in 1937, the United States and Britain had supplied material aid to China via the Burma road and Japan was now determined to close that life-giving supply line.

Alexander arrived at Calcutta in early March, 1942, where he was briefed on the situation by Sir Archibald Wavell who stressed the importance of holding Rangoon. Loss of its port facilities would deny the ability to supply the British forces opposing the Japanese.

On March 5, Alexander arrived in Rangoon and went forward to Seventeenth Division Headquarters to meet with its commanders. He was informed that the Japanese were across the Sittang River in force and approaching the British lines. Alexander felt that there were but two options available: reinforce the British forces so they might be strong enough to cut off the Japanese across the Sittang, or abandon Rangoon entirely. He knew that he had to attempt the first option. Thus, he devised a counteroffensive, ordering the Seventeenth Division to attack in a northeasterly direction towards the Sittang River in conjunction with an attack by the First Burma Division southward. Initially, the Seventeenth Division experienced some local success, but by evening of March 6, they found themselves in danger of being cut off by the enemy. Reports received at Alexander's headquarters revealed the approach of Japanese amphibious forces near the mouth of the Rangoon River, while larger forces approached the city itself by land. The latter would soon have the effect of severing Rangoon's road and rail link to the north. Alexander now realized that he faced the inevitable; Rangoon could not be saved. It was necessary, he felt, to order the demolition of the port facilities and oil refineries. He further realized that once these facilities were destroyed, saving the city would be a useless chore, for no reinforcements could be sent to the city by sea. In the late afternoon of March 6, a mere twenty-four hours after assuming command, he ordered the city evacuated and the demolition plan implemented. The Seventeenth Division was then ordered to withdraw to Prome, on the Irrawaddy River.

The swift movement of the Japanese, however, blocked the escape route and cut off the Seventeenth Division which had been involved in the abortive attack towards the Sittang. In addition, not only was this division cut off, but so was Alexander and his headquarters. Several attempts were made to clear the Japanese from the road, but to no avail as the enemy proved too strong. Alexander then decided to mount a full scale attack against the roadblock at dawn of the following day. However, just as the British were about to launch this attack, one of their advance patrols found that, mysteriously, the Japanese had abandoned their roadblock. Why?

Higher headquarters had ordered the Japanese Thirty-third Division to advance around to the north of Rangoon in order to attack the city from the northwest. Secrecy was essential. In order to ensure this secrecy, the Japanese commander responsible for the outflanking movement, Colonel Sakumo, removed his roadblock as soon as his forces were safely across the road.

Although the Japanese had indeed achieved total surprise, when they reached Rangoon no British garrison was found. Alexander and his forces had made good their escape. What might have been total annihilation turned into yet another successful retreat for Alexander. At this point he must have wondered how many more successful retreats would he be called on to conduct.

Following the battle, in a dispatch, Alexander records:

> Having failed in my primary task of holding Rangoon, I now had to consider my secondary task which was the retention of upper Burma.[6]

He now saw as his primary aim the delaying of the northern advance of the Japanese as long as possible to allow India the time it needed to strengthen her defenses and to keep open the channel to the Chinese, who would be totally isolated should the enemy be successful in conquering central and northern Burma.

As at Dunkirk, Alexander was again responsible for fighting a delaying action, but this time it was to be contested on some of the worst terrain in the world. Besides having to fight in this ungodly terrain, Alexander was also struggling with a complicated command structure. Chiang Kai-shek was the supreme commander of the Chinese forces and had as his deputy supreme commander, the American general, Joseph Stilwell, a very capable but caustic individual, who made no attempt to camouflage his dislike for anything or anyone British. Alexander and "Vinegar Joe" met for the first time on March 13, at Maymyo, east of Mandalay. Maymyo was quite hilly and suitable for Alexander's headquarters. In Stilwell's diary he records his first impression of Alexander,

> Alexander arrived. Very cautious. Long sharp nose. Rather brusque and standoffish. Astonished to find me—mere me, a goddam American—in command of Chinese troops. "Extrawdinery." Looked me over as if I had crawled out from under a rock.[7]

Obviously, with Stilwell's attitude, things were going to be difficult.

Stilwell announced to Alexander his proposals. First he stated that he was to assume command of the Fifth and Sixth Chinese armies. Secondly, he went on, he would work with Alexander as his coequal commander of the Imperial forces in Burma. Alexander graciously accepted.

A week later, Alexander flew to Chungking, China's wartime capital, where he paid his respects to Chiang Kai-shek. He was warmly greeted by Chiang and his wife and received from Chiang his acceptance of a simplified command structure for Burma. The Chinese leader, to Alexander's delight, even changed his mind about his original objection of allowing Chinese troops to serve under a British commander. Returning to Maymyo, Alexander informed Stilwell that Chiang had asked him to accept overall command of Imperial and Chinese forces in Burma. Stilwell agreed to abide by these terms though with reservations. Thus, Alexander now controlled all operations in Burma. Stilwell, however, retained direct command of the Chinese forces.

Alexander now found himself overwhelmed by the heavy responsibilities thrust upon him. As theatre commander, he was responsible for both political and military issues and desired to simplify even further the command structure. So he recommended that a corps headquarters be established combining both the First Burma Division and the Seventeenth Indian Division. This corps headquarters, designated Burma Corps, would be responsible for the day-to-day military planning and leave Alexander free to deal with the total situation. As commander of this corps, he recommended the very capable Gen. Sir William Slim.

Analyzing the situation, Alexander realized that the Japanese were in much better position than he. They had superior equipment and were more easily reinforced than the British. Alexander knew that he needed time and that time could only be bought by trading space. So, reviewing a map of Burma, he planned his strategic withdrawals, knowing full well that it was imperative that these retreats be timed so that they caused the greatest amount of damage with the least amount of casualties. Encirclement by the Japanese was to be avoided at all cost and he therefore ordered that a line not be held too long.

Meanwhile, as Alexander was trying to buy this precious time, the Japanese were being reinforced in both men and air power. As the Japanese prepared to move north, their air forces struck the air forces of the Allies, decimating them, and leaving the Japanese with complete domination of the air space over Burma. Without air support or the means to conduct aerial reconnaissance, Alexander and his commanders were reduced to fighting blindly.

Morale dwindled as the Japanese air attacks struck without opposition. The enemy then resumed the offensive north of Rangoon on March 15. Chiang ordered Alexander to mount an offensive as soon as possible in order to relieve pressure on the Chinese forces. Unfortunately, Slim was not yet ready to mount such an attack, and like Alexander, doubted the value of such an attack. However, orders were orders.

On March 29, Slim mounted an attack with British

forces sweeping down the east side of the Irrawaddy. In the absence of aerial reconnaissance, Slim could not have known that at the same time the Japanese had launched an offensive northwards on both sides of the river. The Japanese almost managed to encircle the Seventeenth Division but the British avoided the trap only after they cleared a Japanese roadblock with the loss of ten tanks and over three hundred men. The British offensive was a dismal failure.

Toungoo was now lost and the Japanese rapidly approached Prome. Alexander then authorized a further withdrawal with the concurrence of Wavell, who on April 1, visited Burma and accompanied Alexander to Slim's headquarters so that he could observe firsthand the precarious situation.

Slim's position was indeed insecure. The retreat line assigned his troops was much too large for the number of men available. Reinforcements were desperately needed but none were forthcoming. Every operation Burma Corps mounted seemed to go wrong: there were too few units for the front; they suffered from lack of reinforcements, were overtired and stretched to their limit; they operated in areas where the local population was hostile and the terrain appalling; and overall, the morale among the defenders sunk lower and lower each day.

Though directed to save the oil fields, Slim had no choice but to order their demolition on April 14. Subsequently, the Japanese struck the British at Taungdwingji and managed to penetrate the defensive line. The British stubbornly tried to hold on but the Japanese attack was overwhelming.

Wavell sent a directive to Alexander informing the

latter of the importance of maintaining contact with the Chinese but in the same breath cautioned Alexander that his prime directive was to keep his forces intact for an eventual reconquest of Burma. For Alexander, it was history repeating itself.

The situation continued to deteriorate and went from bad to worse until finally, Alexander realized that the evacuation of Burma was now the only alternative. On April 25, he therefore issued orders for the withdrawal of his forces and for the final evacuation of supplies from Mandalay to India over the Irrawaddy to begin immediately. His chief aim now was to reach India with as much of the Burma Corps as possible before the coming of the monsoon which was due about May 15.

To insure the successful retreat of the forces to Assam in India, supplies were required, and Alexander ordered that stocks be sent along the jungle tracks. Wavell worked from the other end of the route doing the same. It was estimated that it would take at least a week to stockpile the necessary supplies to sustain a retreat. Could Alexander's forces buy that week?

The withdrawal over the Irrawaddy was conducted with great skill depicting the ability of the man responsible for carrying it out, William Slim. By midnight of April 30, the Ava Bridge over the Irrawaddy was demolished and the Battle of Mandalay over. Alexander ordered the wounded and Indian refugees to go first followed by the fighting forces. Their final destination was Imphal. Slim was ordered to provide the rear guard for the retreat. There was now little else Alexander could do but hope that the monsoon would hold off long enough to allow the troops to reach India in safety.

On May 12, the monsoon struck but the British had already reached India successfully. Eight days later, on May 20, Alexander handed over command of the Burmese army units to IV Indian Corps Command which had been ordered by Wavell to defend Assam. Alexander's first major operational command had come to a disappointing end.

Wavell reported to Churchill that Alexander had accomplished a fine feat in bringing the army back. He performed his duty in the way he always performed his duty, with dignity, skill and professionalism. The task must have been disheartening for him—another retreat following Dunkirk by only two years. Yet, Alexander's calmness during the retreat was infectious. Found in the divisional histories of the units engaged in Burma are Alexander's soothing words: "It's O.K. lads." The confidence he engendered was a blessing during those most trying days.

As for his generalship, Alexander would be criticized for not having any clear-cut defined objectives. Slim, in *Defeat Into Victory*, states that very fact and complains that the aim of the campaign was not clearly defined. In Alexander's defense it must be remembered that he was thrust into a situation that was anything but ideal. He was collaborating with an ally that was virtually unknown to him—the Chinese. His relationship with Stilwell was anything but ideal (nobody's was), his troops were not adequately trained, and the Japanese were in total command of the sky. Furthermore, it appears that Burma was written off by higher British authorities long before

Alexander arrived to make an attempt at salvaging the situation (witness Churchill's comments about the dispatch of Alexander in the first place). With that in mind, it is remarkable that he managed to save what he did. Rather than be criticized, he should be open to the highest praise for his magnificent handling of a most trying situation in a most reasonable and sound manner. Though forced to suffer through another retreat his reputation remained intact and both Churchill and Alan Brooke, chief of the Imperial General Staff never lost confidence in him.

The Prime Minister admired Alexander and began to place a blind faith in him. In this belief, Churchill was wholly supported by Brooke. By 1942, the British were in desperate need of a hero. Their military reputation was suffering on all fronts, but nowhere did it suffer more than in the desert of North Africa. There, a remarkably resourceful and cunning German general by the name of Erwin Rommel was causing the British a tremendous amount of humiliation. The British went through one commander after another searching for the one who could destroy the Axis forces in North Africa. As each successive commander failed to live up to the standards of Winston Churchill, he was rudely sacked. Wavell failed in 1941 so Churchill tried Auchinleck. The Prime Minister found Auchinleck lacking and so was ready to try the man who had distinguished himself as the commander of two successful retreats, Harold Alexander. Before Alexander was assigned to the position desired by Churchill, however, Brooke had expressed other plans.

With America now into the fray, the big question

was where and when the decisive blow would be struck against Germany. After much political haggling and hair-splitting, an invasion of French North Africa was finally agreed upon by both sides. Alexander was appointed to command the British Task Force for the invasion of this objective. As supreme commander, the Allies agreed upon the American general, Dwight D. Eisenhower. Alexander's first meeting with the supreme commander was recorded by Eisenhower's naval aide, Capt. Harry Butcher:

> Ike had General Sir Harold R. L. G. Alexander to lunch at the apartment alone. He has been designated by the British as ground commander for the push for Tunisia after the landings are made in the Mediterranean . . . This was an important luncheon, for with Ike junior to General Alexander in rank, with no actual battle experience. . . . there was the touchy question of how acceptable Ike might be to Alexander. . . . When Ike returned from lunch his first comment was, "That guy's good! He ought to be Commander-in-Chief instead of me."[8]

Meanwhile, events in the western desert took a drastic turn for the worse. After the defeat at Gazala culminating with the loss of Tobruk and the retirement to El Alamein, Churchill lost confidence in Auchinleck. Though the latter managed to halt Rommel at Alamein, it was not enough for Churchill. Victory was what he desired and he wanted it quickly. Therefore he searched for a commander who could deliver just that. The choice fell on Alexander. To command Eighth Army, General Gott was chosen, but as fate would have it, he was tragically killed enroute to his new command and so Bernard L. Montgomery was summoned from England to take command of Eighth Army. Brooke, Alexander, and Montgomery together again. The same team which had held the center of the British line in France in 1940. The Alexander-Montgomery tandem was activated on August 15, 1942.

Montgomery and Alexander complemented each other beautifully. The latter of course was gifted with great charm together with years of military experience and proven military judgment; a man who commanded respect and who guided his subordinates more by suggestion rather than by direct order. Montgomery was strong-willed, opinionated and egocentric; but one who had the rare ability to inspire his men. One might liken the Alexander-Montgomery team to a corporation with Alexander as chairman of the board and Montgomery as the managing director.

On August 9, Alexander arrived in Cairo where he was handed a directive from Churchill.

> Your prime and main duty will be to take or destroy at the earliest possible opportunity the German-Italian Army commanded by Field Marshal Rommel together with all its supplies and establishments in Egypt and Libya.[9]

The success, when achieved, would unquestionably be thanks to the efforts of Alexander. His style of command, that of noninterference and command by persuasion, was the only style of command that could keep the wheels of the team well-oiled and operating efficiently. Montgomery was not an easy subordinate;

if anything, just the opposite. At times he could prove most exasperating. Alexander, however, knew just how to avoid overpowering his subordinate and allowed him broad freedom to develop his skills. This was Alexander's greatest asset. He let Montgomery grasp the reins of command which he himself held very lightly.

Immediately upon assumption of command Alexander sensed that the desert forces lacked confidence and decided that if such confidence was to be instilled in his troops, then they must be made to understand that the new team meant business. Therefore, he issued instructions stating firmly that no further withdrawals were contemplated. Both Alexander and Montgomery continued their attempts to instill confidence, a task at which the new Eighth Army commander was superb. In quick order a Montgomery legend was born. He dressed uniquely, donning different style hats and adorning them with various regimental crests. His flair rapidly became a counterweight to Rommel's "Desert Fox" legend, which had haunted the British forces for over a year and a half.

The two generals used other methods to bolster Eighth Army's confidence. One of these methods was to move the main headquarters nearer the fighting front. Alexander, as a former front line soldier, knew how important it was for the soldier to be aware of the presence of higher commanders near the front.

The only truly effective way to build confidence, however, and both commanders were acutely aware of this, was to once and forever burst the Rommel myth. That opportunity was soon to be presented. Rommel was no fool and was very aware that the

Eighth Army would inevitably be reinforced, while his own forces gradually became weaker through natural attrition. He realized that it was imperative for him to attack before it was too late. Thus, Rommel planned an offensive for the latter part of August with the aim of slicing through the southern end of the El Alamein line from whence he could turn north to the coast. This was a duplication of the remarkably successful strategy used at Gazala the previous June.

Thanks to the Allied code-breaking ability (Ultra), Alexander and Montgomery became privy to this information and planned, through deception and surprise, to lay a trap for their formidable opponent.

On August 31, Rommel struck and suffered a serious setback. The Battle of Alam el Halfa, as this battle is known, has been referred to by some historians as the Stalingrad of the desert. Rommel's losses were severe as his forces were pounded by both the RAF and Eighth Army artillery situated on the Alam el Halfa Ridge. The Desert Fox had met his match and could ill-afford these losses, and by September 2, he was forced to call a retreat after having suffered a major setback. The way was now clear for a systematic defeat of Rommel's entire force but miraculously for the Axis, Montgomery failed to pursue the crestfallen Rommel. Instead, he stuck to his "master plan" (a term closely associated with him) and did not commit Eighth Army to a major attack before it was fully trained and prepared. He insisted that the master plan be adhered to. Alexander concurred with his subordinate. Montgomery had, however, achieved the immediate goal; the Rommel legend was shattered forever and Eighth Army's confidence soared.

Alexander and Montgomery now set about preparing for a major offensive designed to oust the Axis from Egypt and Africa for good. As he had done previously with a succession of commanders, Churchill began to apply pressure to initiate the offensive immediately before Eisenhower's forces could land in French North Africa.

After months of training, October 23 was finally selected as the fixed date for the proposed offensive. Though Churchill continued to lobby for an earlier date Alexander and Montgomery refused to be swayed and the Prime Minister had little choice but to go along with his commanders.

Planning for the offensive involved the talents of both generals. Deception and subterfuge were to play a great part in it. Millions of mines were sowed by both sides turning the land along that forty-mile stretch between the coast and the Qattara Depression into one of the world's largest killing zones.

Montgomery's plan was first of all to convince the Germans that he would attack from the southern section of the Alamein line when in reality his main assault was contrived to go through the northern portion. The final plan was to fall into three phases. In the first phase, which Monty called the break-in, two British corps would drive their armour through dual corridors into the Axis line. The second phase, designated the dog fight, called for British forces to blast the Axis line to pieces. This phase was most reminiscent of the set piece battles of the First World War and the phase that Montgomery considered the most difficult. The third and final phase was the proposed breakout and pursuit of the collapsed Axis army. (See Map 13)

Battle commenced on October 23, 1942 while Rommel was away in Germany recovering from an assortment of ailments acquired in the desert. The assault was preceded by heavy artillery heretofore unseen in the desert. Then, Gen. Oliver Leese's XXX Corps and General Lumsden's X Corps moved into the harried German-Italian line. Montgomery originally wanted to replace Lumsden with a man of his own choosing but Alexander, aware that Lumsden had compiled a steady reputation in the desert, refused to allow Montgomery to summarily dispense with the services of an experienced armoured commander. The battle soon devolved into one of attrition with heavy casualties incurred on both sides. Enormously outnumbered from the beginning in both men and material, Rommel's forces could not hope to survive a war of attrition. Rommel, who had quickly returned to the desert, knew that the vast resources of the British would inevitably lead to defeat. He thus began to contemplate a withdrawal.

The Second Battle of El Alamein was over by November 4, with the British in possession of the field, but only after some period of doubt that the Alexander-Montgomery team too would go the way of previous British commanders who allowed themselves to succumb to the wiles of the Desert Fox. In one last push, codenamed "Supercharge," Montgomery managed to push his army through the Axis line and cause Rommel to fall back. Though he received a direct order from Hitler not to fall back one step, Rommel chose to ignore the order. Within twenty-

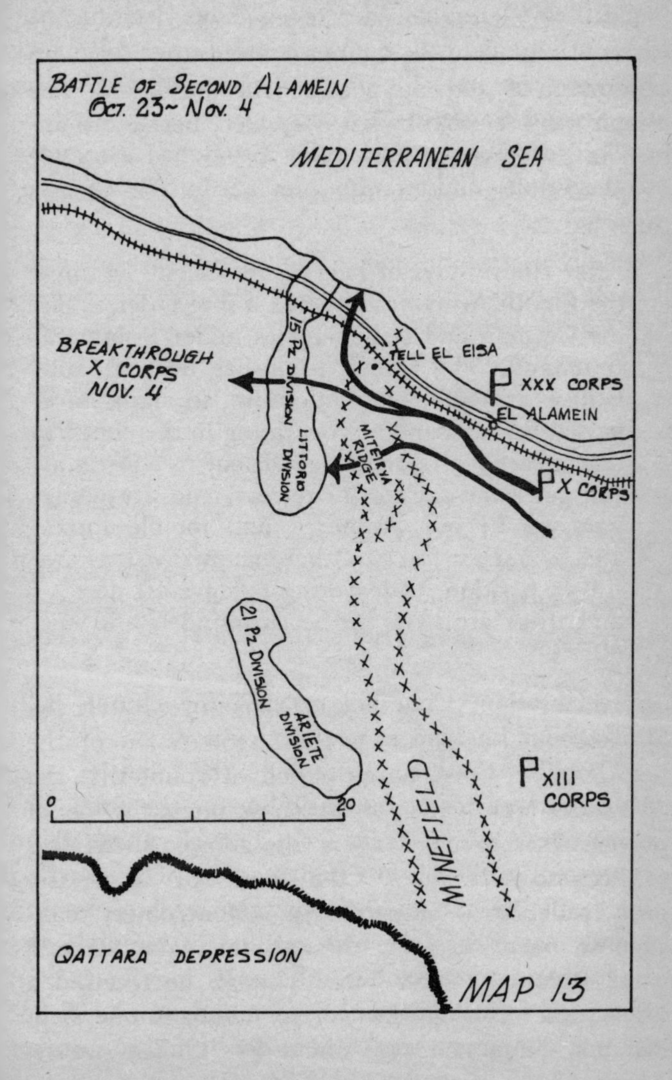
BATTLE OF SECOND ALAMEIN
OCT. 23~ NOV. 4
MEDITERRANEAN SEA
BREAKTHROUGH
X CORPS
NOV. 4
15 Pz DIVISION
LITTORIO DIVISION
TELL EL EISA
XXX CORPS
EL ALAMEIN
MITEIRYA RIDGE
X CORPS
21 Pz DIVISION
ARIETE DIVISION
MINEFIELD
XIII CORPS
0
20
QATTARA DEPRESSION
MAP 13

four hours of receiving the stand fast order, Rommel managed to convince Hitler that the demands were folly. The German leader reversed his decision, but not until many of the nonmechanized units, primarily Italian, were lost. Eighth Army had decisively won the Second Battle of El Alamein.

On November 4, Alexander dispatched a message to the Prime Minister who quotes it in *The Hinge of Fate*:

> After twelve days of heavy and violent fighting the Eighth Army has inflicted a severe defeat on the German and Italian forces under Rommel's command. The enemy front has broken, and British armoured formations in strength have passed through and are operating in the enemy's rear areas. Such portions of the enemy's forces as can get away are in full retreat, and are being harassed by our armoured and mobile forces and by our air forces. Other enemy divisions are still in position, endeavoring to stave off defeat, and these are likely to be surrounded and cut off.[10]

In celebration, Churchill ordered the church bells throughout England to peal for victory.

Though the conduct of the battle was Montgomery's forte, responsibility for the final outcome was as much Alexander's. Though not totally in agreement with the attrition method of conducting the battle, he had allowed Montgomery free rein and found that it was the best method of handling the Eighth Army commander. Alexander may be faulted for giving in to Montgomery's demands so readily but success at Alamein was without doubt and so justified

Alexander's methods. Unfortunately, Rommel eluded entrapment and exposed Alexander's method to be a potential problem. Sicily would put the system to its severest test.

In itself, the Battle of El Alamein was a total victory for the British but a successful battle of annihilation eluded them. Rommel was irrevocably stopped and the myth of his invincibility cracked once and for all, but as indicated, there was a certain hollowness to the victory: Rommel's escape. The Eighth Army's pursuit, methodical to a fault, according to Montgomery's master plan for a set piece battle, allowed the wily Desert Fox to retreat all the way to Tunisia where he stood to fight again with devastating results. (See Map 14)

In conjuction with the British victory at El Alamein, a combined Anglo-American force landed in northwest French Africa under General Eisenhower. After a few days of struggle, the Vichy French capitulated allowing the Allies to proceed to Tunisia. Poor roads and a lethargic Allied advance allowed the Axis to fashion a bridgehead around Bizerta and Tunis. The Allies now approached this bridgehead from the west while the Eighth Army pursued Rommel, who gradually reached this same Tunisian bridgehead from the east. (See Map 15)

Alexander's next appointment had already been decided during a high level meeting held at Casablanca in January of 1943. Roosevelt and Churchill were both in attendance along with their chiefs of staff, Marshall for the Americans and Alan Brooke of the Imperial General Staff. At this conference the leaders made the decision that an invasion of Sicily

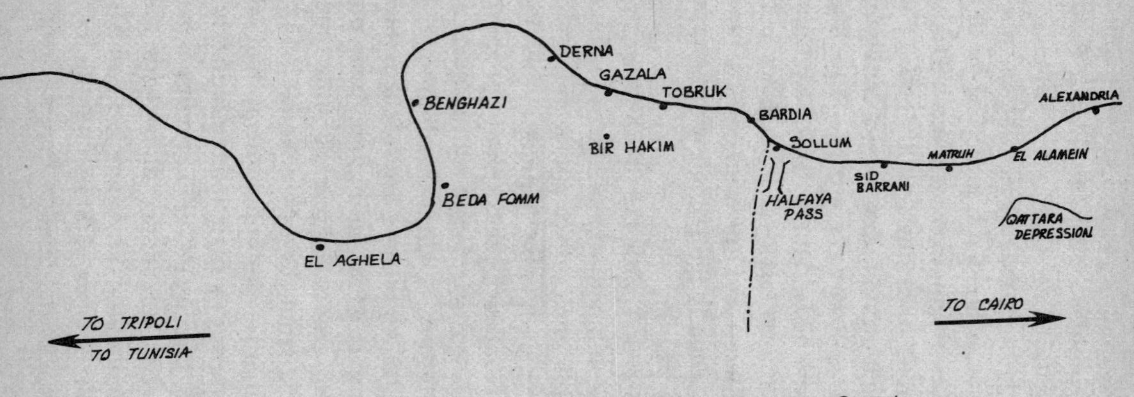
MEDITERRANEAN SEA
DERNA
GAZALA
TOBRUK
BARDIA
SOLLUM
ALEXANDRIA
BENGHAZI
BIR HAKIM
MATRUH
EL ALAMEIN
SID BARRANI
HALFAYA PASS
QATTARA DEPRESSION
BEDA FOMM
EL AGHELA
TO TRIPOLI
TO TUNISIA
TO CAIRO

MAP 14

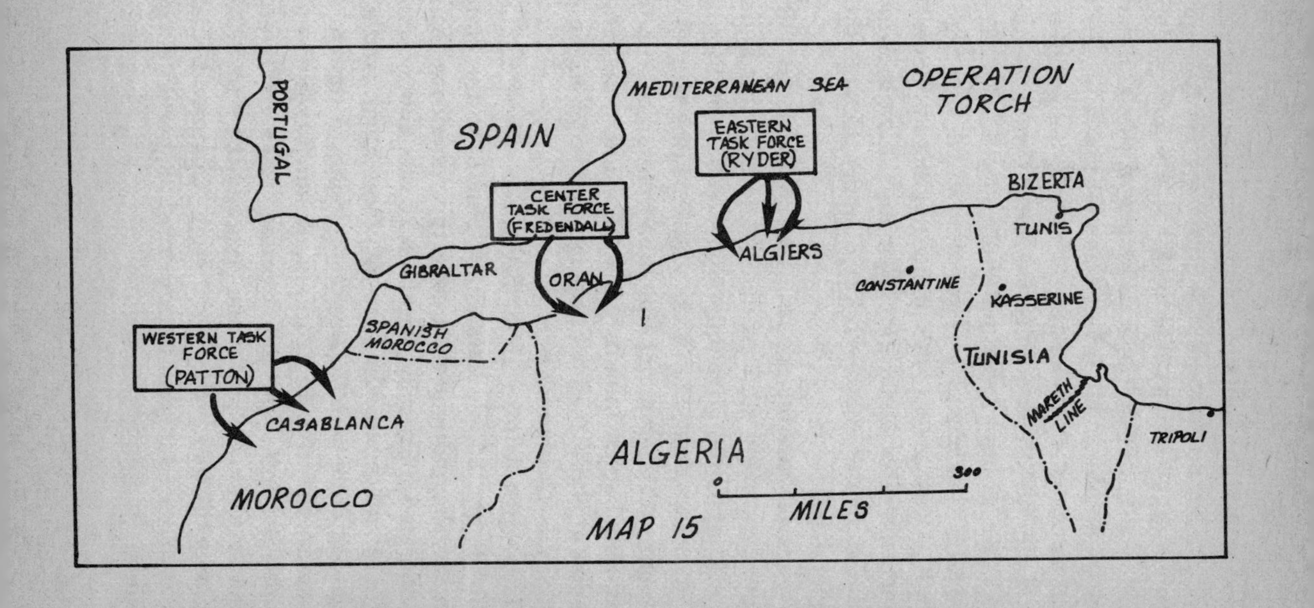
OPERATION
TORCH
MEDITERRANEAN SEA
PORTUGAL
SPAIN
EASTERN
TASK FORCE
(RYDER)
CENTER
TASK FORCE
(FREDENDALL)
BIZERTA
TUNIS
ALGIERS
GIBRALTAR
ORAN
CONSTANTINE
KASSERINE
SPANISH
MOROCCO
WESTERN TASK
FORCE
(PATTON)
TUNISIA
MARETH
LINE
CASABLANCA
TRIPOLI
ALGERIA
0
300
MILES
MOROCCO
MAP 15

would take place once the Axis forces in North Africa were defeated. Alexander was chosen to be commander of all land forces in Sicily. It was further decided that during the final stages of the Tunisian campaign, Alexander would assume command of all land forces in this theatre. This would take effect once the Eighth Army crossed the Libyan frontier and came within supporting distance of Eisenhower's forces. His headquarters was designated the Eighteenth Army group and included British General Anderson's First Army, Montgomery's Eighth Army and the United States II Corps under Gen. Lloyd Fredendall.

Alexander arrived in Algeria on February 18, where he and his staff created the hub of this Eighteen Army Group Headquarters. His first night was spent in discussing the future and renewing the relationship with Eisenhower which had been so abruptly interrupted seven months previously. The remaining portion of the Tunisian campaign also received close scrutiny at this conference.

The North African winter had taken its toll on the Allied forces. Supply lines were stretched to the limit and morale, particularly among the Americans, had deteriorated drastically. Meanwhile, the Axis powers made a concerted effort to reinforce their troops. This was done with relative ease owing to the close proximity of Sicily. In February, Rommel crossed the Tunisian border thereby creating an even larger reservoir of personnel for the Axis. By the middle of the month then, the Axis High Command had achieved a dangerous numerical superiority in Tunisia.

On February 14, before Alexander left Cairo to establish his headquarters in Algeria, the Germans overwhelmed American and French troops holding the southern portion of Tunisia's eastern dorsal. Gen. Jurgen von Arnim, commanding the right arm of a pincer, broke through the American defenses at the Faid Pass while Rommel and Panzerarmee Afrika, forming the left arm, overran El Guettar and Gafsa and promptly headed towards the American position at Kasserine Pass.

At this inauspicious time, Alexander came to Tunisia. There he found a confused command structure with nationalities indiscriminately intermingled, units split up and fighting in scattered groups, general disorganization from top to bottom, and a loss of confidence, especially among the Americans.

February 19 and 20 bode ill in the annals of American military history. On those days the Germans drove the Americans off the Kasserine Pass in the western dorsal and burst open the doorway to Tebessa, LeKef, and the great supply depots of the Allies. Thanks, however, to friction within the Axis command structure, Rommel was forced to disengage his forces on February 22 and order them back to the eastern dorsal where he established a defensive system and prepared to await the methodical approach of Montgomery to the Mareth line.*

Upon assuming command, Alexander said, "The general situation is far from satisfactory." He was particularly anxious about the poor performance of the

*A twenty-two mile line established by the French to prevent incursions of Italians years before the war and now utilized by the Germans to halt the British.

Americans. In a letter to Churchill and Brooke (now contained in the official British history of the campaign) Alexander noted his anxiety. In essence, two themes ran through that letter: first, the total lack of an intelligible plan; and second, the disappointing performance of the American troops. It would be a long time before these bad impressions left Alexander. He was still left with a bad feeling from his earlier dealings with Stilwell in Burma, and now the shaken, demoralized troops of the II Corps implanted in him a lack of faith in the American man of arms. Howe, in the official United States history of the North African campaign claims that General Alexander's impression of the poor fighting quality of the Americans lingered for quite a while and influenced him to depend much more heavily upon the seasoned British units.

Thus, Alexander was faced with some difficult considerations. Allied air superiority was foremost among these. Without it, the Axis could easily continue to reinforce their units from Sicily and make the Allied goals more difficult to achieve. Knowing that his adversary was Rommel, the wily and crafty Desert Fox, did not set too easily with him. He realized that if the Fox was to be brought to bay, the various Allied forces in Tunisia must be unified so that they could fight effectively. One way, he rationalized, was to organize the front into national sections where each national group could fight as divisions for objectives that were within their capabilities. If confidence was needed, this was the way to restore it. By giving units too much to accomplish beyond the realm of feasibility, depression and loss of morale resulted if the task was not accomplished.

On March 14, Alexander moved his army group headquarters forward from Constantine to Ein Beida, northwest of Tebessa. This location placed him directly between Montgomery to the south and Anderson in the north. He then handed each commander their assignment.

Montgomery's major task was to mount one of his famous set piece battles against the Mareth line. Gen. George Patton, who had replaced Fredendall as II Corps commander, was given the role of supporting Montgomery by drawing reserves away from the Mareth line. Anderson was to attack in the north and attempt to regain that territory which von Arnim had seized in an earlier offensive near Medjez el Bab.

Patton attacked on March 17, three days before Montgomery was due to strike at Mareth. The performance of II Corps went a long way towards modifying Alexander's negative view of the fighting ability of the American soldier.

On March 20, Montgomery hit the Mareth line. The fighting was especially brutal. Though Rommel had left Africa forever on permanent sick leave, the elan of the German soldier was not lacking as they launched counterattacks against Eighth Army attempts to breach the line and against the Americans on their left flank.

Alexander personally directed the campaign, changing Patton's orders when necessary in an attempt to capitalize on opportunities as they unfolded. Alexander's "lightness of touch" was his greatest asset as he sought to iron out Anglo-American difficulties. For the sake of Allied unity, Alexander elected to tread very lightly.

The Tunisian battle finally headed towards a climax. On March 28, Montgomery broke the Mareth line and approached the next defensive position around Wadi Akarit. There the battle lasted thirty-six hours and was characterized by ferocious warfare. On April 11, the First and Eighth Armies joined hands, enabling Montgomery's forces to receive supplies from northwest African ports. (See Map 16)

The Tunisian front now stretched 120 miles. Tunis was seen as the key to victory and thus became the main objective of the Allied drive. The question now confronting Alexander was what would be the best line of attack to achieve that objective. Of the 120 miles, the central part of the Axis front offered the best terrain for a projected assault on Tunis. The Mejdera Valley and the plain of Bou Arada were ideal for armoured warfare and both led to the all-important city.

Anderson's First Army was positioned in the central sector ready to surge forward. Though it was obvious to the Axis that this would be the main Allied attack route, Alexander, through deception, attempted to convince von Arnim that Montgomery's Eighth Army would lead the attack.

By air, sea, and land the noose around the Axis was tightened. Before the final battles were fought, however, Alexander was faced with yet another misunderstanding on the part of his American allies. With Anderson and Montgomery ready for the final push, Alexander felt that the time was ideal to pull the Americans out of the line and send them into reserve for training for the forthcoming Sicilian inva-

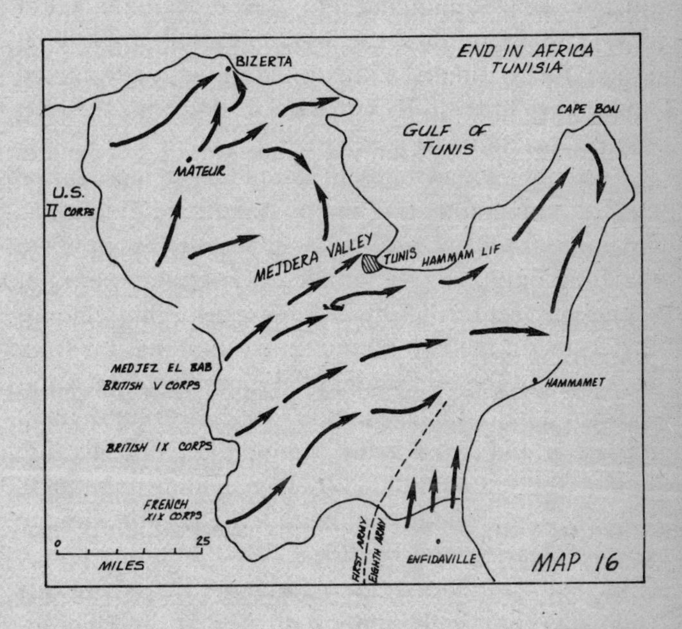
END IN AFRICA
TUNISIA
BIZERTA
CAPE BON
GULF OF
TUNIS
MATEUR
U.S.
II CORPS
MEJDERA VALLEY
TUNIS
HAMMAM LIF
MEDJEZ EL BAB
BRITISH V CORPS
HAMMAMET
BRITISH IX CORPS
FRENCH
XIX CORPS
0
25
MILES
FIRST ARMY
EIGHTH ARMY
ENFIDAVILLE
MAP 16

sion. This created an immediate response from Gen. Omar Bradley, Patton's successor at II Corps. The American commander demanded to know why the United States was to be shut out of the final drive. American public opinion, Bradley reasoned, would not stand for their exclusion and went personally to Alexander to argue his cause. Not satisfied with the outcome, he then appealed to Eisenhower who in turn tossed the ball back to Alexander. The latter then agreed to allow the whole four divisions of II Corps, rather than the one division previously agreed upon, to man the hilly northern section with the port city of Bizerta as its objective.

Alexander found himself in a position most suited for his temperament. Though lacking confidence in American ability, he still allowed them to take part in the final offensive. His problems, however, were not exclusively confined to the Americans. The relationship between the two army commanders was far from harmonious and Alexander's relationship to each was strained to the limit. He was not fully confident of Anderson and was finding Montgomery overbearing. First Army was considered by its neighbor to be inexperienced, and the former considered Eighth Army to be "overbearing and confident."[12]

Late April into early May witnessed the last bloody campaign for the elimination of the Axis bridgehead. On May 7, British forces entered Tunis and were followed shortly thereafter by an American entry into Bizerta. On May 13, the last Axis soldiers laid down their arms and a quarter of a million prisoners marched off to Allied prisoner of war camps.

Alexander looked upon this victory as being most

gratifying. Years later when elevated to the peerage, it was this victory that he elected to have associated with his name. This is not without justification, for he planned the strategy and organized the talents of such spunky and diversified personalities as Patton and Montgomery. Upon arriving in the midst of chaos, he organized these forces and led them to ultimate victory. "It was his leadership rather than his generalship that was his great contribution to the Allied cause."[13] He set the pieces in motion and created harmony, where prior to his arrival, the forces resembled a band out of tune. Though he initially doubted the ability of the Americans, he came to respect them before the campaign ended, thanks to the superb generalship of both Patton and Bradley. The years of experience that molded this man helped bring about the first great Anglo-American victory. He was without doubt the right choice for the most difficult task.

Victory! But what did the victory mean? The Germans still held an iron grip on the continent, with the English Channel and the Mediterranean Sea separating the Allies from the Nazis. The Germans were still deep into Russia and showing signs of rejuvenation after the debacle of Stalingrad. Before the Allies could truly celebrate victory, the great water barriers had to be conquered; the continent had to be invaded.

At Casablanca it was decided that a cross-Channel invasion would take place in the spring of 1944, but in order to keep the Allied forces occupied in weakening the Axis stranglehold on Europe, it was decreed that after the elimination of the Axis hold on Africa,

Sicily would be the next objective in the Mediterranean.

Alexander plunged himself into the planning for Husky, the code name for the invasion of Sicily. As deputy supreme commander for the Sicilian invasion, he found himself thrust into the middle of personal rivalries and strategic differences. The Americans had, since the beginning of their involvement in the war, distrusted British ambitions in the Mediterranean. For the Americans, British interests harkened to the days of imperialistic claims. The former insisted that the swiftest way to defeat Germany was via a cross-Channel invasion; not in the Mediterranean. For their part, the British were convinced that the Mediterranean offered the quickest route to defeat the Axis and that it offered the most strategic opportunities. Alexander was forced to plan amid these political differences.

Added to this difficulty was the reputation of the two flamboyant, egotistical commanders slated to command the invading armies; George Patton of the American Seventh Army and of course, Bernard L. Montgomery, commander of the cocky British Eighth Army. Both were concerned about their personal reputations and both wanted to play the decisive role in the campaign. Each of these commanders were prima donnas. In later years, Alexander would view this period as the most disagreeable of his entire career.

Alexander was now faced with a unique opportunity. Up until the Sicilian campaign, he had been given commands that he had to salvage from imminent disaster; Burma, Egypt, Dunkirk and Tunisia. Now his position was totally different. No longer was he the leader of a crestfallen, unsure army. Instead, he now led professional armies staffed by soldiers who shared the glories of victory and who were fully confident of future ones. His tasks were now modified; his was now more an exercise of professional judgment of what was practical with the resources available under current conditions. He could assume more the role of a chairman of the board, leaving the actual conduct to the commanders in the field.

Alexander was given three objectives for the post-North African campaigns. First the conquest of Sicily, second, the elimination of Italy from the war, and finally, the tying down of German forces in Italy and the attracting of more German troops from France to insure the success of Operation Overlord, the invasion of Normandy. The last was as yet undefined when Sicily was invaded but subsequently became the prime objective of the entire Italian campaign.

As initially presented to Alexander, the Husky plan called for Patton's Seventh Army to land at Palermo and Montgomery to come ashore at Catania on Sicily's east coast. This plan aroused great debates among Allied air and naval forces regarding the practicality of two widely dispersed landings. The most emphatic objection to the plan came from none other than the Eighth Army commander, General Montgomery. He disagreed with the original plan because he felt it divided the effort equally between him and Patton. Instead, always the superb salesman, Montgomery attempted to convince the Allied leadership that a broad front in Sicily was overly ambitious and dangerous. As an alternative, he proposed a landing by Eighth Army over the beaches of southeastern

Sicily, near Pachino, while Patton's Seventh Army landed further west near Gela and Licata. Patton's role would therefore be the security of Montgomery's flank, allowing him to drive swiftly to Syracuse, capturing its port through which his army could be supplied. (See Map 17)

Montgomery persuaded Eisenhower and Alexander to accept his plan. All Patton's prior plans were scrapped and he was directed to take over the Gela-Licata landings. His tasks now became the capture of the Ponte Olivo-Comiso group of airfields and the protection of Montgomery's flank and rear as the British advanced on Messina. Playing second fiddle to Montgomery was a hard pill for Patton to swallow, but as a soldier he was prepared to obey. When Alexander informed Patton of his new assignment, the American merely saluted, obeyed, and to the surprise of Alexander, stated that he always believed in following orders.

Sicily was invaded on July 10, 1943 and was conquered in thirty-eight days. In a sense, however, the victory can be attributed as much to Field Marshal Kesselring's order to evacuate all German forces after Mussolini's fall on July 25, as it was to Allied force of arms. Alexander led the victorious forces but the Germans escaped making for yet another hollow victory.

The Sicilian campaign was fought with friction among the Allies all the way as Montgomery and Patton competed for the laurels. Patton, who loathed playing second fiddle to Montgomery, waited for the opportunity to fulfill his destiny while the latter seemed not to mind who he stepped on in order to accomplish his chosen task.

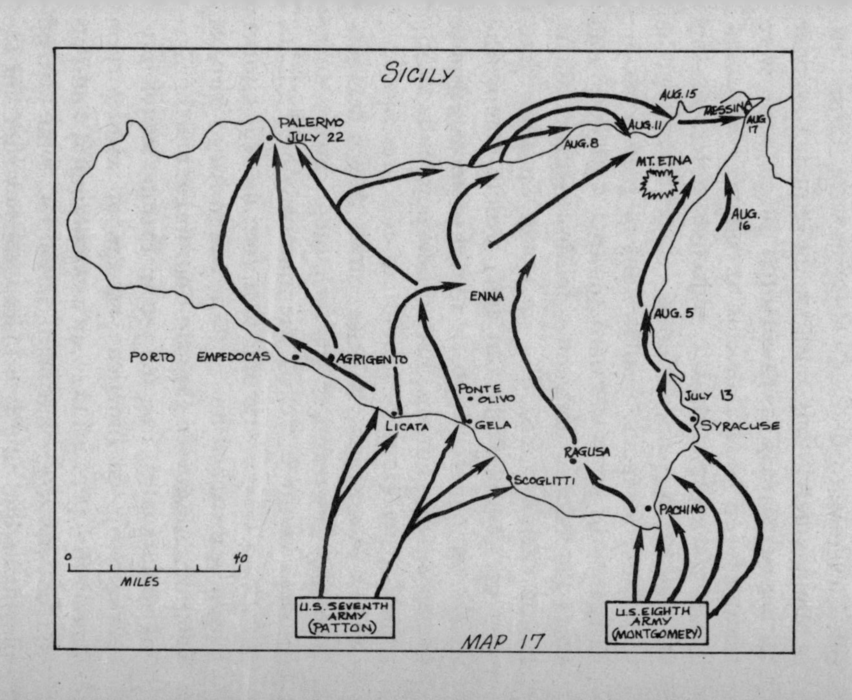
SICILY
PALERMO
JULY 22
AUG. 15
MESSINA
AUG. 17
AUG. 11
AUG. 8
MT. ETNA
AUG. 16
ENNA
AUG. 5
PORTO EMPEDOCAS
AGRIGENTO
PONTE OLIVO
JULY 13
LICATA
GELA
SYRACUSE
RAGUSA
SCOGLITTI
PACHINO
0
40
MILES
U.S. SEVENTH ARMY (PATTON)
U.S. EIGHTH ARMY (MONTGOMERY)
MAP 17

By July 13, Patton saw his chance. His forces were continually squeezed westward because of Montgomery's requirements. The British commander was facing heavy opposition along the coast and in order to enable him to bypass the German strongpoints, key roads assigned to Bradley's II Corps were transferred to Montgomery, thus pushing the Americans even further westward. This gave Patton the chance he was waiting for. Seeking far fields to conquer, he turned his attention towards the objective stated in the original Husky plan; Palermo. Patton persuaded a reluctant Alexander to allow him to send a reconnasissance in force westward towards Agrigento and Porto Empedocle. Both towns fell in swift succession. Patton then assumed that he would be allowed to clear up western Sicily, but again orders were issued which reemphasized his basic role of protecting Montgomery's flank. Furious, Patton flew personally to Fifteenth Army group headquarters and presented his case to Alexander. By this time, Alexander was becoming increasingly disenchanted with Montgomery's failure to deliver the promised "bold strokes and rapid drives." He was therefore intrigued when Patton approached him with a request for a drive on Palermo. Alexander gave his approval readily.

Five days later, Palermo was in Patton's hands. Encouraged by the American success, Alexander then gave Patton permission to turn eastward and come up on Montgomery's northern flank for a combined assault on the Etna line in conjunction with an advance on Messina via the north coast.

Alexander had progressed a long way from his earlier opinion of the military ability of the

Americans. He now treated them as equals.

Mussolini's fall presented Alexander with an entirely new set of circumstances. Little did he know that a German evacuation of Sicily was in full sway under the capable guidance of Field Marshal Kesselring. The evacuation was a complete success. Not until August 14 did anyone on the Allied side realize that the Germans were evacuating Sicily. The Germans made good their escape, insuring that there would be no large bag of prisoners as at Tunis.

Though Sicily was an Allied victory, Alexander was still plagued by errors of judgment. Foremost among these was allowing Montgomery to change the Husky plan to suit his own means. If the Allies had kept to the original plan, the one Patton had suggested, Messina could have been reached more rapidly and the Axis forces would have been trapped with little room for escape. Secondly, Alexander's unique style of command, though successful in the past, this time caused the victory to be watered down. Montgomery's personality proved too much for Alexander and because of this Patton was given the short end of the stick. To his everlasting credit, Alexander soon saw Montgomery for what he really was and allowed Patton to strike for Palermo and then Messina, which the latter reached hours before the British. But, as we have already seen, squabbling among the Allies allowed the Germans to make good their escape under the very eyes of the British and Americans. However, Alexander did accomplish his primary objective. Sicily was captured quickly and economically.

One incident of the Sicilian campaign stands out as a classic example of Alexander's style of command.

During Seventh Army's advance from Palermo to Messina, General Patton opened Pandora's box when he stopped at an American field hospital. While visiting the wounded he slapped an American soldier whom he felt was malingering. The chief surgeon of the hospital unit saw fit to compose a lengthy report of the incident and forward it through the chain of command. When this report reached Alexander's desk, the latter simply pigeon-holed it and refused to become involved in what he considered to be a trivial and strictly American incident. Instead of becoming embroiled in a controversy that could have portrayed Patton in a bad light in comparison to his fellow countryman, Montgomery, Alexander simply elected to ignore the entire thing.

Unfortunately, a copy of the report also reached Eisenhower's headquarters where it fell into the hands of an unscrupulous journalist who exposed the matter to the entire world. The resulting furor nearly cost Patton his command, which would have sent him to the sidelines for the duration of the war. Only the intervention of Eisenhower and Roosevelt saved Patton, but had Alexander had his way, the incident would have simply been forgotten with but a slight admonishment.

After the overthrow of Mussolini's government, active negotiations between the new Italian government under Marshal Badoglio and Eisenhower's staff began in earnest. Alexander played no part in these negotiations but it was obvious that an Italian surrender would make his subsequent moves easier.

Allied plans after Sicily were heavily debated months before the invasion even took place. The

Americans were not in favor of continuing operations in the Mediterranean, but the British forcefully presented the benefits to the Allied cause of an invasion of Italy proper following the fall of Sicily. Reluctantly, the Americans acquiesced and a planning staff was organized to prepare for this invasion of the Italian mainland.

Where to land was the first priority. Alexander, after his experience in Sicily, realized the importance of ports and airfields and these dominated his considerations in the planning. Air Marshal Tedder could guarantee fighter protection only as far north as the Sorrento Peninsula. Thus, this limited Alexander's choices of invasion points. Though an invasion nearer Rome or north of Naples appeared more desirable, the fact that air support was unavailable mitigated against a landing that far north. The need for a port therefore forced Alexander to consider an invasion near a major Italian seafront city. Consequently, he settled on the Bay of Salerno for the invasion point. Though his decision was not unanimously accepted, he refused to be swayed. Mark Clark, the American Fifth Army commander and the man slated to command the landing, continued to lobby for a landing north of Naples. Montgomery too disagreed with Salerno for many of the same objections that he had put forth prior to Sicily. His army was slated to land on the toe of Italy itself, directly across from Sicily, and could hardly be expected to provide mutual support for a landing at Salerno. Clark's and Montgomery's objections were taken into consideration and quickly overruled. (See Map 18)

The Salerno operation was codenamed Avalanche.

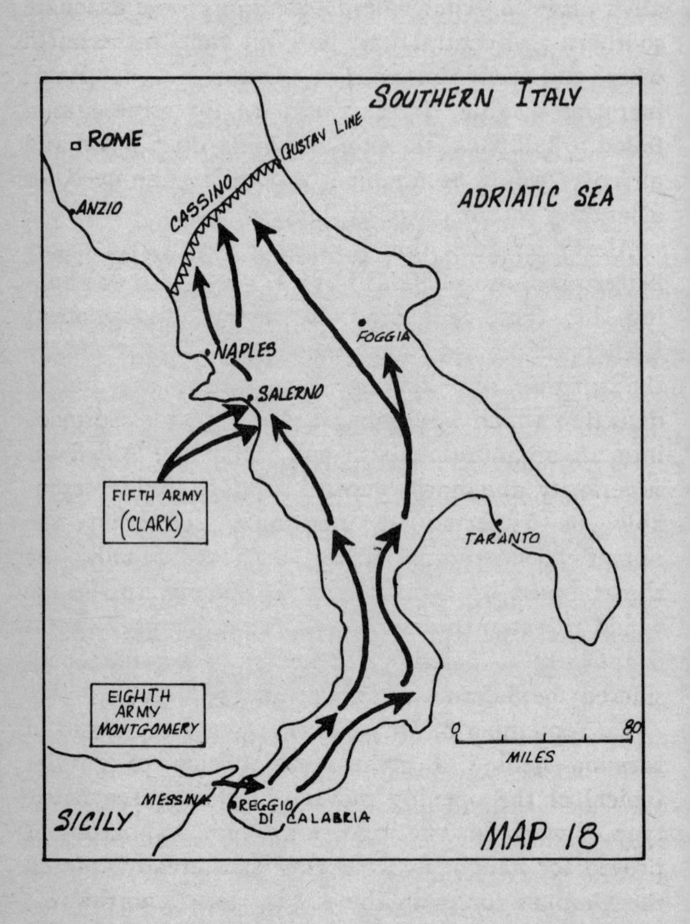
SOUTHERN ITALY
ROME
GUSTAV LINE
CASSINO
ANZIO
ADRIATIC SEA
FOGGIA
NAPLES
SALERNO
FIFTH ARMY
(CLARK)
TARANTO
EIGHTH
ARMY
MONTGOMERY
0
80
MILES
MESSINA
REGGIO
DI CALABRIA
SICILY
MAP 18

It was hoped that an Italian surrender would precede the operation, thus making the odds of success that much more in the Allies' favor. Alexander expected that once the Germans got wind of their erstwhile ally's plans to switch sides, Kesselring would evacuate southern and central Italy and fall back to the north where the newly formed Army Group B under Rommel was waiting. If the Germans for some reason failed to fall back, then the need for Allied naval and air cover would be doubled, reinforcing the need for a landing within range of fighters.

Alexander knew that Kesselring was in a tactically better position to defend Italy. However, he was hoping that three factors would prevent his opponent from opposing the Salerno landings. First would be the surprise and confusion caused by the Italian defection which was expected to throw the Germans into an organizational turmoil. Secondly, Allied air superiority and naval gunfire support could reasonably be expected to neutralize somewhat the numerical superiority of the Germans. Finally, the threat posed by Eighth Army advancing up the toe would threaten the rear of the German forces opposing Clark at Salerno. Therefore, Alexander considered the Salerno risk worth taking.

On September 3, Montgomery crossed the Straits of Messina behind a great concentration of gunfire typical of the opening moves of his set piece battle type of warfare. The massive artillery bombardment proved for naught as Kesselring had already ordered the German forces in the toe to retreat northward, methodically delaying the Eighth Army's pace by the sowing of mines and the time-tested use of demolitions. Ironically, Montgomery was hampered more by the destruction caused by his excessive reliance on gunfire than by the enemy.

On the evening of September 8, when the Italian surrender was finally announced, it wasn't the Germans who found themselves confused, but rather the Italians themselves. Many were shocked at the treachery of their own government. The Germans already possessed a contingency plan covering just such an eventuality and without hesitating, Kesselring ordered the Italian army disarmed immediately. So, when Clark burst ashore on September 9, it was not into the arms of an Italian reception committee, but smack into Kesselring's troops who had a nasty surprise awaiting Fifth Army. The Italian surrender had failed to give the Allies any advantage at all.

The Battle of Salerno lasted for nine days with fierce fighting characterizing each one of them. Alexander personally visited the battlefield on September 15 where his very presence heartened his subordinates. Clark, at one point, was all for evacuating the beachhead, but Alexander never lost his poise.

> Alexander's unruffled confidence, the obvious soundness of the instructions he gave to meet the crisis which bore no stamp of alarm, and the calming effect of his immaculate appearance, had a decisive effect on men's minds.[14]

The scales were finally tipped on September 16 when Allied air and naval forces came to the aid of the troops on shore. The crisis had finally begun to subside and Kesselring began a strategic withdrawal to the hills north of Naples.

Alexander felt confident that he would be able to move northward rapidly and destroy the German forces. However, within a month, disillusionment and utter frustration came home to him. From coast to coast the Germans established an elaborate defensive system utilizing the topography of Italy to its optimum. Consequently, Alexander now faced what he most dreaded; a stalemate. With the advent of autumn, these fears soon became reality.

The day-to-day fighting in the Italian countryside is amply covered in many excellent volumes and so need not be covered in detail. Rather, the command abilities of Alexander as he conducted this long, drawn-out, attritional campaign merits scrutiny. Why did Alexander find himself in this stalemated position? Certainly it did not stem from anything he had done wrong, but instead can be attributed to the stubbornness and capabilities of one of Germany's greats, Field Marshal Albert Kesselring.* During the month following the Allied invasion, he had attempted to explain to Hitler the importance of containing the Allies as far south as possible. He was convinced that to evacuate the whole of Italy and defend the Reich from positions in the Alps would be against the best interests of Germany, for it would give the Allies unlimited freedom of movement in either the direction of France or the Balkans. It would also mean sacrificing an indispensable deep battle zone; thus opening up southern Germany and Austria to a devastating air campaign from northern Italy. Consequently, Kesselring felt that the battle for Italy was

*See Volume 1.

not only justified, military common sense demanded it.

After Salerno, Kesselring did withdraw northward; not to the north of Italy as Hitler desired, but just north of Naples. Though forced to relinquish ground, Kesselring was enthusiastically optimistic over the possibility of going over to the defensive south of Rome, using the terrain there as his ally. By using the spiny backbone of Italy, he deemed it possible to establish impenetrable defensive lines stretching from east coast to west. Hitler gradually came to accept Kesselring's logic and saw the benefit to be gained by adopting a policy of gradual withdrawal with one successful delaying action following another.

The first delaying action the Germans established after their retreat north of Naples was on the Volturno River. There, the Germans bought time while they prepared their massive defensive barrier, the Gustav line, further north around the town of Cassino. The United States official history records what the Allies faced at the Gustav line.

> The line was rooted in the high ground backing the Gargliano and Rapido rivers. In the hills behind the Gargliano in the Saint Ambrogio area, on the steep and barren slopes of Monte Cassino, and among the jumbled mountain peaks near the source of the Rapido, the Germans had blasted and dug weapons pits, built concrete bunkers and steel turreted machine gun emplacements, strung bands of barbed wire and planted mine fields—making lavish use of the box mine, which was difficult to detect because it had almost no metallic parts, to block the few natural avenues of advance. They had sited

mortars on reverse slopes and placed automatic weapons to cover the forward slopes.[15]

Alexander and his subordinate commanders were faced with a deep sense of frustration. Rome, which at first appeared ripe for the picking, now loomed as an elusive goal. Instead, Alexander gradually came to realize that the ultimate goal of the Italian campaign was the containment of those German forces in Italy and the drawing of more from France and other fronts. His army group was destined to become an auxiliary to Overlord, the invasion of Normandy.

Bogged down in the Italian hills with the autumn mud, the weary troops began to show signs of battle fatigue. Added to this was the start of the reduction of Alexander's army group for the preparation of Overlord, "the tyranny of Overlord," as the British preferred to call it. Diminished Allied resources meant reduced pressure on the Germans, which in turn gave them more time to build even more formidable defenses. At this time, with morale fading rapidly, Alexander came down with jaundice.

Eisenhower and the Allied planners had for some time discussed an amphibious operation along the west coast designed to circumvent the German defenses. Through political wrangling and string pulling, a plan was formulated which was designed to land an Allied corps at Anzio, thirty miles south of Rome. This, it was felt, would put the Allies in an excellent position to bypass the Gustav line and threaten not only Rome, but the rear of the German line as well.

While this planning and debating was proceeding,

bigger plans and operations were being designed, the invasion of Normandy chief among them. There was naturally a need to assign a man to the position of supreme commander for Overlord. Alexander's name was discussed as one of the possibilities but the choice fell instead to Eisenhower. Alexander then became the obvious candidate to fill Eisenhower's shoes in the Mediterranean theatre. Brooke, his own countryman, voiced objections so Gen. Sir Henry Maitland Wilson, commander in charge of the Middle East was chosen to succeed Eisenhower.

Montgomery was slated to leave the theatre and return to England to prepare for the big invasion. Eisenhower had proposed that instead of Montgomery assuming command of the Twenty-first Army Group for Overlord, Alexander be given that command, leaving the former to fill Alexander's vacant command in the Mediterranean. That however was not to be. Churchill, Montgomery's champion, would not hear of it.

> Alexander was to stay in Italy while all the rest of the battle experienced first team returned to England to command the forces assembling for Overlord.[16]

Alexander must have felt a deep sense of disappointment. His job was relegated to being one of diverting the Germans. Yet he still was expecting to fight with vim and vigor. He also had to keep his men inspired; men from many different races and creeds. He was also expected to keep their morale up even though they were fighting in a theatre which was obviously considered second rate. Lady Astor was even touring Italy calling the men fighting in Italy the D-Day Dodgers. Secondary theatre or not, Alexander was determined to pursue the campaign in the only way he knew how, with complete victory as the only goal.

At the Tehran Conference held in November of 1943, Roosevelt, Stalin, and Churchill discussed the upcoming Allied strategy. There Roosevelt presented the Overlord plan to Stalin. The Soviet leader who harbored many suspicions about Allied intentions was glad to finally see the invasion plans. The president also placed before him a proposal for a simultaneous landing in southern France (Operation Anvil) to coincide with the Normandy landing. Churchill fought bitterly against Anvil for he felt it was a waste of Allied Mediterranean strength. Why open yet a third front to divert the Germans when already the forces in Italy were achieving this? Why not instead, strengthen those forces in Italy to help them destroy the Germans and quickly proceed north into Austria and central Europe, then turn east into the Balkans? Roosevelt, always the pragmatist, saw Anvil as the surest way to victory, while Churchill's plans smacked too much of British imperialistic policies. At Tehran, Churchill was overruled. Anvil would proceed as scheduled much to the relief of Stalin and the eventual dismay and grief of the democratic nations of the world. The last thing Stalin desired was Allied forces beating him to central and eastern Europe.

For Alexander, the one positive benefit of Anvil was the need to retain amphibious vehicles to support the operation in the Mediterranean. This gave Brooke and Churchill the necessary "in" to push the Anzio landing. Since the landing vehicles were already in the theatre, why not put them to use in expediting the capture of Rome. They received the go-ahead from the Combined Chiefs of Staff.

When the Allies landed at Anzio on January 22, 1944, it proved a momentary embarrassment for Kesselring. However, he immediately grasped the situation, and thanks to the hesitancy of the American VI Corps commander, General Lucas, a respite was granted. Lucas gave priority to the building up of the beachhead before advancing on the Alban Hills where he could sever the access routes of the German Tenth Army manning the Gustav line. This latter should have been his prime objective.

Although complete surprise was achieved at Anzio and Rome stood undefended and ripe for the picking, Lucas threw away his advantage and elected to mark time on the beach. This allowed Kesselring time to form a new army, the Fourteenth, under the battle tested veteran of the Russian front, General von Mackensen. Von Mackensen slammed the door in Lucas' face at Anzio and rammed home the bolt. Consequently, when the latter was finally ready to move, he faced an irresistible force. (See Map 19)

Although Anzio failed to achieve its major objective, Alexander, in his memoirs, does give it a place of prominence.

> Anzio played a vital role in the capture of Rome by giving me the means to employ a double-handed punch—from the beachhead and from Cassino—which caught the Germans in a pincer movement. Without this double-handed punch I do not believe we should ever have been able to

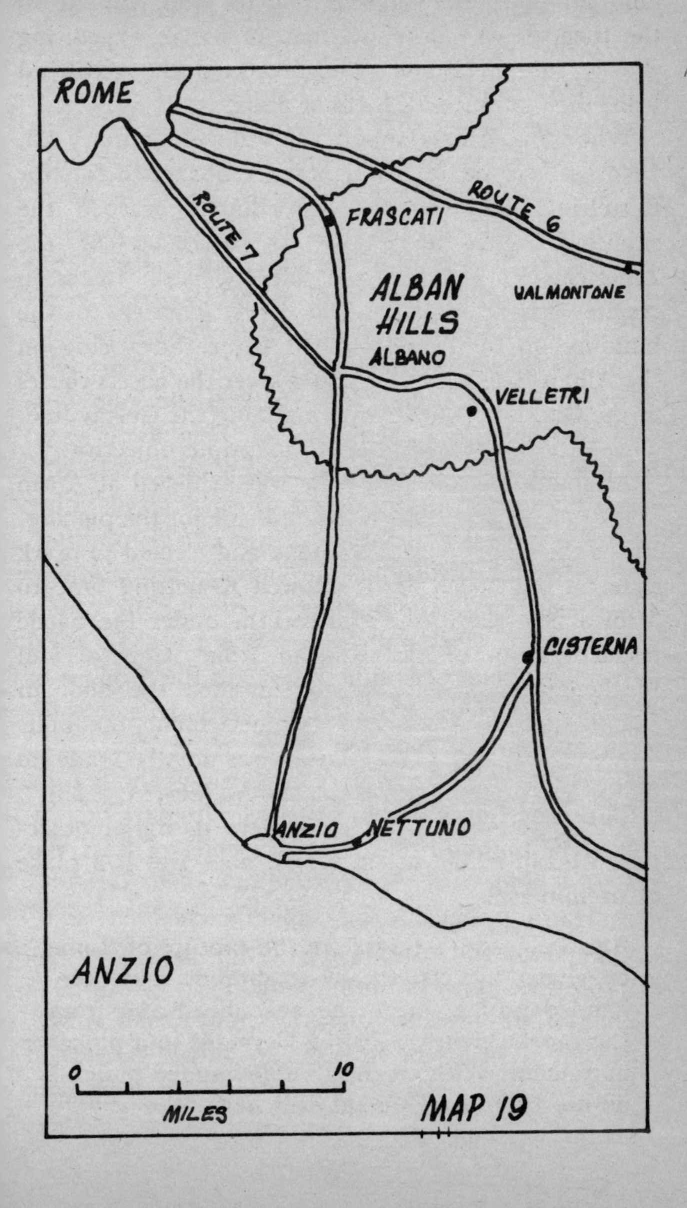
ROME
ROUTE 7
ROUTE 6
FRASCATI
ALBAN
HILLS
VALMONTONE
ALBANO
VELLETRI
CISTERNA
ANZIO
NETTUNO
ANZIO
0
10
MILES
MAP 19

> break through the German defences at Cassino.[17]

Though Alexander justifies the importance of Anzio, it cannot be denied that it was a failure as far as its original objective was concerned, and Alexander must accept part of the blame. By no stretch of the imagination however, can the total blame be laid at Alexander's feet. Lucas must shoulder his share of the responsibility and above all, the Fifth Army commander, Mark Clark, must not be allowed escape with his image intact. Many historians and authors who knew Alexander rather well, General Jackson and Field Marshal Carver being two of them, both agree that Alexander needed a good chief of staff. When he lacked one, his strategy faulted. During the planning for Anzio he was without an officer in this position. This deficiency was evident throughout the campaign as well as prior to the landing. Contradictory orders were issued to Clark and Lucas. Was Lucas to build up his beachhead or was he to exploit the element of surprise? The fact that his subordinates did not know exactly what was expected of them is Alexander's fault. However, supposedly competent generals such as Clark and Lucas should have been prepared to exploit any situation. The lack of a chief of staff was remedied before the actual landings when Gen. Sir John Harding became Alexander's chief of staff. Though he assumed this post prior to Anzio, the operation was not Harding's plan.

The failure of the Anzio landing was however, somewhat offset by the strategic advantage gained. In order to defend both the Gustav line and eliminate the Anzio beachhead, Hitler was forced to pour in streams of reinforcements thus denuding various other battle fronts, especially France.

The last days of January were spent by Alexander in constant visits to the two fronts, advising and directing when necessary. On both fronts he found the Germans too difficult to budge and on Anzio, he found himself faced with the imminent threat of a massive German counterattack.

Alexander switched his methods to that of a fighter now that he had two fronts to be concerned with. He decided to attack on his right (Cassino) to relieve the pressure on his left (Anzio). In conjunction with that policy, on February 15 he ordered an offensive at Cassino in order to draw pressure off the German counterattack at Anzio. Coincidentally at this time, under pressure from his subordinates, Alexander gave his consent for the bombing of the historic monastery of Monte Cassino. German propaganda portrayed the Allies and particularly Alexander as barbarians for the wanton destruction of this holy shrine. Alexander, however, had little choice, the welfare of his men came first. The famous monastery overlooked the only practical road to Rome. On top of this hill (but not in the monastery itself), the Germans had established an excellent observation post. To open that road, Alexander's men had to take that hill in order to secure the surrounding ground. The German positions on that hill simply had to be eliminated.

> How could a structure which dominated the fighting field be allowed to stand? The Monastery had to be destroyed.[18]

Alexander continues:

> Was the destruction of the monastery a military necessity? Was it morally wrong to destroy it? The answer to the first question is 'yes'. It was necessary more for the effect it would have on the morale of the attackers than for purely material reasons. The answer to the second question is this: When soldiers are fighting for a just cause and are prepared to suffer death and mutilation in the process, bricks and mortar, no matter how venerable, cannot be allowed to weigh against human lives. Every good commander must consider the morale and feelings of his fighting men.[19]

Still, the Gustav line held. But so did Anzio, even though at one point Lucas found himself fighting from his final defensive line.

In late February the Germans again tried to eliminate the Anzio beachhead. Gen. Lucian Truscott who now replaced Lucas, halted the drive of the Germans who were then forced to go over to the defensive.

On March 15, the Allies made one more attempt to take Cassino. A week later after no apparent results, Alexander called off the offensive. Thus ended the winter battles. From March 24, when the winter battles ceased, till May 11, when Alexander's next offensive (Diadem) commenced, preparations for the spring offensive went ahead full steam.

The plan called for the Eighth Army to cross the Apennines and act as the main striking force of Cassino. The main Fifth Army effort would be from Anzio while the balance of this army would support

Eighth Army's efforts. Diadem was designed to take place in three phases. The first phase was the breaking into the Gustav line. The second phase would be Eighth Army's destruction of the next defensive line, the Hitler line. It was hoped that the third phase would then result in the final crushing of Kesselring's forces by the combined efforts of Fifth and Eighth Armies.

On May 11, Diadem began. The fighting was fierce and desperate as the Germans bravely defended their positions. In the long run, however, they proved unable to hold on against superior Allied forces. The Germans were taken by surprise. Faulty intelligence caused Kesselring to send three divisions north to Leghorn to protect against a potential amphibious landing. In addition, five more divisions were dispatched to Fourteenth Army at Anzio and two others sent into reserve, leaving only nine divisions on the Gustav line opposing fifteen of the Allies'.

By May 19, it was obvious that the Tenth Army required immediate reinforcement if the Gustav line was going to hold. So Kesselring transferred the Twenty-ninth Panzer Grenadiers from Fourteenth Army. Von Mackensen opposed the transfer and Kesselring had to convince him of the importance of the transfer. The move, however, came too late. The Germans were forced to fall back from the Gustav line to the next line of prepared defenses, the Senger line formally the Hitler line. Again the Germans employed the tactics for which they had become famous and earned valuable time by delaying the Allies.

Then, on May 22, the Anzio forces under Truscott,

broke loose from their shackles. The following day, the Canadians on Eighth Army's front cracked the Senger line and poured up the Liri Valley with the French keeping pace on their left and the Americans along the coast seeking to link up with the forces striking out of Anzio.

With the outbreak at Anzio, Kesselring's forces now faced disaster. Thanks to the ambitions of Mark Clark, however, the Germans were handed a respite and avoided complete annihilation. Alexander ordered Clark to send VI Corps to Valmontone which would sever the escape route of the German Tenth Army if successful. Instead, Clark sought immortality as the conqueror of Rome and decided to head for that city. Altering Alexander's orders to suit his own purpose, he sent a token force to Valmontone and directed the bulk of VI Corps to make for Rome.

Alexander's critics point to the Valmontone debacle as an excellent example of the weakness of his style of command. Clark changed his direction without any real authority. Alexander's instructions to and conversations with Clark during the battle were indefinite. It must be remembered that Alexander preferred to command by persuasion. Clark paid lip service to Alexander's directive in that he could state that he was maintaining pressure on the Valmontone axis while he massed his main effort for a direct thrust at Rome up Route 7. If Clark had kept to the proper objective, Valmontone, most of the German Tenth Army would have been destroyed. By keeping Route 6 at Valmontone open, von Vietinghoff's army, fleeing from the collapsed Gustav line, escaped falling into the Allied bag. As it was, the route was left open and most of the German troops made good their escape. Clark had Rome and his page in the history books, but Kesselring still had his Tenth Army north of Rome virtually intact.

The Eternal City fell, but the victory was incomplete. Alexander made no attempt to share the triumph with Clark. It was the American general's day of glory. Churchill, however, knew who the triumph belonged to and rewarded Alexander with a Field Marshal's baton. Rome, elusive Rome, was finally in Allied hands just in the nick of time. Two days after Clark's triumphal entry into the city, Overlord was launched on the shores of Normandy and Clark's achievement was relegated to the back pages of the newspapers.

Alexander's pressure in the Italian theatre left twenty-three fewer divisions in France, units which could possibly have been used against the Normandy landings. During the initial stages of Overlord the Allied toehold on Europe proper was tenuous at best. Those twenty-three divisions might have tipped the scales in Germany's favor and heaven only knows when another successful one could have been launched. Furthermore, of those twenty-three divisions, many no longer existed, having been chewed up and destroyed during the previous six months fighting in Italy. Though Kesselring and his forces escaped to fight another day, the Allies had taken a severe mauling.

As the invasion of northwest Europe proceeded, it appeared that Alexander's work was now over. Rome had been taken, why proceed further north? Particularly in light of the fact that most of the necessary goods of war were being diverted from his theatre to feed the voracious appetites of Eisenhower's forces. Further action seemed to serve little or no purpose. But there was still the need to maintain in the Italian theatre. The drawing off of German troops, keeping Germany off balance and overextended still warranted consideration. (See Map 20)

Alexander struggled to retain his optimism. He never lost faith despite vague objectives and the loss of enthusiasm among Churchill and Brooke. His ever present enthusiasm became infectious, and what could have devolved into a demoralized dejected Allied Army Group, instead continued to be a fighting force which retained its elan, vigor, and zeal.

Alexander still maintained that his theatre could serve more of a purpose than merely drawing off German troops from other fronts. He hoped that ultimately he would be allowed to exploit his victory at Rome and head rapidly north where he could cross the Italian border and capture Vienna. One major obstacle stood in his way. Not the enemy, but instead his ally.

Operation Anvil, which was scheduled to become a reality in August after its earlier postponement, presented Alexander with yet another hurdle to overcome. Troops from his army group would have to be used in this invasion of southern France, troops that for the most part constituted the most experienced, battle-hardened units and were the best trained. If he were allowed to exploit the Diadem victory it would have to be at the expense of Anvil which in turn would have to be cancelled. Mark Clark also favored the cancellation of Anvil, but then Clark was never

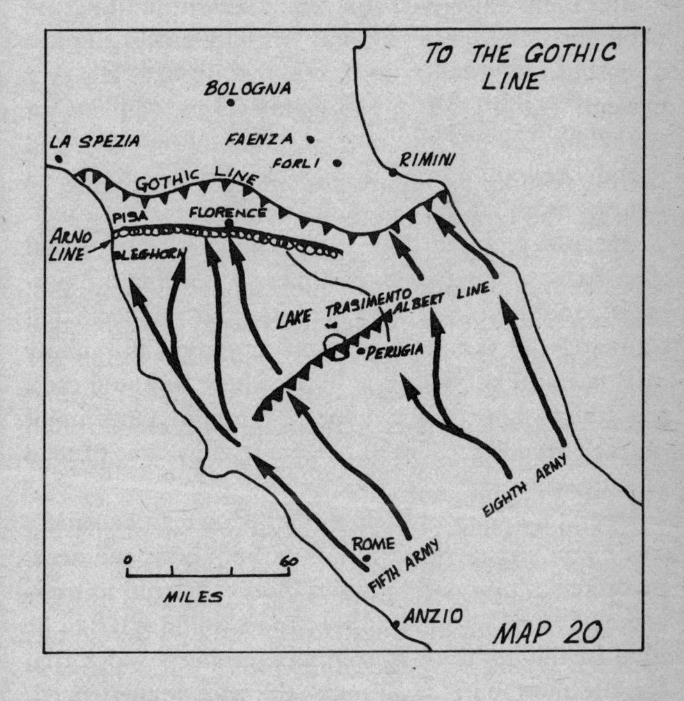
TO THE GOTHIC LINE
BOLOGNA
LA SPEZIA
FAENZA
FORLI
RIMINI
GOTHIC LINE
PISA
FLORENCE
ARNO LINE
LEGHORN
LAKE TRASIMENTO
ALBERT LINE
PERUGIA
EIGHTH ARMY
ROME
FIFTH ARMY
0
60
MILES
ANZIO
MAP 20

in favor of any operation that did not feature himself in a key role. He saw great opportunities on the horizon for Fifth Army, if only Anvil would not interfere.

> There was no question in my mind that day that we could soon destroy the enemy in Italy and drive him beyond the Alps and go on to whatever objective was set for us . . . That, however, was not the way it worked out. For various reasons . . . our team was broken up and the Fifth Army was sapped of a great part of its strength.[20]

Both Alexander and Clark pushed their plans forward despite "the tyranny of Anvil."

The key to success lay in the rapid breach of the new German defense line which stretched from Pisa to Rimini. Again the master defensive genius, Kesselring, had a barrier constructed, this time using the spiny back of the Northern Apennines. This new line was called the Gothic line. If the Allies broke through the line, the flat, wide Po Valley would be open for armoured exploitation.

Alexander's chief of staff, Harding, in preparing plans for a breakthrough of the Gothic line, recognized three potential avenues of advance. The first was up the Ligurian Coast in the west. This course, however, would leave the Allied forces with no significant strategic objective. The next possibility was on the east coast, via Rimini, northward into the Romagna Plain. This route did have potential strategic objectives; Venice, Trieste, the Lyubyana Gap, and ultimately, Vienna. The final approach ran through the center of the German defenses but led to the vital Po Valley through the cities of Bologna, Inola, Faenza and Foili. This final approach would prove by far the most difficult. However, through deception Alexander hoped to bluff Kesselring into believing that the main Allied effort would indeed be on the east coast. Therefore, should Kesselring send his forces to this point it could only be at the expense of weakening his center. Then Clark's army could strike.

This then was the proposed plan, but it was up to the Combined Chiefs of Staff whether to adopt it or not. Anvil was rapidly approaching and with it the timetable for Alexander to relinquish command of those units destined for southern France but also desperately required for an attack into the heart of the Gothic line.

Brooke saw that Alexander's arguments for the cancellation of Anvil were rather attractive. The possibility of opening up Central Europe and the Balkans was most appealing. However, he also knew that this plan would be repugnant to the anti-imperialist sentiments of the Americans who continued to fully advocate Anvil's role in furthering the exploitation of Overlord. Nevertheless, the British chiefs of staff, led by Brooke despite some reservations, backed Alexander's plan using as a lure to the Americans the fact that this plan was a better way of weakening German resistance by drawing more troops to Italy than the Anvil landings could ever hope to do. All this could be accomplished without having to mount yet another hazardous amphibious operation.

Still the Americans continued to be violently opposed and in the end the British gave way in the interest of Allied unity. It must be remembered that the fall of 1944 was presidential election time. Roosevelt wanted to present the American electorate with a great victory. Anvil, he felt, could provide the key to that victory. On the other hand, Alexander's plan could lead to great political controversy in the vast maze of central and southeastern Europe. General Marshall opposed Alexander's plans on the grounds that Kesselring would just retreat into the Alps with the advent of an Allied breakthrough. By doing this, he could then free more German soldiers to oppose Eisenhower rather than actually draw more away from western Europe.

Anvil was thus given new life and Alexander was ordered to give up two corps, the crack veteran VI Corps of Salerno and Anzio, and the mountain-trained French Expeditionary Corps whose troops had fought so gallantly on the slopes of Monte Cassino. This obviously had a dampening effect of the enthusiasm of the army group commander.

Alexander always expressed a deep admiration for Eisenhower and this admiration never wavered. Still, Alexander placed the blame for Anvil squarely on the supreme commander's shoulders. In his memoirs, Alexander points an accusing finger.

> I must record—without any bitterness—that he alone was responsible for halting the triumphant advance of my armies in Italy at a key moment in that campaign.
>
> Why then do I charge Ike alone with having delivered a bodyblow at the Italian campaign despite Winston's powerful advocacy? Because,

> as he records, the United States Chiefs of Staff declined to interfere with the conclusions of the commander in the field. Thus the decision lay solely with Ike, who, as I say, felt no concern about the future of the Italian campaign; and as much as I admire him I cannot believe that the ultimate formation of the United States Sixth Army Group following the "Anvil-Dragoon" operation, represented anything other than an unwise dispersal of force.[21]

In approaching the Gothic line, Alexander was required to break down German delaying positions, first at Lake Trasimene, then around Arezzo. At this point, the two veteran corps were dispatched. Anvil, now renamed Dragoon, was being readied. Even lacking the two corps, Alexander carried on. His instructions still held the clause that the main job was the destruction of the German army even if the resources for accomplishing that job were withdrawn.

Ironically, while Alexander's forces were weakened, Kesselring's were strengthened. Alexander found himself required to accomplish a job and at the same time seeing the tools required to accomplish it snatched away. He was ordered to proceed despite a now numerical inferiority.

With the transfer of the two disputed corps, particularly the French mountain corps who were designated to break the Gothic line in the center, Alexander was forced to modify his plans. Gen. Oliver Leese, the man who inherited Eighth Army from Montgomery, proposed that his army now be given the major attack role with its direction on the east coast past Pesaro, Coriano, and Rimini. Alexander accepted this idea but still wanted Fifth Army to strike at the center; the one-two punch combination which he had used successfully at Cassino and Anzio. Fifth Army was therefore directed to hit in the middle of the Gothic line. Hopefully, Kesselring would believe this to be the major Allied thrust. Then, Eighth Army would launch their attack.

Kesselring hoped he would not have to shuffle troops from one front to another and cause a general weakness, thus allowing for an Allied exploitation.

Leese's plan was codenamed "Oliver." At first the Gothic defenses were quickly overun on the east coast, but just as Eighth Army was about to break free of the mountains south of Rimini, Kesselring was able to halt the offensive. As August turned into September, the battles around Coriano were as fierce as any fought in the entire Italian campaign. Kesselring had managed to scrape together enough troops to stop Leese just short of the Romagna Plain. Shortage of troops hindered Leese dearly.

Alexander realized that Kesselring had used up his reserve in opposing Eighth Army so he ordered Clark to open an offensive in the center, north of Florence. The Germans were caught totally unprepared and it appeared for a while as if Clark was going to break through. But, like Leese before him, Clark lacked sufficient fresh troops required to tip the balance. Kesselring, the master craftsman of defense, stopped Clark dead in his tracks just as he had done with Leese earlier. If only Anvil had been cancelled, then those desperately needed fresh troops would have been available to bring Alexander a great victory, opening up to him the vast northern Italian plain before the onset of winter.

Leese finally managed to break through to Rimini on September 21, but just as he approached the Romagna Plain the heavy autumn rains broke and turned the plain into a gigantic sea of mud. Alexander's stroke had come too late. He would have to wait for spring before achieving final victory.

The fighting in the fall of 1944 was marked by heavy casualties. Alexander spent much of his time moving from front to front monitoring conditions and the state of morale among the men.

Originally, Alexander had set November 15 as the cutoff date for offensive operations in Clark's area. Wherever Fifth Army stood at that time was to be their winter line. He later extended the date in hopes that perhaps a little more effort would break the mountain barrier and expose the Po Valley. It would be immensely better to await spring in the valley rather than have to stay in the mountains for the season. German resistance, however, was simply too stiff. On December 30, Alexander finally called a halt to all operations. With this decision, all hopes of advancing into Yugoslavia and Austria faded away.

On December 12, 1944, Alexander reached the highest military position short of chief of the Imperial General Staff; he was named supreme commander for the Mediterranean Theatre upon the transfer of Jumbo Wilson to Washington. Clark moved up to Fifteenth Army Group commander and Truscott became commander of Fifth Army.

Immediately, Alexander's responsibilities broadened. The day before assuming the position of supreme commander, he was sent to Athens to bolster a noncommunist Greek government struggling against communist guerrillas who for years had been fighting the Germans and now demanded political power. While his armoured car was driving through Athens he was fired upon by armed rebels but was unhurt. With the arrival of British troops, the communists were defeated but the overall situation in Greece remained unstable. Alexander did, however, accomplish the de-escalation of the civil war. In time, the Greek monarchy reestablished itself and brought about some semblance of stability.

Back in Italy plans were laid for the spring offensive. Allied divisions now numbered seventeen as opposed to the German's nineteen. Clark handled all the details.

The campaign opened on April 9. Again it was a two punch operation with Eighth and Fifth Armies meeting on the Po, north of Bologna. Kesselring, Alexander's respected adversary for the past two years, had been transferred to command all German troops in the west, so the Germans in Italy were now commanded by the former Tenth Army commander, von Vietinghoff. The latter tried desperately to halt the Allied steamroller but the combined pressure of two Allied armies under the complete dominance of Allied air power was too much. Most of Vietinghoff's Army Group C was either killed or captured south of the Po.

The Germans in Italy then urgently sought an end to the slaughter. SS Gen. Karl Wolff had for some time been meeting with a representative of the OSS*

*Office of Strategic Services, forerunner of the current CIA.

in Switzerland, Alan Dulles, in an attempt to conclude a separate peace. Finally, the talks reached a successful conclusion and on May 2, 1945, German forces in Italy laid down their arms.

With war's conclusion, Brooke desired that Alexander succeed him as chief of the Imperial General Staff. At Potsdam, however, when Alexander arrived to participate in the final Allied War Council, Churchill ushered him aside and said that Canada had requested that he be its next governor general. Alexander graciously accepted.

In 1946 he was made a viscount by a grateful government. After serving with great distinction in Canada where the populace adored his charm and grace, he returned to England in 1952 and was created First Earl Alexander of Tunis. That same year Churchill offered him the position of minister of defense in his second government. Alexander remained in this position for two and one-half years but was uneasy and did not really enjoy the political forum. In October, 1954, he retired from public life. During his remaining years he painted, gardened, enjoyed leisure time with his family, collaborated in the writing of his memoirs and dispatches, and served as director of various companies. Alexander died in June, 1969.

> A commander is a man who can inspire men at every level to work together in the common cause.[22]

That statement by the noted historian W. F. G. Jackson most accurately describes Sir Harold Alexander or "Alex," as he was affectionately called. He was a man of great personal integrity, enthusiasm and humanity. Most assuredly he projected the image of a true gentleman.

As a strategist and tactician, though his policies were usually sound, they were rarely outstanding. However, he was well chosen to chair the position he held. At El Alamein he provided a stabilizing influence. In the Mediterranean theatre he was able to draw together the military and political leaders of many nations and bring out the best in all of them. He was superb in handling the many problems that such a great mixture of nationalities brought.

Alexander though, was not infallible and did misjudge and underestimate. His stereotyping of the Americans in Tunisia was not one of his finest hours and his handling of the Patton-Montgomery conflict in Sicily left something to be desired.

No one will discount the fact that Alexander was brilliant, but not as a strategist. He foundered without a good chief of staff. When one was not present, as was the case between the planning for Sicily and January 1944, his plans contained many strategic mistakes. His unique style of command demanded the presence of a strong chief of staff able to forcefully handle subordinates. Alexander was simply too much of a gentleman to exercise a strong hand.

In Italy, Alexander accomplished what he set out to do. He drew German strength to his theatre and exploited his successes as best he could with the material available. His softness of manner tarnished the complete success of Diadem when Clark was allowed to advance on Rome rather than Valmontone. But the postponement of Anvil from June to

August was one of the great debating successes in his eternal struggle with the Combined Chiefs. The fact that he failed to have this operation cancelled completely represented one of his most dismal failures.

One sign indicative of Alexander's ability was the total number of casualties for the Italian campaign. Traditionally, the attacker suffers a much higher percentage of casualties when attacking fixed defenses. It is usually the defender who comes off better despite the final outcome of the battle. In Italy, the tally was 312,000 Allied casualties as opposed to the 536,000 suffered by the Germans.

Though uniquely suited for the position he was placed in, it was a shame that he was then required to fight with such restraints. Given the proper tools of war, Alexander would surely have put them to good use. His remarkable talents could have, and should have, been utilized in Overlord. The greatest mistake made by the Combined Chiefs was the appointment of Montgomery to assume command of the Twenty-first Army Group while Alexander was left to languish in Italy. It should have been the other way around.

It is even more interesting to theorize what might have transpired had Alexander been named supreme commander in lieu of Eisenhower. Alexander's knowledge and keen sense of traditional European foibles would most certainly have resulted in a drastically altered postwar European map. Surely his personality, charm, and ability to mold various nationalities into a cohesive team warranted his appointment to this position. Unfortunately, historians are now reduced to speculation.

It is in the art of command that Alexander made

his greatest contribution to the war effort. In the art of leadership he had few, if any, peers. Successive generations fortunate enough to study this remarkable man should feel towards him the same way his subordinates, and the authors, feel towards the man who shall forever be affectionately known as "Alex."

Field Marshal Sir Bernard Law Montgomery

Chapter 5

In today's modern English language there exists a virtual litany of words that can be appropriately utilized to describe the personality of Field Marshal Sir Bernard Law Montgomery, Earl of Alamein. Obnoxious, churlish, vain, arrogant, egocentric, and thoroughly unpleasant come to mind immediately, and have all been used by historians, critics, and even his own military colleagues when speaking of the British leader. One fact is absolutely certain: he was without doubt the most overrated general of the entire war. One of America's finest commanders, Gen. Omar Bradley, has this to say of Montgomery:

> Montgomery is a third rate general and he never did anything or won any battle that any other general could not have won as well or better.[1]

These words are not meant to convey the fact that he was not one of the great commanders, or to be more specific, one of the great leaders of the war. He was. It is merely that when discussing the relative merits of Montgomery one must carefully walk that fine line and be constantly aware of the distinction between commander and leader. Few can dispute Monty's gift for leadership when it came to inspiring troops or subordinates. In addition, his incredible portrayal of the image of a successful officer was of incalculable value to a victory-starved English populace. Consequently Britain's most famous commander of the twentieth century, Montgomery of Alamein, rates membership in that select group of individuals considered to be the great commanders of World War II.

Who was this complex character? Was he the champion that finally brought the "Desert Fox" to bay in the sands of El Alamein or was he the selfish glory seeker who consigned the British Airborne forces to their annihilation at Arnhem? Could he have been the methodical strategist, master of the set piece battle who left nothing to chance but then threw away the victory at Antwerp because he failed to take into consideration the dominating German presence on the Schledt Estuary? Perhaps the riddle of Montgomery's personality accompanied him to the grave and will forever be shrouded in mystery. But of one thing we can be absolutely certain; as long as men insist on waging war, his memory will be forever entwined with the glorious military history of the British Empire.

It has been said by biographers that Montgomery had an unhappy childhood, and although this may be true, it appears that any unhappiness associated with his adolescence was entirely of his own making. Even as a child he was rebellious towards authority and disinclined to associate with his siblings. His frequent indiscretions incurred the wrath of not only his brothers and sisters, but of his parents as well.

The most dominating influence of his early years was without doubt his mother. When Bernard was but a babe, his clergyman father was appointed Bishop of Tasmania and the family was uprooted and transported halfway around the world. His father's position demanded frequent lengthy absences from home, leaving his young wife with sole responsibility for the upbringing of the children. Montgomery's few references to her in later years were laced with hostility and bitterness for obviously she was rather strict and domineering. As a young lad, Montgomery rebelled frequently against her authority and found himself constantly being punished for his behavior. In later years, after he joined the army, he saw as little of her as possible and even refused to attend her funeral. To the day he died, Montgomery harbored bitter memories of his mother. As for his brothers and sisters, they too became alienated from him and except for one sister, Bernard saw less and less of them in his adult life. Eventually, this sister too became a stranger as Montgomery withdrew into the cocoon of his profession.

When the family returned home to England, Bernard was thirteen and had earned a well-deserved reputation as a bully and unruly child. As soon as he entered public school he made up his mind to enter the military and become a soldier. Although far from a brilliant scholar, Montgomery entered Sandhurst in 1907. Almost immediately his qualities of leadership were recognized and he was soon given a stripe and promoted to command of a student company. Montgomery soon turned his company into a marauding band of thugs and bullies before his brief command ended ingloriously after he set fire to another cadet. When the unfortunate brunt of his bullying tactics was seriously burnt, Montgomery was reduced to the lowest rank possible and remained there for the balance of his tenure at Sandhurst.

Because he was not a gentleman of private means, Montgomery's goal was to join the Indian Army after graduation. Unfortunately, only the top thirty of each graduating class were considered for vacancies in this organization and when the final standings were posted, Montgomery stood thirty-sixth despite having concentrated heavily on his studies. The fact that he even ranked that high was remarkable insofar as he was considered to possess only average intelligence. However, his financial situation precluded an active social life, and thanks to the unpleasant memory of his mother, he was totally uninterested in women. Therefore, unlike many of his classmates, he devoted full-time to his studies, although he did manage to make time for games at which he excelled. Masking his severe disappointment, Montgomery then opted for a commission in the Royal Warwickshires, and much to his delight, found himself in India anyway as the regiment was transferred to that station. During this period, two other young officers held commissions similiar to that of Montgomery. Both William Slim and Cyril Newell would later have illustrious careers in World War II.

While in India, Montgomery totally immersed himself in his work and was puzzled by the attitude of his comrades when they preferred to discuss matters other than military when off duty. They, in turn, considered Montgomery to be somewhat stuffy, odd, and completely lacking in the social graces. Also, during this time Montgomery's often insubordinate character began to surface most notably during a football match with sailors of the visiting German cruiser, *Gneisenau*. As battalion sport officer, Montgomery was told to go easy on the Germans. Instead, he did the very opposite and administered a humiliating defeat on the guests to the chagrin of his superiors who were determined to play the gracious host. Montgomery was severely chastised for his actions and was marked down as an officer who was not above disobeying orders.

The Warwickshires returned to England early in 1913 and Montgomery plunged himself into the study of the art of warfare. Heretofore he had confined his attention to becoming an outstanding regimental officer. His new interest consumed his attention, and as he had few outside interests, he was closely observed and soon earned a reputation as somewhat of a forward thinker.

World War I brought an abrupt end to parade ground soldiering and the Warwickshires were sent to France in August of 1914, just in time to participate in the Battle of Mons which became an Allied rout. Then followed the bloodbath known as the Battle of Ypres during which Montgomery, by now a captain, personally led his platoon against enemy held positions. Eventually, his reckless bravery was rewarded with a bullet in the chest, later followed by another wound in the knee as he lay bleeding and mortally wounded in a no-man's-land. His platoon feared for their commander but were unable to offer assistance until nightfall. When he was finally rescued from his

*Distinguished Service Order

plight he was all but given up for dead. Fortunately, his determination and will to live won out and he recovered in time to receive the D.S.O.,* a decoration usually reserved for officers much higher in rank than a mere captain.

When he was sufficiently recovered, Montgomery returned to France as a staff officer and learned many valuable lessons which were to serve him well in later years. Staff work fascinated him thus he apparently found his niche as his work proved superior in all ways. In later years, he excelled in staff work although his battlefield performance left something to be desired.

The end of World War I brought a return to the boredom of peacetime soldiering for the professional officers of the British army, but for Montgomery it was merely another assignment to be carried out with vigour. After all, soldiering was his chosen profession so how could it be boring? One valuable lesson while a staff officer was that troops were the tool of any officer and to foolishly waste these tools was to court disaster. For the rest of his active career he was to court disaster. For the rest of his active career he remained firmly loyal to this theory, which probably accounts for the fact that during World War II, his men held him in almost Godlike esteem.

Montgomery's newly acquired interest in staff work caused him to apply for the Staff College at Camberley upon his return to England in 1919. He knew that a course at the Staff College was a prerequisite for those officers aspiring to higher command. One of three things was necessary to earn appointment to the staff course; above average intelligence, favoritism, or influential contacts. Montgomery, of course, possessed none of these and thus failed to earn appointment for the 1920 course. He was determined not to allow himself to be passed over. To insure this, he curried the favor of the influential Gen. Sir William Robertson and just prior to the beginning of the course, Montgomery's name was added to the list.

Students at Camberley were not graded insofar as final exams were concerned so it is virtually impossible for historians to assess Montgomery's performance at the staff college. Typically, Major Montgomery made no effort to mask his impression that his knowledge was superior to that of his instructors. He was beginning to justify his already unpopular personality.

Upon completion of the one year course, Montgomery was sent as brigade major to Cork, Ireland. The Easter rebellion of 1916 was still fresh in memory and the spark of rebellion continued to smolder throughout the Emerald Isle. Wicklow, Carle, Donegal, and Cork, among others, were hotbeds of rebellion merely awaiting the time when the breeze would fan the spark into the flame of open revolt. It was a typical guerrilla war but Montgomery refused to be intimidated. His effective method of suppression was to fight fire with fire and the ruthless side of the man surfaced during this period. When the Irish crisis was finally resolved in 1922, he returned to England as G.S.O., 2, of the Third Division, responsible for training. He continued to serve in various staff positions until the beginning of 1926 when he returned to Camberley as an instructor. Among the students who attended his lectures were future generals Leese, Harding, Dempsey, and the man later destined to be his superior in World War II, Harold Alexander. One can but wonder if any of Montgomery's students thought that they knew more than their instructor just as Montgomery had earlier thought. Fortunately, Montgomery possessed a thorough knowledge of his subject and was for the most part an interesting speaker.

During the period at Camberley, Montgomery met, courted, and married Betty Carver, widow of an officer slain in World War I and sister of the armoured authority, Percy Hobart. She was the only female Montgomery ever felt affection for and he remained completely devoted to her until her untimely death in 1937.

Montgomery still held the rank of major and was a rather senior one at that. It seemed to him as if his career was at a standstill until he was appointed to command his former regiment, the Warwickshires, and set off to Palestine with his unit in 1930. As lieutenant colonel of the regiment, this was his first independent command.

A year later, the regiment was transferred to Alexandria, Egypt, where he again proceeded to run afoul of his superiors. To the puritanical Montgomery, the temptation of the fleshpots and vice dens of the city represented a Satan's den. He instituted regulations aimed at discouraging the troops from relieving their boredom. Violations were harshly punished with the result that morale in the regiment sank to a dangerously low level. These actions were in contrast to the method of a man who would later place such a high degree of emphasis on the ordinary soldier. Fortunately, Montgomery's superiors stepped in, chastised him, and smoothed matters over. Still, Montgomery failed to profit from his experiences with higher authority. When the army in Egypt began to experiment with night maneuvers, Montgomery was highly critical and vocal in his opposition. So much so that eventually he was told to shut up and just obey orders. Consequently, he threw himself wholeheartedly into the experiment and performed so successfully that he became an instant convert.

In 1937, Montgomery received command of the Ninth Brigade, Third Division at Portsmouth. This division was part of Southern Command under General Wavell. The Montgomery legend continued to grow. On one occasion, after he excitedly reported to Wavell on the success of a landing operation, he climbed into his car and drove full speed into a dung heap. On another, he rented government out to raise money for the Brigade Welfare fund. For this, he received a severe dressing down from his superiors. Nonetheless, Wavell formed a high opinion of his eccentric subordinate.

> Strange fellow, Montgomery. One of the most capable officers we have but for some reason not popular with senior officers.[2]

The following year, Montgomery returned to Palestine to take command of the Eighth Division. The country was in turmoil as quotas established on Jewish immigration led to hostile feelings against the British occupation forces. Instead of one regiment, the police action now required the use of two full divisions, Montgomery's in the north and Sir Richard

O'Connor's in the south of the country. The rebels were highly active and it was unsafe for the occupation troops and officers to travel without escort. Montgomery's dispositions soon restored order and the crisis ebbed.

In 1939, a vacancy occurred for a commander for the Third Division in England. This division was part of Wavell's Southern Command, and when asked who he would like to have for the Third's new commander, the latter unhesitatingly replied Montgomery. In Wavell's own words:

> There was something like a sigh of relief from the other Army Commanders and instant acquiescence. Monty's name had come up several times before in front of the selection board; everyone agreed that he ought to be promoted, but every other commander who had a vacancy for a major-general had always excellent reasons for finding someone more suitable than Monty. I never had any doubts about his ability and I also liked him and was not afraid of his independent ideas and ways, which I could control.[3]

Archibald Wavell was one of England's brightest and most illustrious commanders of World War II, but his high opinion of Montgomery must be taken to task.

That Montgomery was a superb trainer of troops was without doubt. Unfortunately, his ideas for practical use of these troops was not revolutionary. If anything, they were very conservative. During the twenties, Montgomery had written a couple of brochures on infantry tactics. These he forwarded to the military theorist Basil Liddell-Hart, who pointed out that although the principle of attack had been brilliantly handled, there was no mention of exploiting a breakthrough. Montgomery excused this by saying that he did not want to teach too much all at once. But, in the early thirties he rewrote the infantry manual for the British army and again failed to include exploitation. One must then wonder where he earned the reputation as an independent and forward thinker. Wavell's assessment of him therefore must be an indictment of the outmoded methods of the prewar British army and may explain why the Germans ran circles around them for the first two years of the war.

Montgomery was scheduled to assume command of the Third Division in August, 1939, but before leaving the Middle East he fell seriously ill and the physicians feared for his life. Although he was placed aboard ship for passage to England, few thought that he would survive the trip. Only Montgomery himself was convinced that he would regain his health. When the ship docked in England, Montgomery was able to walk ashore jauntily only to be informed that due to mobilization for the war threat, all changes in command were cancelled. Supremely confident that he was the best man for the job, he badgered the War Office until they relented and he got his way. Late in August he assumed command. A few weeks later, before he had time to become acquainted with his command, the Third Division was sent off to France as part of the BEF.*

The BEF consisted of two corps. I Corps, under Sir

*British Expeditionary Force

John Dill contained First and Second Divisions, the former under General Alexander. General Alan Brooke's II Corps included the Third and Fourth Divisions.

During the bleak winter of 1939-40, Montgomery continued to acquaint himself with his command. Training was not neglected as Montgomery was a firm believer in maintaining the alert fighting trim of his troops.

On May 10, 1940, when Guderian's panzers smashed into the French positions near Sedan, the BEF was defending the left of the Allied line with only the French Seventh Army between it and the sea. French Gen. Maurice Gamelin was in overall command of the Allied forces and his grand strategy (Dyle Plan) called for the BEF to advance into Belgium and defend the River Dyle line against a German attack through the lowlands.

Third Division advanced to a position east of Brussels and prepared to dig in. On the fourteenth, the Dutch surrendered and Guderian's armoured formations crossed the Meuse and dashed for the Allied rear. The next day, Third Division made contact with the enemy. Montgomery's division managed to hold but a few days later, the BEF was ordered to withdraw toward the channel. By the twenty-third, II Corps was back in the positions in which they had spent the winter. However, by now the situation was critical as they fought to establish defensive positions. As the end of May drew near, the British found themselves squeezed into a rapidly shrinking pocket near the coast. Adding to the dilemma was the surrender of the Belgian army, exposing the left flank of the British line. The German advance threatened to cut the road to Dunkirk on the coast. Montgomery was ordered to reposition his division and plug the yawning gap. This entailed pulling it out of line at night, loading it aboard transport, moving close in the rear of the hard-pressed Fifth Division, and having it in position by morning ready to fight. At this type of maneuver Montgomery was a master and carried it off brilliantly. Brooke wrote this comment in his diary about Monty's feat:

> Found he had, as usual, accomplished almost the impossible and had marched from Roubaix to north of Ypres. A flank march past the front of attack, and was firmly established on the line.[4]

As the situation continued to deteriorate it became obvious that the battle was lost. Churchill therefore ordered Brooke and Dill to turn over their commands and return home to begin preparations for defending Britain itself. Brooke confidently turned II Corps over to Montgomery but when Dill selected Lieutenant General Barker to succeed him, Montgomery suggested that the I Corps commander was making a grave error. Such audacity was typical of Montgomery. Here he was, a relatively junior major-general, impudently suggesting that Dill had made an error in judgment. Montgomery went on to recommend that Harold Alexander be chosen instead. Incredibly, Dill agreed. Whatever one might say of Montgomery's unusual behavior in this matter, the choice of Alexander was fortuitous. He brilliantly conducted the evacuation of Dunkirk and was one of the last British officers off the beach (Montgomery and his corps left on May 31).

The War Office had intended to return troops to the continent to assist France in its final agonizing struggle against the Germans. The only division suitably equipped for this endeavor was the Third. Fortunately for England, before Montgomery could prepare his division for a return to the fray, France sued for peace.

As Britain settled down to await the imminent invasion, the generals made feverish preparations for defense. The Third Division was the most battle worthy and was thus held back from the front in order to preserve it as a mobile reserve for use in whatever area the attack came. Although the division was to act as a mobile reserve, it was actually immobile due to lack of sufficient transport. Undeterred, Montgomery persuaded his superiors to requisition all available civilian buses for his use. Armed with this unusual method of transportation, the Third Division prepared to defend the homeland.

In July, Montgomery was promoted to command of V Corps in Auchinleck's Southern Command. Curiously, he seemed to go out of his way to antagonize his immediate superior and developed an intense dislike for "The Auk" which did not abate throughout the war or even afterward. This was puzzling for Auchinleck was most affable and a popular commander. Montgomery's behavior under Auchinleck amounted to nothing less than rank insubordination and blatant disrespect. He was constantly going over Auchinleck's head with matters on which he did not agree and went so far as to ridicule the commander of Southern Command.* Were it not for the fact that Auchinleck was truly a gentleman, a quality that Montgomery knew little or nothing of, he would have been sacked. But Auchinleck was indeed a gentleman and although Montgomery attempted to chastise his insubordinate V Corps commander, a lesser man would have fired Montgomery and demanded that charges be brought by virtue of the latter's irregular behavior. Auchinleck was greatly relieved to return to India at the end of the year and leave the problem of Montgomery to some other unfortunate commander. Monty had made life truly miserable. In his postwar memoirs, Montgomery has this to say of his period under Auchinleck's command:

> I cannot recall that we ever agreed on anything.[5]

As the war progressed, rising generals in the British army were plucked from England and sent off to active command in the Far and Middle East. Not so Montgomery. He was left behind to train and develop troops.

The raid on Dieppe in August of 1942 still remains shrouded in controversy. As G.O.C. of Southern Command, Montgomery was involved because the raid set off from his area of responsibility. Many erroneous decisions were made during the planning stages for the operation and Montgomery certainly made his share of those. However, the blame for failure should not be laid at his doorstep for there were too many others involved more deeply. Besides, before leaving to take over the Eighth Army, Mont-

*See Chapter 3

gomery recommended that the entire operation be scrapped. He was probably correct.

In midsummer of 1942, England's fortunes in North Africa reached a low ebb. All the gains of the previous fall's Operation Crusader were rudely nullified by Rommel's amazing string of victories at Gazala, Tobruk, and Mersa Matruh. Tobruk had fallen during the third week in June and Eighth Army had been routed and put to flight. Rommel pursued the British across the Egyptian border and approached the Nile. The great naval base at Alexandria was evacuated and the Suez Canal was in danger of falling.

The commander in charge of the Middle East, Sir Claude Auchinleck, finally halted the Germans at a defensive line hastily thrown up near a whistle stop known as El Alamein. From the time that defeat in the western desert became obvious, Auchinleck had considered making a last ditch stand in this position so as to take advantage of the natural terrain. The impassable Qattara Depression in the south and the Mediterranean Sea in the north provided a relatively narrow stretch of land to defend and precluded wide flanking movements. Thus, Rommel would be required to attack on a narrow front and would be unable to outflank the British positions as he had done so many times in the past.

On June 30, Rommel hit the Alamein line. By then, Auchinleck had assumed personal command and his brilliant use of the natural terrain blunted the Axis attack. Two days later, Eighth Army went over to the offensive and drove the vaunted Axis forces back. Unfortunately, Eighth Army was too weak to sustain the offensive, but for three weeks their aggressive behavior held Rommel at bay until the German commander was forced to call a halt. The First Battle of El Alamein ended in a British victory.

Auchinleck's inability to launch a full scale offensive accelerated the already deteriorating relationship between him and Churchill. Consequently, the prime minister, always clamoring for an attack, traveled to Egypt to see for himself why Auchinleck had decided to go on the defensive. On August 3, Churchill and Brooke, by now chief of the Imperial General Staff, arrived in Cairo. After a round of talks and tours, Churchill and Brooke decided upon a change in command. Alexander was chosen to become the new commander in charge of the Middle East, and General Gott, veteran commander of the Seventh Armoured Division, was designated the new commander of Eighth Army. Enroute to take up his new command, Gott's plane was shot down and the general lost his life. A replacement was required immediately.

Montgomery was still holding down a training command in England at this time although he had been selected to command the British effort in the joint US-British assault on French North Africa (Operation Torch). An urgent call went out from Cairo ordering him to report immediately to Egypt and take up command of the Eighth Army. On August 12, Montgomery arrived in the desert.

That same morning, Montgomery met with Auchinleck and was familiarized with the situation. Montgomery later claimed that at this meeting Auchinleck admitted to making preparations for a further retreat to the Nile. Nothing could have been further from the truth. Any commander worth his salt possesses a contingency plan and Auchinleck had developed one that called for a withdrawal to the Nile prior to First Alamein. He was determined not to let Eighth Army stand and fight to the last man thereby sealing the fate of the entire Middle East. His spectacular victory over Rommel later caused these plans to be shelved. After the war, the outcry of General Dorman-Smith, Auchinleck's chief of staff, caused Montgomery to retract his degrading statement.

Shortly after noon on the thirteenth, Montgomery usurped his authority and assumed command of Eighth Army, two days before his appointment was to become official. Such behavior was inexcusable but Monty's ego convinced him that he had been sent as saviour of the entire Middle East and could therefore not afford to leave the army in the hands of incompetents. He immediately began a purge of key Eighth Army personnel and sent for his "own men" to fill these positions. He always insisted on having subordinates whose theories and thinking paralleled his. So Brian Horrocks and Oliver Leese arrived to command XIII and XXX Corps.

Now began the process of revitalizing the command. Montgomery set about visiting the front, addressing junior officers, NCOs and ordinary soldiers. He made it a point to speak to all ranks and was very candid about his future plans. Above all, he emphasized that retreat was out of the question and that from now on the only direction would be forward. Morale soared and Eighth Army found itself mesmerized by the eccentric little general.

Montgomery also decided that he needed to project

an image. Therefore, in order to give himself a distinctive appearance, he donned a bush hat and adorned it with a regimental badge from every unit that he visited. Although this was later abandoned in favor of a beret with but two badges, the effort worked. He also curried the favor of the press and openly discussed his plans with them thus making valuable friends who were eager to publicize Montgomery.

Montgomery was also fortunate to have as his superior Sir Harold Alexander, one of the gentlest and most easy going commanders of the entire war. Although "Alex" considered Montgomery's methods to be somewhat unorthodox, he was willing to live with them provided the latter delivered the goods.

Montgomery's first test came during the Battle of Alam Halfa. From intelligence sources (Ultra), he was made aware of Rommel's intention to launch another offensive. Montgomery was also aware that Rommel would try to repeat his earlier tactic of attempting a breakthrough in the south followed by a swing northward in the British rear. As Auchinleck had defeated a similar thrust a month earlier, Montgomery had a ready made and tested plan available. Although he later claimed that the plan was entirely his own, in reality he merely made a few modifications to the original. Even Alexander's statements contradict Montgomery's claim.

> The plan was to hold as strongly as possible the area between the sea and Ruweisat Ridge and to threaten from the flank any enemy advance south of the ridge from a strongly defended posi-

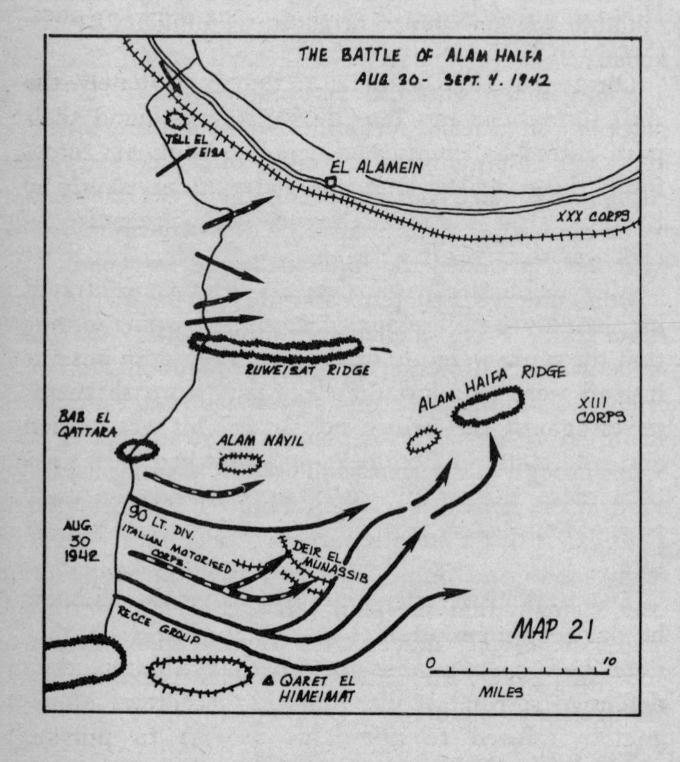
THE BATTLE OF ALAM HALFA
AUG. 30- SEPT. 4. 1942
TELL EL EISA
EL ALAMEIN
XXX CORPS
RUWEISAT RIDGE
ALAM HALFA RIDGE
XIII CORPS
BAB EL QATTARA
ALAM NAYIL
AUG. 30 1942
90 LT. DIV.
ITALIAN MOTORISED CORPS.
DEIR EL MUNASSIB
RECCE GROUP
MAP 21
0
10
MILES
QARET EL HIMEIMAT

> tion on the Alam Halfa ridge. General Montgomery, now in command of Eighth Army, accepted this plan in principle, to which I agreed, and hoped that if the enemy should give us enough time he would be able to improve our positions by strengthening the left or southern flank.[6]

However, Montgomery's modifications were key ones. (See Map 21)

On August 30, Rommel attacked. Immediately, the Axis formations ran into difficulty and found their path barred by extensive minefields. Rommel's forces found the going slow and were harassed incessantly by bombing attacks launched by the RAF. The entire attack was thrown off schedule.

Like Auchinleck, Montgomery also concentrated his artillery and armour and issued distinct orders that the tanks were not to abandon their positions but instead were to allow the Germans to smash themselves against the British positions. This was a tried and true tactic of Rommel's, one that had been used by him so successfully so many times in the past. Now, Montgomery was using his own tactics against him.

Two days later, after little progress, Rommel knew he was beaten and ordered a retreat. The Axis formations had been unable to penetrate Montgomery's defensive screen. While Rommel withdrew, Montgomery refused to allow his armour to pursue, wishing instead to husband his forces for a future offensive. Thus, Montgomery's first battle proved a huge success and the confidence of Eighth Army soared. More importantly, the legendary Rommel had finally been beaten. Alam Halfa was a textbook battle conducted by a master at the set piece battle.

Churchill was suitably impressed and of course began demanding an offensive at the earliest possible date. Montgomery was not about to be badgered into premature action as had been his successors. He bluntly told the prime minister that he, Montgomery, was in charge of Eighth Army and would attack only when he was ready and not before. If this was unacceptable, then a new commander would have to be found and that was that. This firm stand shook Churchill but resulted in the prime minister's interference being drastically reduced. From that point forward, Mr. Churchill's demands and meddling decreased and Montgomery was left to conduct operations on his own.

El Alamein was Montgomery's crowning achievement and the one on which his reputation was built. However, it must be remembered that this victory followed the disasters of Gazala, Tobruk, and Mersa Matruh by less than half a year and that it was earned at the expense of one of the most glorified and romanticized figures of the entire war; Rommel. Therefore, any success at all was bound to draw a disproportionate amount of publicity to the victor even if the victory was incomplete. Montgomery's intense public relations efforts added to the notoriety.

October 23 was the date selected for an offensive aimed at driving the Axis out of North Africa once and for all. Montgomery was determined not to launch an offensive until he was heavily reinforced, the troops were suitably trained, and victory was assured before the battle was even joined.

As Montgomery prepared Eighth Army for the attack, Rommel did likewise to Panzerarmee Afrika, preparing his units for a defensive struggle. The German commander knew that it would be only a matter of time before his opponent attacked and made his dispositions accordingly. Unfortunately for Rommel, his flow of supplies and reinforcements was but a trickle compared to the wealth of men and material pouring into Egypt.

Rommel began by sowing a massive minefield whose depth was unparalleled in the war to date. He then split his two Panzer divisions and sent them to bolster the formations of his Italian allies. Through use of deception, Montgomery hoped to deceive Rommel into believing that the British attack would come in the southern portion of the Alamein line near where Rommel himself had attempted to break through during First Alamein and Alam Halfa. The British began laying a dummy pipeline southward into the desert. The rate of progress of this pipeline acted to deceive Rommel into concluding that the British offensive was scheduled for a much later date than it actually was. Dummy trucks, tanks, and other support vehicles were positioned in this sector while the real ones were brilliantly camouflaged in the north. As the date for the offensive approached, Montgomery's superiority continued to grow. He possessed a two to one superiority in tanks, transport, and artillery, and a four to one superiority over the German troops. Finally, Malta was making its presence known astride the Axis supply lines. Axis convoys bringing supplies to Rommel were attacked with great success, and as a result, Rommel was dreadfully short of fuel and equipment. The last straw was when Rommel, ill and exhausted, left the desert a few weeks prior to the attack. He was badly in need of a rest. His place was taken by Gen. George Stumme.

Montgomery's original plan called for a dual offensive by X and XXX Corps in the north and XIII Corps in the south. Later, he decided that this was too risky so he altered the plan and proposed instead that the southern attack be little more than a feint. Liddell-Hart criticizes this plan:

> This cautiously limited plan led to a protracted and costly struggle, which might have been avoided by the bolder original plan—taking account of the Eighth Army's immense superiority in strength.[7]

Montgomery placed the bulk of his strength in the north opposite the Fifteenth Panzer and Littorio (Italian) Divisions. Rommel held Ninetieth Light in reserve near the coast. Facing these were the First South African, Ninth Australian, Fifty-first Highland, New Zealand Division and two armoured divisions, the First and Tenth.

Early in the evening of October 23, after seeing to it that all preparations were final, Montgomery returned to his headquarters and retired for the night. At 10:00 P.M., over one thousand Eighth Army artillery pieces opened fire on the German positions. The barrage continued for a quarter of an hour. Immediately afterward, the infantry units began to clear a path through the minefields. (See Map 22)

The British had underestimated the depth of the

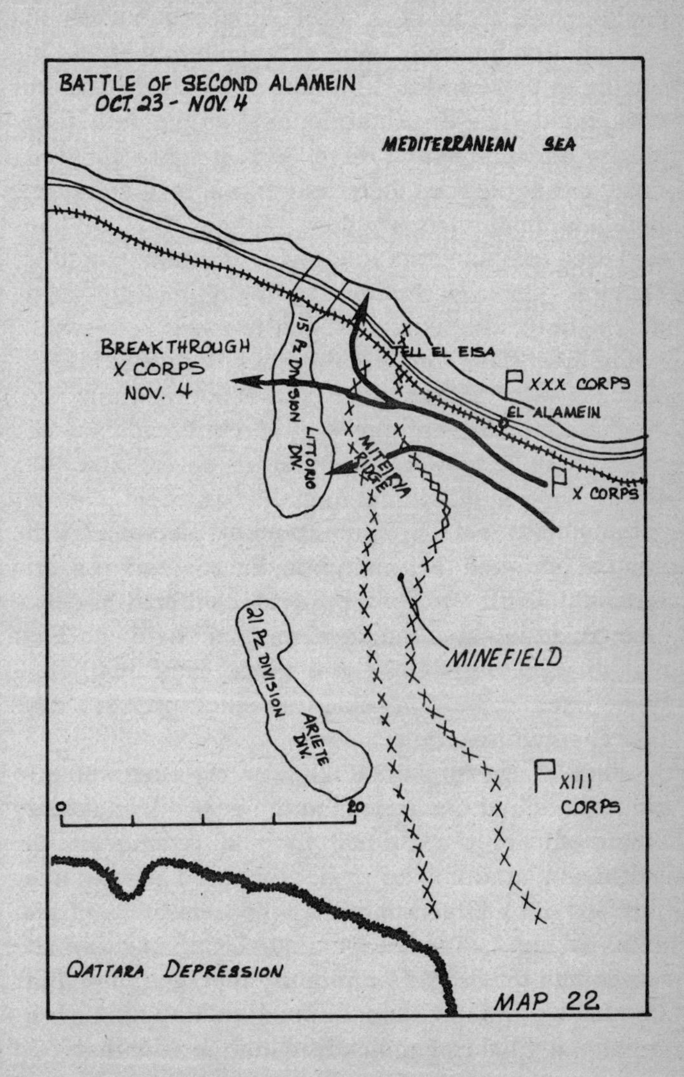
BATTLE OF SECOND ALAMEIN
OCT. 23 - NOV. 4
MEDITERRANEAN SEA
BREAKTHROUGH
X CORPS
NOV. 4
15 Pz DIVISION
LITTORIO DIV.
TELL EL EISA
XXX CORPS
EL ALAMEIN
MITEIRYA RIDGE
X CORPS
MINEFIELD
21 Pz DIVISION
ARIETE DIV.
XIII CORPS
0
20
QATTARA DEPRESSION
MAP 22

Axis minefields and could not clear a path all the way through. As morning dawned over the desert, one could behold an awesome sight. Stretched out behind the infantry for miles were long columns of tanks, unable to move forward because the minefields were not cleared. The British armour sat on the battlefield all day under fire from the enemy. It was their good fortune that the Axis batteries were short of ammunition and unable to lay down a heavy fire. When darkness fell, the infantry divisions again trundled forward. A small corridor was finally made through which the British armour began to move.

The next day, Rommel's armour counterattacked. The Axis formations were handicapped from the beginning by their low fuel supply, the broad expanse of territory they were required to cover, and the British control of the skies over the battlefield. Consequently, Rommel's armour attacked piecemeal and the concentrated British firepower beat off the attacks. Fifteenth Panzer in particular suffered heavily. The battle lasted throughout most of the day. Horrock's attack with XIII Corps in the south met with determined opposition and was called off that day (the twenty-fifth).

When dawn broke on the twenty-sixth, Montgomery ordered the armour to move forward. To the amazement of the British, they were immediately halted aby a curtain of steel. Rommel had used the previous day's attack to mask a concentration of his antitank guns. The wedge that Eighth Army had driven into the defenses was now under heavy fire and the British advance was stopped cold. The Eighth Army was further handicapped by the fact that the corridor through the minefield was much too narrow. As a result, it was difficult to push more armour forward, armour that might have tipped the scales. On the twenty-eighth, Montgomery attempted to shift the axis of attack to the northwest. Ninth Australian Division launched an attack towards the coast. Rommel moved Ninetieth Light in from reserve and blunted the enemy spearheads, aided once more by the massive belt of mines.

Montgomery now decided to revert to the original plan and stick with it. Whatever else one might say of his conduct of operations, he demonstrated his flexibility and refused to panic. He therefore ordered all offensive operations to cease temporarily until Eighth Army could regroup. He also transferred the Seventh Armoured Division from Horrocks and added its weight to the attack in the north.

Monty's decision to halt reverberated all the way back to England. Brooke, Montgomery's champion, was fearful of yet another defeat, as was Churchill. Nevertheless, Brooke managed to smooth things over and dispel the notion that Rommel had used up yet another British general. Brooke recorded his feelings:

> Personally . . . I had my own doubts and anxieties as to the course of events, but these had to be kept entirely to myself. On returning to my office I paced up and down suffering from a desperate feeling of loneliness. I had told them [Smuts and Churchill]* what I thought Monty must be doing, and I knew him well, but there was just that possibility that I was wrong and

*Author's brackets

that Monty was beat.[8]

His fears were unjustified.

On November 2, Montgomery renewed the attack. By daylight, the antitank screen had still not been penetrated but Montgomery maintained the pressure. The armour poured through the gaps but was checked by a determined effort on the part of Twenty-first Panzer. By nightfall, Eighth Army had lost over two hundred tanks. Now, even the supremely confident Montgomery began to harbor reservations. That same night, Rommel, his forces reduced to a mere shell of their former self, with little or no prospect of significant reinforcement, decided to withdraw.

When Montgomery realized that Rommel was abandoning the battlefield, he sent Fifty-first Highland and Fourth Indian Divisions against the gap between the German and Italian units. A breakthrough occurred shortly thereafter through which Montgomery pushed all three armoured divisions with orders to swing north and cut off the German retreat. The advance was slow and cautious and by the time the British reached the coastal road, the quarry had fled. Now began the long pursuit across the desert.

The Battle of El Alamein had been an epic struggle from which the British unquestionably emerged the victor. But they failed to exploit their success. A golden opportunity to destroy Panzerarmee Afrika once and for all was sacrificed to excessive caution. At times, during the retreat, Rommel's fuel situation became so critical that he was obliged to order a complete halt. Whenever this occurred, Montgomery halted too, waited for a buildup of supplies, concentrated his forces, and vacillated just long enough for his crafty opponent to scrape together enough fuel to resume the retreat. By the time Montgomery got ready to attack, Rommel had moved on. At Fuka, Mersa Matruh, Sollum, and Mersa Brega the Germans managed to postpone judgment day. Even though Rommel's effective tank strength was reduced to less than fifty, Montgomery was reluctant to gamble. Once more, he failed to grasp the significance of a breakthrough. To Montgomery's credit, however, the pursuit kept pace with the retreating enemy and never once were the Axis formations allowed to shake off their tenacious pursuers. Consequently, Rommel was unable to gain breathing space and turn on his tormentors as he had done so many times previously. On the other hand, Montgomery also kept a tight rein on his forces and his refusal to unleash them allowed Rommel to conduct a brilliant withdrawal all the way to Tunisia.

Rommel reached the Mareth line in Tunisia early in February. Once behind the fortified positions of this line, he felt a slight measure of security. By this time he had the measure of his opponent and sensed that Montgomery would not be anxious to launch an attack immediately. Therefore, he confidently turned on the green American forces at Kasserine Pass and administered a serious beating to the U.S. That operation successfully carrried out, he again moved into the Mareth line. (See Map 23)

As Montgomery approached Mareth, he again settled down until he was sure in his own mind that he could achieve victory. While he waited for his sup-

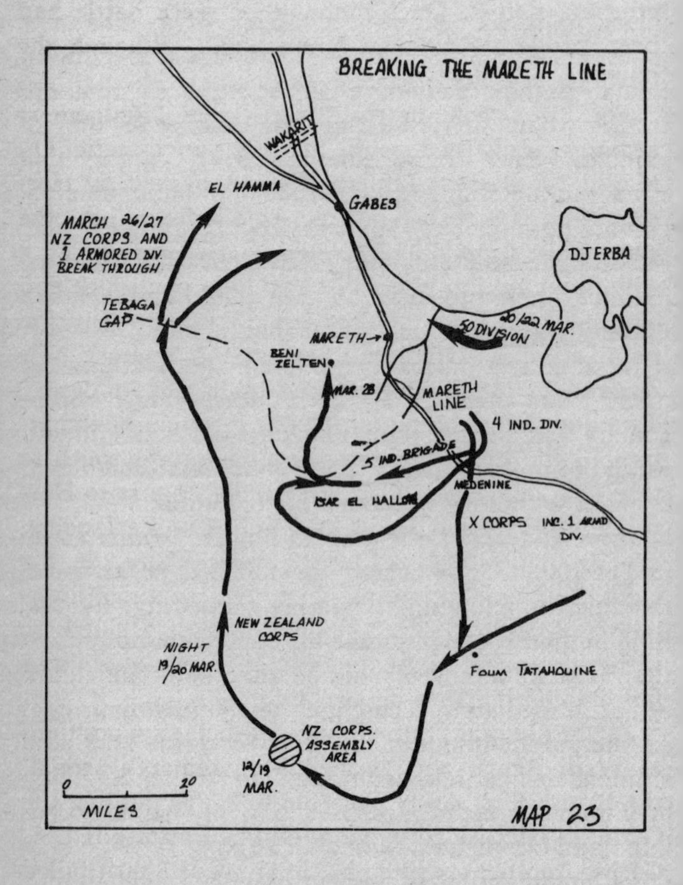
BREAKING THE MARETH LINE
WAKARIT
EL HAMMA
GABES
MARCH 26/27
NZ CORPS AND
1 ARMORED DIV.
BREAK THROUGH
DJERBA
TEBAGA
GAP
20/22 MAR.
50 DIVISION
MARETH
BENI
ZELTEN
MAR. 28
MARETH
LINE
4 IND. DIV.
5 IND. BRIGADE
MEDENINE
KSAR EL HALLOUF
X CORPS
INC. 1 ARMD
DIV.
NEW ZEALAND
CORPS
NIGHT
19/20 MAR.
FOUM TATAHOUINE
NZ CORPS.
ASSEMBLY
AREA
12/19
MAR.
0
20
MILES
MAP 23

plies to be built up, Rommel, fresh from his victory at Kasserine, attacked. But this time Montgomery had anticipated him. In a brief battle around Medenine on March 6, the Germans battered themselves against Montgomery's massed artillery and suffered a crushing defeat. Once more, a set piece battle had been brilliantly won by Montgomery, although the Germans still held the Mareth line.

For his attack on the Mareth line Montgomery again decided to adopt the one-two punch tactic. On March 20, he sent Fiftieth Division backed by Horrock's XXX Corps against the fixed defenses near the coast while a provisional New Zealand corps began a wide flanking movement around the open south end of the line. Both attacks failed. Fiftieth Division found its way barred by heavy defenses and the New Zealand corps was sluggish and made little progress. Two days later, Monty ordered a cessation of the attack in the north and sent Brian Horrocks south to take charge of operations. Eventually, thanks to Horrock's inspirational leadership, the New Zealanders, Sir Brian leading personally, broke through the enemy defenses and swung north; but this time, Rommel's successor, General von Arnim, decided to withdraw to Wadi Akarit and once more the trap failed to spring shut on the Axis.

As the Germans settled down in their new positions at Wadi Akarit and awaited Montgomery's arrival, the British First Army from the west was pushing the Germans back aided by Gen. George Patton's II U.S. Corps. Another set piece battle at Wadi Akarit failed to trap the Axis formations who once more made good their escape. Finally, however, II U.S. Corps (now commanded by Omar Bradley), along with the First and Eighth Armies, combined to push the Germans back to Cape Bon where they surrendered with losses rivaling those of Stalingrad. But by now Montgomery had other things on his mind. The Allies had decided to invade Sicily.

A variety of plans were considered for the invasion of Sicily, foremost among them being a plan for separate British and American landings at Catania and Palermo respectively. Air Marshal Tedder and Admiral Cunningham favored this plan because it provided for a dispersal of forces.

Another plan called for both Montgomery's Eighth Army and Patton's Seventh Army to invade over open beaches in the south, thus making it easier to supply both armies. Montgomery rejected this plan because he was reluctant to spread his formations out over the large area called for in the plan. He therefore countered with his own plan. Why not land both on the southeastern section of the island. In this way, he argued, Patton's forces could provide protection for the flank and rear of Eighth Army while the latter executed a "rapid thrust" up the east coast culminating in a "swift drive" on Messina, trapping the Axis formations on the island. Alexander was not present at the meeting where Montgomery made his proposal to the Allied planners but Patton, Tedder, and Cunningham were. All three fumed. Patton, because he would be relegated to a secondary role while Montgomery stole the show. Furthermore, the Seventh Army commander had seen enough of Montgomery's "speed" in Tunisia and Libya to cause him to have reservations about the Britisher's ability to do anything rapidly. Tedder and Cunningham were opposed because the plan meant a concentration of force which would allow the enemy to concentrate in turn. This could possibly lead to severe Axis reprisals against the concentrated Allied naval and air forces.

Once convinced, Montgomery refused to have it any way but his own. To him it was unthinkable that anyone but he could author a successful plan and he was determined to stop at nothing to have his plan adopted. He still considered the Americans to be rank amateurs at the art of war. Of all places, he cornered Eisenhower's chief of staff, Bedell Smith, in a lavatory and sold the plan to Ike's right-hand man. Smith agreed to intercede with his boss, and true to his word, Smith delivered. Montgomery's plan was approved. (See Map 24)

On July 10, 1943, the invasion of Sicily proceeded with the British XIII Corps landing on the east coast of Sicily approximately ten miles south of Syracuse. At the same time, XXX Corps under Leese landed on both sides of the Pachino Peninsula. Simultaneously, Patton's Seventh Army waded ashore further west in the Gulf of Gela and immediately ran into heavy opposition. The U.S. Forty-fifth Division, aided by naval gunfire from offshore, just barely beat off a determined attack by the Hermann Goering Panzer Division.

In contrast, Eighth Army's landings were virtually unopposed and by evening of the first day, Syracuse was in British hands. Dempsey promptly pushed his units beyond the port in the direction of Augusta, but a hastily assembled German combat group, Group Schmalz, stopped the XIII Corps advance halfway

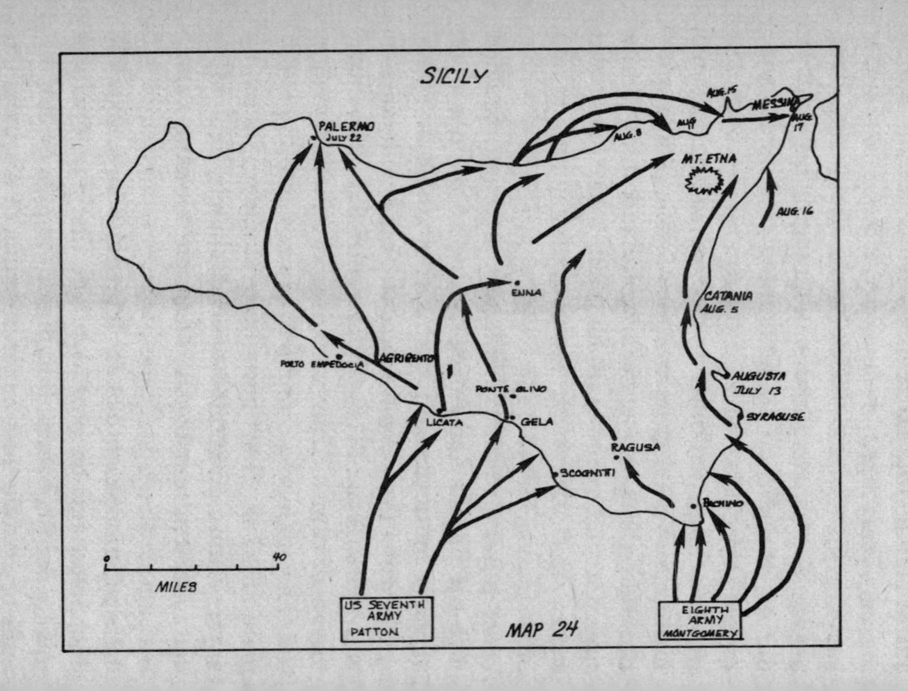
SICILY
PALERMO
JULY 22
AUG. 15
MESSINA
AUG. 17
AUG. 11
AUG. 8
MT. ETNA
AUG. 16
ENNA
CATANIA
AUG. 5
PORTO EMPEDOCLA
AGRIGENTO
PONTE OLIVO
AUGUSTA
JULY 13
LICATA
GELA
SYRACUSE
RAGUSA
SCOGLITTI
PACHINO
0
40
MILES
US SEVENTH
ARMY
PATTON
EIGHTH
ARMY
MONTGOMERY

MAP 24

between Syracuse and Augusta. On the twelfth, Group Schmalz, assisted by an Italian division, counterattacked. Dempsey immediately went over to the defensive and managed to beat off the attack. What he failed to realize was that, far from being a determined offensive, the German attack's primary goal was to cover a withdrawal to a series of fixed defensive positions around Lentini. This withdrawal opened the port of Augusta which was rapidly occupied by Eighth Army, giving Montgomery two useful ports through which to bring supplies ashore. Even with both ports now open, Montgomery found himself bogged down and unable to break the German line at Lentini. An alternative would have to be found.

As previously mentioned, Patton's official directive ordered him to protect Montgomery's flank and rear. The overall plan called for Bradley's II Corps to advance due north and cut off any opposition approaching from the west. To help Bradley accomplish this, the key road to the north, Highway 124, was assigned to his corps.

Montgomery now decided that XIII Corps would be unable to break through the German line facing it. He therefore decided to send Leese's XXX Corps on a flanking movement around the west of Lentini and Mt. Etna. In order for Leese to move, however, he needed Highway 124 for his own use. Montgomery had no reservations whatsoever about demanding that Alexander, the overall ground forces commander, order Patton to shift his forces further west and abandon Highway 124 for British use. In fact, even before Alexander's orders were drafted agreeing to Montgomery's demand, units of XXX Corps were moving along the road.

When he was informed of the latest directive, Bradley blew his stack and appealed to Patton. However, the latter was anxious to strike his own bargain with Alexander and merely tried to mollify Bradley. The end result was that Montgomery now controlled all key roads to Messina with the exception of Highway 113 running on an east-west axis along the northern coast. It was this road that held Patton's gaze.

Nevertheless, Montgomery's grand plan backfired. The pressure on the Hermann Goering Division facing Bradley eased as the American commander pulled his Forty-fifth Division out of line and side-stepped it around the rear of First Division to make way for the British. This enabled the Germans to move their forces eastward directly in the path of XXX Corps and slam the door in the British faces.

The German commander in chief of the south, Field Marshal Kesselring, never had intended to hold onto Sicily forever and was determined to keep an escape hatch open at Messina until all German troops could be safely evacuated from the island. Kesselring was nobody's fool* and knew that Allied superiority would eventually win out. Therefore, he sent to Sicily only enough reinforcements necessary to fight a successful delaying action and placed them in the capable hands of Gen. Hans Hube. In addition, both German commanders could easily see that Montgomery had by far the shortest route to Messina, so all available strength was put directly in the path of the British. Montgomery was stalled and Patton began to run wild in the western portion of the island.

*See volume I, chapter 5

On the evening of the thirteenth, Montgomery attempted to force the issue at Lentini by dropping paratroops behind German lines in an effort to seize key bridges and crossroads for an advance by XIII Corps. Unfortunately, those troops that were dropped in the correct positions fell into the midst of the German First Parachute Division, newly arrived from Italy. The outcome never was in doubt, but small pockets of British held out until eventually overwhelmed. Meanwhile, Dempsey's attack ground to a halt almost as soon as it jumped off. The Germans refused to yield. Another attack by Leese a few days later suffered the same fate and failed to achieve results.

Montgomery decided that now was the time to pause and regroup. Before resuming the offensive, he demanded to be heavily reinforced. German positions around Mt. Etna were considered too strong for the amount of formations available to Eighth Army.

On July 22, leading elements of the Seventh Army entered Palermo, and Alexander, disenchanted with the progress of Eighth Army and Montgomery's promises, put Messina up for grabs and made it plain that the city was now fair game for anyone who could capture it. Unfortunately for Patton, he now found himself at the extreme opposite end of the island. Nevertheless, after pausing to regroup, Seventh Army set off for Messina on July 30, using the northern coastal roads.

Motivated by Alexander's new directive, Montgomery too launched a heavy attack. On the left, the Canadian First Division broke through the German defenses and passed the Seventy-eighth British Division through. This leapfrog tactic paid huge dividends, and by August 3, the key town of Adrano was under fire. Meanwhile, along the coast, Dempsey had been sitting still waiting for the right opportunity. On August 3, the opportunity came. Faced with the imminent fall of Adrano and Patton's advance in the north, Kesselring ordered the withdrawal to begin. Consequently, when Hube began to pull back, Dempsey's XIII Corps swarmed into Catania. The shackles were finally broken and the race for Messina was on.

Montgomery's reluctance to gamble and exploit a breakthrough played right into Patton's hands. Instead of pushing fast-moving mobile forces through the breach, Montgomery elected to follow up the German retreat, snapping at the enemy's heels.

In the face of the two strong Allied attacks, the German evacuation of Sicily was stepped up. By August 16, most of the German troops were safely across the Straits of Messina and on the mainland of Italy. The following day, Patton was accepting the surrender of the city as units of Eighth Army entered from the south. Montgomery's lethargy and insistence on building up his supplies and insuring overwhelming superiority before precipitating battle had cost the British the prize. Fortunately for the Americans, the Sicilian campaign had restored the prestige lost at Kasserine. In addition, it gave credence to Patton's claim that Montgomery was incapable of rapid movement. Italy would lend further credence to that statement.

With Sicily now firmly in Allied hands the invasion of Italy itself was the next order of business. Montgomery, of course, was to lead the way. Eighth Army was ordered to cross the Straits of Messina (Operation

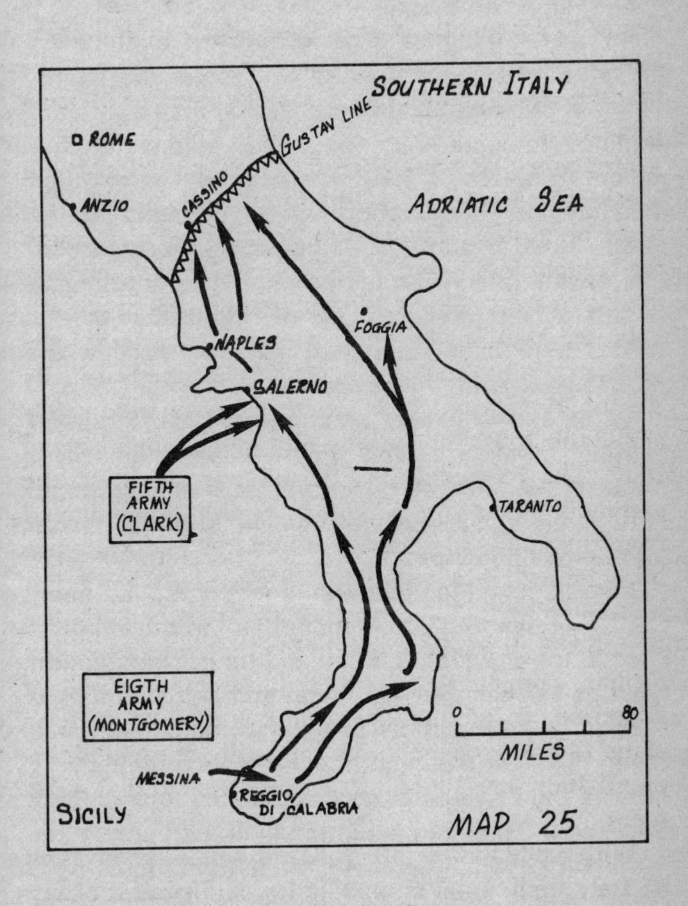
SOUTHERN ITALY
ROME
GUSTAV LINE
ANZIO
CASSINO
ADRIATIC SEA
FOGGIA
NAPLES
SALERNO
FIFTH ARMY (CLARK)
TARANTO
EIGTH ARMY (MONTGOMERY)
0
80
MILES
MESSINA
REGGIO DI CALABRIA
SICILY
MAP 25

Baytown), work its way up the toe of Italy, and link up with the British First Airborne Division from Taranto (Operation Slapstick), and an American landing in the Gulf of Salerno (Operation Avalanche). (See Map 25)

On the evening of September 2, virtually every British gun in Sicily opened fire across the straits. This was followed up the next day by an amphibious landing. Progress was slow once ashore for two reasons. The toe of Italy was relatively narrow and therefore allowed the Germans to defend a rather narrow strip. In addition, Montgomery's insistence on a massive artillery barrage prior to the launching of an attack created such a pile of rubble that the attackers were hard pressed to advance through the ruin. Eighth Army's advance was slow.

Six days after Montgomery jumped the Straits of Messina, Avalanche and Slapstick were launched. Taranto fell without opposition but the American Fifth Army at Salerno led by Gen. Mark Clark ran into fierce opposition.

Thanks to Montgomery's deliberate advance, Kesselring felt confident enough to withdraw units from in front of Eighth Army and threw them against Clark at Salerno. The American and British troops at Salerno hung on grimly in the face of concentrated enemy fire. On the twelfth, a German counterattack hit with full fury and Clark was tempted to re-embark his troops. Throughout the ranks of Fifth Army the word was passed; where was the relieving force from Eighth Army? Finally, two days later, Montgomery's leading elements made contact with Clark's advance units and the siege was lifted.

Kesselring, however, had merely been playing for time. Now he began a systematic withdrawal to the first of a series of defensive positions, culminating in the Gustav line. Pursuit was hardly rapid. Indeed, it was just the opposite. Clark was still licking the wounds received at Salerno and was in no shape to press home an attack. On the other side of the peninsula, Montgomery still preferred the methodical system of advance. As long as he was gaining territory and the enemy was retreating, he seemed content despite constant prodding from Alexander. Finally, in the first week of December, both Clark and Montgomery bumped up against the Gustav line and were rudely halted.

The German line was centered by the mountainous spine of Italy and was anchored in the east by the River Sangro and the Adriatic Sea. In the west, Cassino and the Abbey were the dominating features. In addition, Kesselring had plenty of time to prepare his positions in depth and the line would eventually prove a tough nut to crack. Montgomery's own comments on the Italian campaign give an insight into his constant reliance on overwhelming supply superiority:

> We became involved in a major campaign lacking a predetermined plan of attack. The result was that the administrative machine became unable to exploit our advantage in September and October when operationally a speedy advance to 'Rome' seemed still a feasible proposition. If then we had had the resources to allow us to maintain pressure on the enemy, our superiority in armour and in the air might have enabled us to roll the enemy back to the 'Rome

Line' before the winter began.

If the capture of Rome was then considered an urgent necessity, it could have been ensured only by the allocation of sufficient resources to build up the armies to a strength adequate for the task.[9]

Montgomery was not around for the cracking of the Gustav line.

On Christmas Eve, 1943, Montgomery was handed a dispatch ordering him to return to England to assume command of Twenty-first Army Group for the cross-Channel invasion. On January 30, after a moving farewell address, he turned command of his beloved Eighth Army over to Oliver Leese.

When Eisenhower left the Mediterranean to oversee the planning for the cross-Channel attack on France he was already aware of the need to appoint a British general to command the English forces involved. The supreme commander unhesitatingly requested Alexander to fill this position. Churchill would have none of it. Although he admired and respected Alexander immensely, Churchill (and Brooke) was determined to have Montgomery. The latter's cultivation of the press corps had paid dividends. While his popularity soared in England, Alexander's modest and low key approach to command resulted in his taking a back seat. Consequently, thanks to Montgomery's inflated reputation, Churchill's choice was more one of political expediency than of personal esteem.

True to form, Montgomery immediately found fault with the planner's blueprint for "Operation Overlord." He contended, and rightly so, that the landings were scheduled on too narrow a front and that the area of invasion be enlarged. Naturally, he got his way.

By the first of June, 1944, everything was in readiness for an invasion scheduled for the fifth. Two days later, a severe storm threatened to postpone the invasion indefinitely. When Eisenhower called his leading commanders together and solicited their opinion as to whether the invasion should be put off, Montgomery was the only one who voted to go, but he was in the minority and Eisenhower decided to wait one more day.

Montgomery was placed in overall command of the ground forces assembled for Overlord. These forces included the British Second Army under Miles Dempsey and the American First Army under Omar Bradley. The Canadian First and American Third Armies were scheduled to follow later. This command arrangement was scheduled to remain intact until such time as Eisenhower himself could establish a headquarters on the continent. Then, Montgomery would revert to command of only the British Twenty-first Army Group as a coequal with Bradley, who was slated to assume command of the American Twelfth Army Group. Montgomery was unhappy at the prospect of sharing the command with Bradley and lobbied constantly to be allowed to retain control over the entire show as overall ground commander. (See Map 26)

On June 6, 1944, the greatest amphibious operation the world had ever seen approached the coast of Normandy. On the eastern (left) flank of the assault wave, the British Second Army came ashore over

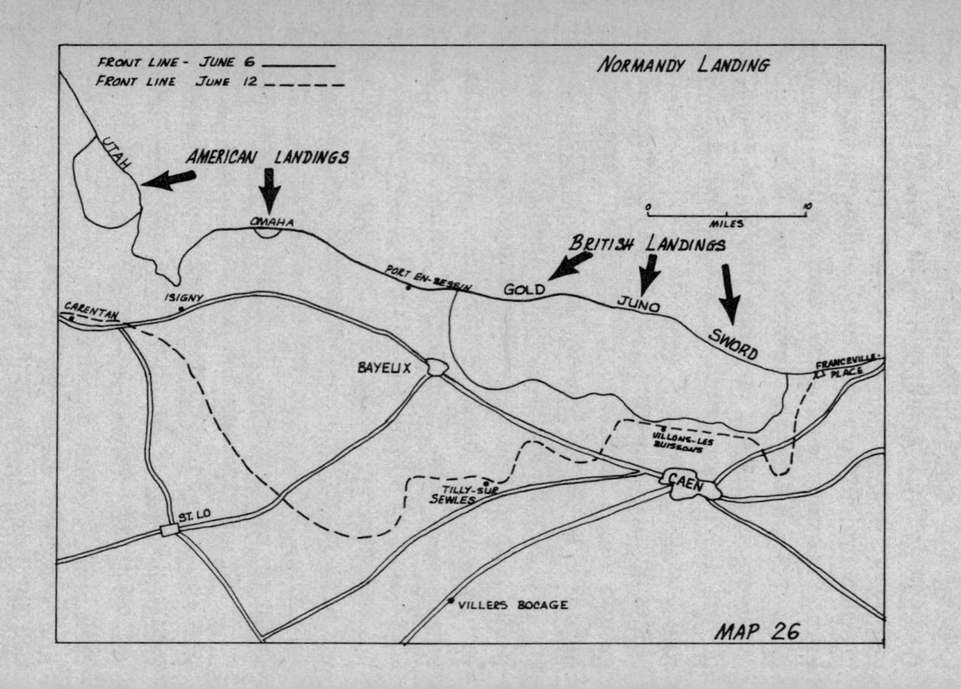
NORMANDY LANDING
FRONT LINE - JUNE 6
FRONT LINE JUNE 12
AMERICAN LANDINGS
UTAH
OMAHA
BRITISH LANDINGS
GOLD
JUNO
SWORD
0
10
MILES
PORT EN-BESSIN
ISIGNY
CARENTAN
BAYEUX
FRANCEVILLE-PLACE
VILLONS-LES BUISSONS
CAEN
TILLY-SUR SEWLES
ST. LO
VILLERS BOCAGE
MAP 26

three beaches; Sword, Juno, and Gold near the city of Caen. Further west, the First American Army stormed ashore at Utah and Omaha beaches near the base of the Cotentin Peninsula. Only at "Bloody Omaha" did the Allies meet stern opposition in the form of a vicious German defense. The Americans suffered severely and were pinned down on the beach for hours before they managed to make their way inland.

On the British front, initial opposition was extremely light but the confusion and dallying on the beach cost the invaders precious time. By the time they began their move inland in mid-afternoon, one of Montgomery's old antagonists from the desert, Twenty-first Panzer Division arrived on the scene and threw back the British thrust. Thus, the first day's objective, the city of Caen, remained in German hands. In addition, a proposed British armoured drive towards Villars-Bocage never materialized despite a relatively clear path devoid of German troops. The next day, the German army commander on the spot, Rommel, moved up additional panzer forces and the British had to be content with settling down to a bloody battle of position around Caen.

As Montgomery maneuvered in an effort to break the bottleneck at Caen, Bradley's First Army was thrusting forward through the hedgerow country to the west. The Germans skillfully took advantage of the natural defensive positions provided by the terrain and contested every yard. Nonetheless, First Army moved slowly but steadily forward, but the rate of progress was unacceptable and no one could venture a guess as to when the Allied armies would break out of Normandy.

June twentieth came and went and still the Canadians had not crossed the Channel. Montgomery was right, the bridgehead was too congested. But, had he acted more promptly and enlarged the bridgehead, the situation would never have existed in the first place.

Montgomery was now under fire by the press and his Allied colleagues. To them it appeared as if the British commander was dragging his feet. Eisenhower and Bradley were both unhappy with the inability of the British to register any significant progress around Caen. The deputy supreme commander, British Air Marshal Tedder was for sacking Montgomery and was totally disenchanted with Eisenhower's coddling of the troublesome British general. Tedder though, had never been a fan of Montgomery's. Earlier in the year he had been heard to remark:

> He is a little fellow of average ability who has had such a buildup that he thinks of himself as Napoleon. He is not.[10]

Despite Montgomery's hesitancy one thing was absolutely certain; he had managed to draw the bulk of the German armour onto his front and was successfully tying it down. Thus, some of the pressure on Bradley was eased. He therefore put forth a plan (Operation Goodwood) whereby the British would attempt a breakout, continue to tie down the enemy armour and allow Bradley to mount a strong attack of his own and break out of Normandy in the vicinity of St. Lo.

Facing the two Allied armies were the German

Seventh Army under Waffen SS Gen. Paul Hausser* on Bradley's front and Panzer Group West commanded by Gen. Hans Eberbach. The latter consisted of most of the panzer formations in Normandy including the fanatical SS panzer divisions.

Montgomery held a briefing for his subordinate commanders. It was a typical Montgomery classroom session with the Twenty-first Army Group commander dominating the stage. His sessions were unique for their conduct. Gen. Mark Clark of the United States describes a typical Montgomery session:

> Montgomery: Who's smoking?
> Eisenhower: I am.
> Montgomery: I don't permit smoking in my office.[11]

Neither would he tolerate interruptions for coughing. It was not unusual for him to preface a meeting by allowing the participants a few minutes to cough so that they would not do so during the conference. At the briefing, Dempsey, commander of the Second British Army was ordered to limit his objective to the high ground south of Caen. West of the city II, XII, and XXX Corps were to make a feint attack while O'Connor's VIII Corps of three armoured divisions was directed to advance on the opposite side of the city and break into the German defenses. Despite what he had told Eisenhower and the other Allied commanders, Montgomery obviously had no intention of exploiting any breakthrough with a dash towards the Seine.

*See Volume I, Chapter 6

Unknown to Montgomery, Rommel and Eberbach anticipated that the main weight of the attack would strike east of Caen. They therefore constructed a heavily fortified and deep defensive zone. As a result, VIII Corps was due to attack the strongest point of the German positions.

On July 15, XII and XXX Corps launched strong attacks on their front. Progress was measured in yards as the SS panzer troopers bitterly resisted all efforts to puncture their front. Foot by foot the British advance moved forward.

During the night of July 17, O'Connor's three armoured divisions moved up to their jumping off point. Early the next morning, the German positions were bombarded by over one thousand RAF bombers. This attack was followed immediately by a bombardment from the heavy caliber guns of three Royal Navy ships steaming offshore. After one and a half hours, the naval gunfire subsided as another thousand planes this time from the USAAF took over. The severe pounding had stunned, deafened, and driven men mad on the German side but failed to destroy their fighting capability.

As the last of the bombers returned to England, the Seventh, Eleventh and Guards Armoured Divisions moved forward supported by two infantry divisions. The fanatical resistance encountered slowed the British advance to a crawl but they continued the advance until nightfall. At evening, precious little ground had been gained. That same evening, Montgomery broadcast a message stating that the operation had been a complete success. In fact, none of the British formations had reached their objectives.

The following morning, the battle resumed in full fury all along the line. The determined SS troopers threw back every British attack and by day's end, the British had but naught to show for the terrible losses they had incurred. All three armoured divisions suffered terribly and after two days found themselves severely understrength.

Montgomery refused to concede. On the twentieth, yet another heavy attack was mounted, but shortly after it began, heavy rains forced its cancellation. Although by this time most of Caen was in British hands, the major objectives were largely unrealized and thought of a breakout was abandoned. Still, the British had managed to draw the bulk of the German armour to their front. Montgomery recognized this and continued to make offensive overtures in order to keep the Germans from withdrawing this armour to oppose Bradley. In this he succeeded.

On July 25, Bradley launched Operation Cobra on the First Army front in the vicinity of St. Lo and Coutances. The attack moved steadily forward and a few days later, on July 30, Patton's Third Army was officially activated and blew open the gateway from Normandy at Avranches. George Patton at the head of no less than three corps was loose in the German rear. On August 1, Bradley assumed command of the U.S. Twelfth Army Group but Montgomery was allowed to retain overall responsibility for ground operations temporarily.

In Berlin, Hitler ordered his commanders in Normandy to attack and sever the neck of Patton's breakthrough and cut the American forces off from their supplies. The ill-fated Mortain offensive failed to achieve this goal and by August 8, Third Army's XV Corps was deep in the German rear at LeMans. Suddenly it was obvious to the principal Allied commanders that Patton had handed them a fantastic opportunity. Montgomery, Bradley, and Patton all recognized the potential for destroying the German forces in Normandy.

Taking advantage of the Ultra system, the Allied commanders joyfully read the intercepts that ordered von Kluge, the German commander in charge of the west to continue the Mortain offensive against Patton's supply line. The U.S. First Army (now under Courtney Hodges) was effectively handling the German attack and the concern in the Allied camp was minimized. Hitler did not realize that von Kluge was moving deeper and deeper into a trap.

Montgomery suggested that a British attack towards Falaise be launched into the German rear. Bradley, suspicious of Montgomery's motives and skeptical of the British general's ability to move swiftly, went him one better. He suggested that Patton move up from the south to join hands with the British attack coming down from Falaise.

On August 7, Montgomery sent the newly landed First Canadian Army forward along the road from Caen to Falaise behind a wall of tanks. Once more the attack was preceded by a massive bombing attack. A few hours later Wade Haislip turned his U.S. XV Corps around at LeMans and raced towards a linkup with the Canadians. Five days later, he was in Argentan and anxious to continue on to Falaise. To Haislip's eternal disgust, Bradley, through Patton, ordered XV Corps to halt at Argentan and await the arrival of the Canadians.

As XV Corps was racing headlong for Argentan, the Canadian attack was having difficulties and was brought to a halt abruptly by Kurt Meyer's Twelfth SS Panzer Division dug in astride the Caen-Falaise road. The Germans refused to budge. Continuous Canadian attacks proved fruitless. Nevertheless, Montgomery still insisted that his units could reach Falaise in time. Armed with this assurance, Bradley refused to take the wraps off XV Corps for he argued that the Americans and Canadians would collide and fire on each other. Thus, Haislip sat idle while the Germans, who began to recognize the threat, began to slip out of the grasp of the Allies.

On August 16, the Canadians finally managed a breakthrough on their front. The desperate Germans conducted a most skillfull rearguard action, and not until the nineteenth did the Canadians reach Chambois. A three-mile-wide gap still existed in the pocket and through this gap streamed thousands of German troops. The pocket was not sealed until August 22. In the interim, a golden opportunity for total annihilation of the German forces in Normandy was lost. Montgomery's reluctance to share the limelight with Patton (or with anyone for that matter) was an expensive sop to vanity.

Montgomery never had agreed with Eisenhower's broad front strategy that called for all Allied armies to advance on a wide front towards Germany. As they were closing the trap at Falaise, Montgomery was badgering the supreme commander with ideas of his own. He still clung to the belief that one strong thrust along a single axis was the best method of defeating the enemy. Therefore, he proposed that he be allowed to launch a swift attack northwards, capture Antwerp and open up another port, and thrust rapidly into the industrial heartland of Germany, the Ruhr.

At first Eisenhower disagreed. Then he took a closer look at the supply situation and had second thoughts. Although supplies in England were plentiful, the Allies were unable to bring them ashore in large quantities and move them forward to keep pace with the far ranging armies. The deep water port of Antwerp was a tempting prize and one that could go a long way towards alleviating the Allied supply problems. Through there, supplies could be brought ashore more rapidly and in larger quantities. Accordingly, Eisenhower changed his mind and gave in to Montgomery. Unfortunately, there were catches to the deal.

Montgomery's demands did not sit well with the Americans. The British commander requested that a number of American divisions be placed under his command to assist in the forthcoming drive. He also requested that First Army support and secure his right flank. Finally, he requested that the bulk of the supplies coming ashore over the beaches be allocated to his command with a smaller share given to Hodges. Patton and Third Army would have to make do. This naturally aroused the ire of both Bradley and Patton. Both Americans generals were doubtful that Montgomery could move rapidly and they knew that Montgomery was a hoarder who always insured that he had more than enough supplies. As a result of Montgomery's demands, Patton's advance towards the Saar was effectively stalled.

On September 1, the day that he relinquished overall ground command to Eisenhower, Monty was promoted to the rank of Field Marshal. He now outranked his boss, Eisenhower.

Towards the end of August, Montgomery launched his attack into Belgium. The British Second Army was ordered to drive towards Antwerp and beyond to the Ruhr while the Canadian First Army cleared the Channel coast. In the path of the Canadians, sat the V-2 launching sites that were raining death and destruction on England.

When the Allies landed in Normandy, Hitler had refused to commit the German Fifteenth Army to the battle. The German leader was not convinced that the Normandy landings were the main invasion. He still harbored fears that an invasion of the Pas de Calais, where sat the Fifteenth Army, was possible. This same Fifteenth now faced Montgomery.

On August 28, XXX Corps crossed the Seine and headed for Antwerp. Montgomery was fond of using this formation to spearhead his attacks. One reason being that it was commanded by an outstanding general and one of Montgomery's favorites, Brian Horrocks. Second Army made excellent progress and moved rapidly past the flank of the enemy Fifteenth Army. By the first of September, the Canadians had reached Dieppe and XX Corps was at Arras. Horrocks then sent his armour surging forward. On the third, the Guards Armoured Division liberated Brussels and the following day, Eleven Armoured reached Antwerp.

The drive to Antwerp was atypical of Montgomery's

previous campaigns. Heretofore, he conducted methodical set piece battles in which his overwhelming superiority guaranteed victory, (El Alamein, Mareth, and Mt. Etna). His operations against an enemy whose strength more equally paralleled his own left something to be desired, (Caen and Falaise). Furthermore, in prior battles he was reluctant to expose his armour with slashing, swift moving drives. This had allowed Rommel to flee clear across North Africa. Therefore, the drive on Antwerp exposed a weakness in the man. He was simply incapable of conducting a fast moving campaign. Perhaps Montgomery suspected all along that the weakness was there. Meanwhile, the Canadian First Army was moving steadily along the coast, clearing the channel ports and driving the German Fifteenth Army steadily back towards Belgium and Holland.

Eleven Armoured's dash took the Germans completely by surprise. In their haste to retreat, they left the port facilities undamaged. Docks, cranes, and warehouses fell intact to the British. Unfortunately, it was a while before the Allies could take advantage of the coup.

The city of Antwerp lies approximately fifty miles from the North Sea. The waterway approach to the port is along a progressively narrowing stretch of water known as the Scheldt Estuary. The northern Scheldt is dominated by the South Beveland Peninsula which is connected to Walcheren Island by a narrow causeway. The southern bank of the estuary is the mainland of Belgium. Control of this vital approach is essential to the availability of the port itself. When Eleventh Armoured Division drove into Antwerp, instead of immediately seizing the bridges over the Albert Canal and continuing the drive northward, it paused to rest and regroup although enough supplies and petrol was available to continue the drive for many more miles. In fairness, though, it must be recalled that the division had just completed a long drive and had not paused to rest for almost a week. Consequently, the troops were bone weary.

While XXX Corps dashed to Antwerp, von Zangen's army retreated steadily along the Channel coast in the face of pressure by the Canadians. The pause at Antwerp allowed von Zangen to evacuate his force across the Scheldt, march east across the path of the British advance, and settle them down into defensive positions near the Ruhr. The commander in chief of the west, von Rundstedt sensed that Montgomery would pause at Antwerp, thus the orders to von Zangen to use the Scheldt as an escape route. Individual units were left behind to defend the Scheldt and prevent the Allies from making use of the port. The failure to capture Antwerp completely was one of the great errors of the war. In the words of Liddell-Hart, "It was a multiple lapse—by four commanders from Montgomery on down."[12] The American historian, Charles MacDonald calls it: "One of the great tactical mistakes of the war.[13] In his memoirs, Sir Brian Horrocks graciously attempts to shoulder the responsibility.

> My excuse is that my eyes were fixed entirely on the Rhine and everything else seemed of subsidiary importance. It never entered my head that the Scheldt would be mined or that we

> would not be able to use Antwerp until the channel had been swept and the Germans cleared from the coastlines on either side . . . Napoleon would, no doubt, have realized these things but Horrocks didn't.[14]

Montgomery should have. His obsession with making a quick dash to justify his contention that Eisenhower's broad front strategy was wrong and that his own was correct, coupled with his intense desire to have the key role played by his army group at the expense of Patton, gave credence that he was not capable of executing rapid drives.

Brian Horrocks went on to mention that had Eleventh Armoured jumped the Albert Canal immediately, there was little opposition to contend with for the next one hundred miles. When the British advance did get rolling a few days later, a hastily scraped together German force managed to stall the drive after a dozen or so miles.

During the same week in September, Montgomery met with Prince Bernhard of the Netherlands, commander in chief of the Dutch Army. Intelligence reports received from Dutch Resistance fighters told of a panicky German retreat from that country. Montgomery was full of excuses as to why the liberation of Holland was being delayed. He then informed Bernhard that he was planning an elaborate airborne operation to free Holland from the Nazi yoke. Thus was born one of the most controversial operations of the entire war; Operation Market Garden. (See Map 27)

Montgomery's grandoise plan called for a three and

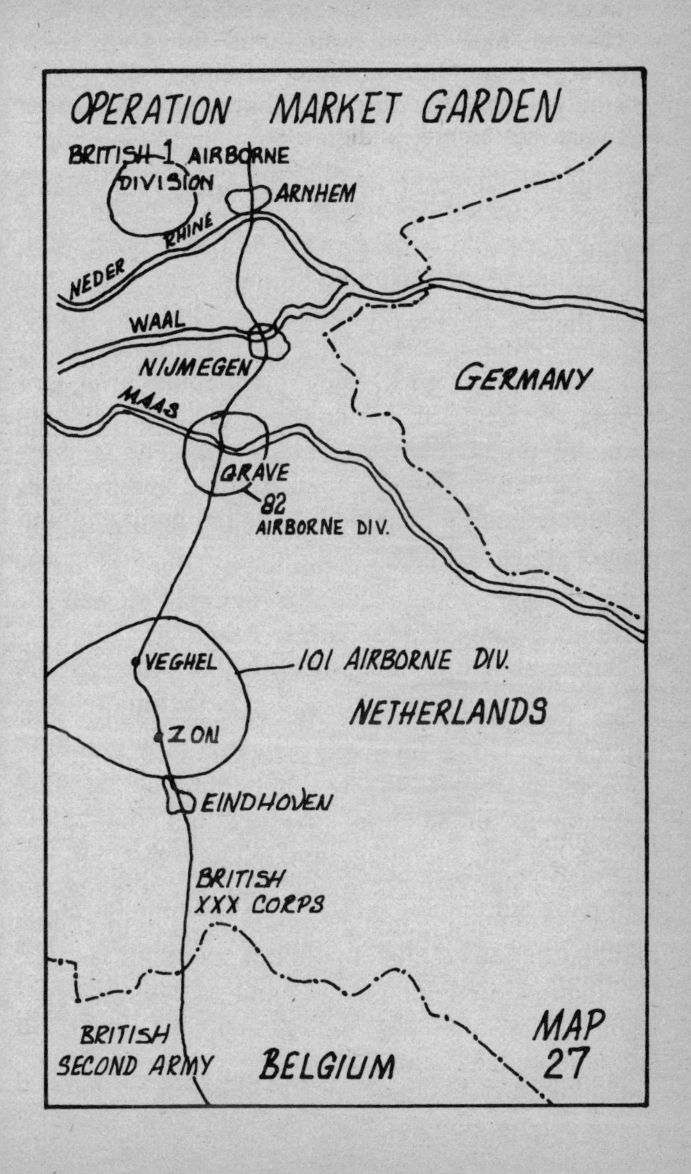
OPERATION MARKET GARDEN
BRITISH 1 AIRBORNE
DIVISION
ARNHEM
NEDER RHINE
WAAL
NIJMEGEN
MAAS
GERMANY
GRAVE
82
AIRBORNE DIV.
VEGHEL
101 AIRBORNE DIV.
NETHERLANDS
ZON
EINDHOVEN
BRITISH
XXX CORPS
BRITISH
SECOND ARMY
BELGIUM
MAP
27

one-half division airborne assault designed to blast a corridor through to and over the Rhine ninety miles away at Arnhem. Along this corridor two American, one British division, and a Polish brigade would be dropped into enemy territory to secure key bridges over the canals and rivers. These units would then be relieved in turn by elements of XXX Corps driving rapidly along the route secured by the paratroopers. The British First Airborne division was given the hardest assignment, the capture of the bridge over the lower Rhine at Arnhem. Once over the Rhine, Montgomery explained, the British could pivot east behind the Siegfried line and into the Ruhr. To say that the project was ambitious would be a gross understatement. When Omar Bradley heard of his British colleague's proposal he was flabbergasted and remarked:

> Had the pious, teetotalling Montgomery wobbled into SHAEF with a hangover I could not have been more astonished.[15]

On September 10, Montgomery met with Eisenhower. In a firm and unpleasant manner he opened the meeting by once more assailing Eisenhower's broad front strategy and that there should be one overall ground commander for the drive, namely him. He curtly informed Eisenhower that the supreme commander would have to choose between Patton or him. Instead of losing his temper, Eisenhower merely placed his hand on Montgomery's knee and said "Steady Monty, I'm your boss. You can't talk to me like that."[16]

Ike derided Montgomery's constant insistence on

one thrust into Germany and maintained that his strategy would remain unaltered with these words.

> What you're proposing is this—if I give you all of the supplies you want, you could go straight to Berlin—right straight to Berlin? Monty, you're nuts. You can't do it. What the hell! If you try a long column like that in a single thrust you'd have to throw off division after division to protect your flank from attack. Now suppose you did get a bridge across the Rhine. You couldn't depend on that one bridge to supply your drive. Monty, you can't do it.[17]

If Guderian had listened to the same type of reasoning prior to Sedan in 1940, the entire Montgomery-Eisenhower argument would have been redundant. Montgomery replied:

> I'll supply them all right. Just give me what I need and I'll reach Berlin and end the war.[18]

The British commander persisted. Finally, he unveiled his plan for Market Garden. Eisenhower was impressed and gave in. If Montgomery thought he could pull it off, why not let him try? The plan seemed imaginative and Ike pledged his full support.

Miles Dempsey, the British First Army commander did not like the plan. Likewise Brian Horrocks of XXX Corps. Montgomery had determined that it would take XXX Corps a mere two days to drive to Arnhem and told this to Gen. Frederick Browning, commander of the I British Airborne Corps. Browning felt that the forces at Arnhem could possibly hold on for four days, but no longer. Dempsey thought that enemy resistance would prove too strong. His staff had concluded that the Germans were moving fresh units into the very place selected for the assault. Horrock's objection was that his corps would be required to advance over a single narrow road to reach their objective. Even the slightest resistance would serve to delay the advance. Montgomery assured them all that the plan would succeed and set September 17th as the date for the attack.

Dempsey was right. The Germans were indeed moving units into the area of Arnhem and Eindhoven. The II SS Panzer Corps, severely mauled at Caen and Falaise was arriving for a refit. The units that Hitler had scraped together for a quick defensive position north of Antwerp was known as the First Parachute Army (in name only) and placed under the command of Germany's airborne expert, Gen. Kurt Student. If anyone knew how to deal with an airborne operation it was this man. In addition, the commander in chief of the German Army Group B, Field Marshal Walther Model, a tenacious bulldog of a commander with a reputation for being an outstanding defensive strategist, had his new headquarters at Oosterbeek, a few miles from Arnhem.

On September 14, Montgomery confirmed the orders for Market Garden. The airborne assault would go in early in the morning (Market) and was to be followed later in the day by the opening of XXX Corps drive (Garden). Ultra intercepts warned both Eisenhower and Montgomery of the presence of II SS Panzer Corps around Arnhem. Ike was so concerned that he sent his chief of staff, Bedell Smith to Montgomery with the information. Smith flew to Montgomery's headquarters and cautioned him of the presence of the Ninth and Tenth SS Panzer Divisions. Montgomery still felt confident of success.

While Smith was enroute to Montgomery's headquarters, an intelligence officer on Browning's staff was reaching the same conclusion. Armed with photographic evidence and resistance reports, he confronted Browning and received the same rebuff. There was nothing to be duly concerned about.

September 17, 1944 will be well remembered by the participants as the day Market Garden began. Overhead roared a vast armada of transports and gliders carrying the paratroops to their deadly rendezvous with destiny while XXX Corps moved up to its starting point. Horrock's attack was spearheaded by the Guards Armoured Divisions, the Irish Guards in the van.

Initially, the Germans were taken by surprise. Near Eindhoven, Gen. Maxwell Taylor's 101st (American) Airborne Division quickly seized their bridge with little opposition. Clearing a road for XXX Corps proved a more difficult task. Shortly after they moved off, the Guards were stopped by a brief but fierce German attack. Although the resistance was quickly overcome, it took time to clear the damaged and destroyed vehicles off the single road. The German attack disrupted the entire schedule. Not until the next day did the Guards link up with Taylor's main element.

Further along, at Grave and Nijmegen it was a different story. Gen. James Gavin's U.S. Eighty-second Airborne ran into stiffer resistance. Although the bridge at Grave fell relatively early, Nijmegen proved more difficult.

The Germans quickly recovered their senses. As reports began to come in telling of the various landings, General Bittrich, the II SS Panzer Corps commander, fit the pieces together and recognized the objective of the attack. Every available unit was swiftly rushed into position around the bridges and along the route from Eindhoven to Arnhem. When Gavin's men attempted to seize the bridge at Nijmegen, they were met with a withering fire from SS troopers stationed on the bridge and along the opposite shore.

Meanwhile, at Arnhem, Roy Urquhart's Red Devils had their hands full to say the least. The division was widely scattered upon landing a few miles from Arnhem and much of their communications were inoperable. Nevertheless, Col. John Frost's battalion quickly moved into town and seized the bridge. However, before the confusion in the British force wore off, the Germans surrounded the town and sealed off Frost. In addition, Urquhart was trapped in a private residence by enemy soldiers and was out of touch with his subordinate commanders and unable to coordinate activities.

Back at Nijmegen, the 101st continued their efforts to capture the crucial bridge. XXX Corps linked up with Gavin's forces near Grave on the nineteenth but could not advance beyond Nijmegen. The next day, Horrocks and Gavin joined forces to capture the key bridge, allowing XXX Corps to continue their drive.

The German stranglehold around Arnhem began to take effect. Those British units unable to break through the ring and into the town were steadily compressed into a pocket around the town of Oosterbeek. On the twenty-first, Frost's battalion at the bridge was overwhelmed with heavy casualties.

The next day, the Polish brigade arrived. Overcast weather in England had prevented their takeoff any earlier. When the gallant Poles and their commander, General Sosabowski, began their descent from the sky, they dropped squarely into a zone occupied by the Germans. The slaughter was terrible and the Poles ceased to be a factor in the battle.

With the British threat securely under control, Bittrich turned his attention to the advance of XXX Corps. The ring of steel around Arnhem was diluted somewhat and placed directly in the path of the Irish Guards. XXX Corps was stopped cold a few miles from Arnhem.

On the twenty-fifth, Montgomery called off the attack. Those units in the pocket still surviving were ordered to break out. Of the more than ten thousand men dropped near Arnhem, less than twenty-five hundred made it back to their own lines. Although a fifty mile corridor had been driven into Holland, Market Garden had been a disastrous failure.

The fiasco of Market Garden behind him, Montgomery paused to lick his wounds and concentrate on clearing the Scheldt. On October 2, the Canadians launched a two pronged offensive against the German defenders. The southern prong of the attack was directed against the German Sixty-fourth Division defending the southern bank of the Scheldt. Squeezed into the "Breskens Pocket," the Germans held on doggedly for a month as the Canadian attack methodically reduced the defensive zones. As October turned to

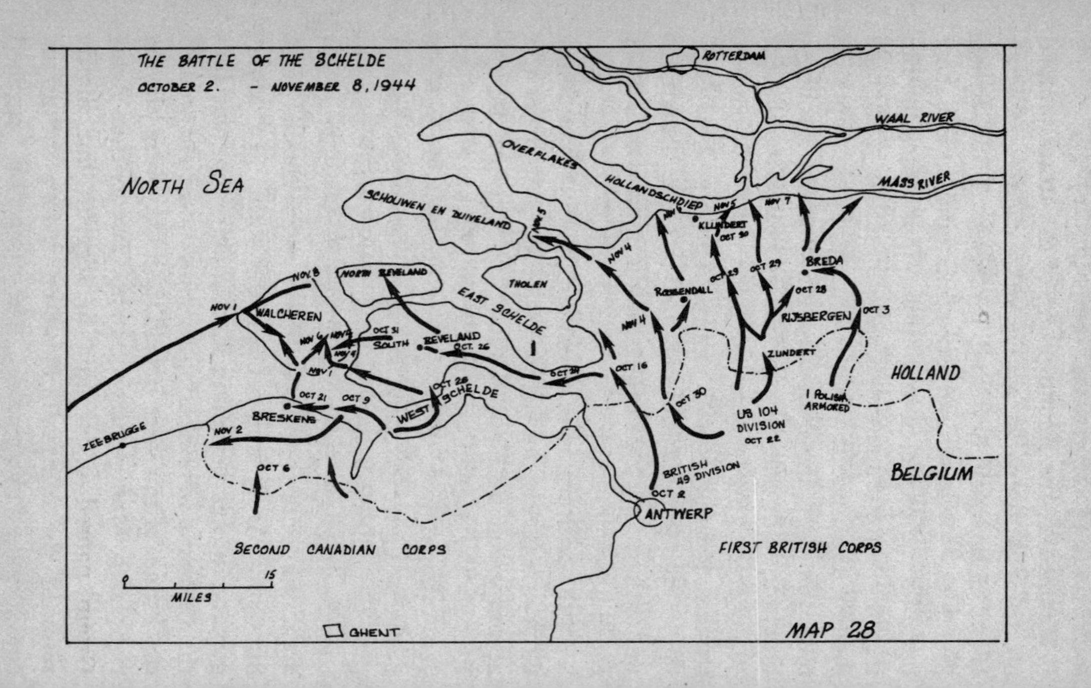
THE BATTLE OF THE SCHELDE
OCTOBER 2. - NOVEMBER 8, 1944
NORTH SEA
ROTTERDAM
WAAL RIVER
MASS RIVER
OVERFLAKES
HOLLANDSCHDIEP
SCHOUWEN EN DUIVELAND
THOLEN
EAST SCHELDE
NORTH BEVELAND
SOUTH BEVELAND
WALCHEREN
WEST SCHELDE
BRESKENS
ZEEBRUGGE
ANTWERP
KLUNDERT
ROOSENDALL
BREDA
RIJSBERGEN
ZUNDERT
HOLLAND
BELGIUM
1 POLISH ARMORED
US 104 DIVISION
OCT 22
BRITISH 49 DIVISION
OCT 2
OCT 3
OCT 6
OCT 9
OCT 16
OCT 21
OCT 24
OCT 26
OCT 28
OCT 29
OCT 30
OCT 31
NOV 1
NOV 2
NOV 4
NOV 5
NOV 6
NOV 7
NOV 8
SECOND CANADIAN CORPS
FIRST BRITISH CORPS
0
15
MILES
GHENT
MAP 28

November, the Canadians completely secured the south bank of the estuary. (See Map 28)

Meanwhile, the second prong of the attack jumped off from Antwerp in an effort to clear Walcheren Island and South Beveland Peninsula. The German Seventieth Division had been manning heavy shore batteries there since late summer. This attack too ran into fierce resistance and the approach to Walcheren did not fall until the last few days of the month. It took the Canadians another week, aided by heavy bombing raids and an amphibious operation, to clear Walcheren. Finally, in the second week of November, the first ships began to unload at Antwerp. The clearing of the Scheldt Estuary had cost the Canadians well over ten thousand casualties, a heavy price to pay for a strategic error.

With Antwerp now open, the Twenty-first Army Group, bolstered by Simpson's Ninth U.S. Army and accompanied by Hodges' First Army, set off for the Rhine. The Canadians on the left flank of the advance were given the objective of Arnhem but the Germans destroyed the dikes in the area and flooded the entire countryside. The Canadians were forced to withdraw. Nevertheless, by December 3, the entire area west of the Maas River was cleared and Simpson's Army approached the Ruhr. To Montgomery, it was becoming increasingly apparent that the Germans were electing to stand and fight west of the Rhine. If this were indeed true, they were playing right into Montgomery's hands. Twenty-first Army Group paused once more to regroup but shortly resumed the offensive. However, before the attack could gain momentum, the Germans stunned everyone in the Allied camp with a full scale attack through the Ardennes.

More commonly known as the Battle of the Bulge, the German offensive was designed to slice right through between the two Allied commands, Montgomery's and Bradley's, and recapture Antwerp. Hitler's generals thought he was mad and that the attack should be limited to the smaller objective of Brussels but their voices fell on deaf ears. The German leader had assembled a strong force for the attack by withdrawing units from in front of Patton and Hodges during Montgomery's drive in the north. In addition, he had reinforced every unit in reserve and gambled everything on one throw of the dice. Two complete panzer armies were assembled for the attack whose flanks were protected by Student's forces opposite Montgomery and another infantry army on Patton's flank. As winter settled over the countryside of northern France, the German attack surged out of the Ardennes and quickly caved in the front of First Army. Although Montgomery continued his attack against the Ruhr, he pulled XXX Corps out of line and sent it to guard the bridges over the Meuse at the rear of the Americans.

Onward came the Germans and by December 19, the entire Allied position in northern Europe was in jeopardy. First Army was pushed rapidly backward and onto the northern shoulder of the German advance by the surprise attack. Eisenhower was forced to adopt drastic measures. That day, he split the Allied command in two. Montgomery was given responsibility for all Allied forces on the north side of the bulge including First Army. Bradley was left with

Patton's Third Army in the south. Montgomery contacted Brooke and reported the situation. He implied that the entire American command was in a state of confusion and inferred that Eisenhower had lost control of the battle.

Shortly after noon on December 20, Montgomery strode into Hodges' headquarters "like Christ coming to cleanse the temple," and met with Hodges and Simpson. His report to Brooke stated

> There were no reserves anywhere behind the front. Morale was very low. They seemed delighted to have someone give them orders.[19]

Despite relishing his role as saviour, he approved most of Hodges' dispositions but suggested that the American forces defending St. Vith withdraw. Montgomery was unaccustomed to having units spread all over the battlefield. He wanted to tidy up the line. He then asked Hodges to designate his best fighting general to prepare for a counterattack. Hodges nominated "Lightning Joe" Collins.

On the twenty-first, as the German steamroller continued to roll inexorably forward, the Americans finally evacuated St. Vith. In Montgomery's own words, "with all honors—they put up a wonderful show."[20] Indeed they had. That handful of Americans at St. Vith had delayed the German attack.

The American commanders seemed concerned with blunting the German spearheads to prevent the capture of the bridges over the Meuse, but Montgomery did not share that concern, knowing full well that Brian Horrocks and XXX Corps were poised there just waiting for the enemy to put in an appearance. However, he delayed Collins' counterattack while a strategic reserve was assembled. On his own recognizance, Hodges turned Collins loose on Christmas Day. The northern wing of the German offensive had been slowed by a tenacious American defense and lack of fuel. Collins' attack was the final straw. The German attack was brought to a halt. The same day, Patton's Third Army made contact with the defenders of Bastogne. Their gallant stand had delayed the southern German pincer.

As the year ended, Eisenhower, Patton, and Bradley were insisting that Montgomery allow First Army to swing over to the offensive. None of the American commanders could fathom the delay in recovery. Finally, on January 3, First Army launched a powerful counterattack against the German salient. Hitler's offensive had shot its bolt. As the weather cleared over Belgium, the Allied air forces operated freely over the battlefield and harassed the Germans along every road. On January 16, First and Third Armies linked up near Houffalize. The Battle of the Bulge was, for all intents and purposes, finished. Hodges' advance had not only acted to surround those Germans still in the pocket, but had also driven First Army back under Bradley's command.

Although the enemy threat subsided, the storm in the Allied camp did not. From the time of the Allies' landing in Normandy, Montgomery would not let go of his agitation at not having an overall ground commander (namely him) to conduct operations. He doggedly lobbied against Eisenhower's broad front strategy. Ike's continued rejection of Montgomery's proposals did little to alleviate the tension. Monty had the ear of the chief of the Imperial Staff, Gen. Alan Brooke and the war minister, Sir James Grigg. Dispatches and telegrams flowed freely and frequently between the battlefield and London. Early in December Montgomery wrote to Grigg:

> Eisenhower's plan for winning the war is quite dreadful. If you want to end the war in any reasonable time you will have to remove Ike's hand from the control of the land battle; and Bradley's hand also.[21]

After the German Ardennes offensive lost steam, he again wrote:

> All is well and the Germans will not now get what they wanted. But they have given the Americans a colossal 'bloody nose' and mucked up all our plans; however, as we have not got a plan I suppose they will say it does not matter!![22]

Curiously, despite his intense rivalry with Patton, Montgomery seldom attempted to degrade the Third Army commander in his dispatches. On the other hand, Bradley frequently was mentioned in the same breath with Eisenhower. Brooke was the recipient of most of this scathing correspondence.

The crisis peaked during the final days of the Battle of the Bulge. On January 7, 1945, Montgomery hosted one of his famous press conferences during which he told the assembled correspondents:

> As soon as I saw what was happening, I took certain steps to insure that if the Germans got to the Meuse they would certainly not get over the

> river. I was thinking ahead. The situation began to deteriorate. . . . national considerations were thrown overboard and General Eisenhower placed me in command of the whole northern front. I employed the whole available power of the British Group of Armies bringing it into play gradually and then finally with a bang so that today, British divisions are fighting hard on the right flank of the United States First Army. The operation was one of the most interesting and tricky I have ever handled.[23]

Not only had he failed to mention that those forces fighting on Hodges' flank were in fact the American Ninth Army and that British units saw little if any fighting in the Battle of the Bulge, but he left the impression that the fate of the entire European venture had been placed in his hands and that he personally had salvaged victory. Perhaps the press distorted the facts somewhat, but there can be no mistaking the implication. Even his supporters will admit that once an operation reached a successful conclusion, Montgomery convinced himself that the entire plan had been his from the very beginning. Alam Halfa and the battles in Normandy support this theory.

The entire American camp flew into a rage after Montgomery's ill timed press conference. Bradley and Patton were so enraged that they both threatened to resign. It took all the diplomatic skills of Eisenhower and Churchill to smooth matters over, but the wound never did heal completely.

Germany's last offensive now history, the Allies regrouped for the final push into Germany. Montgomery was directed to continue his push past the

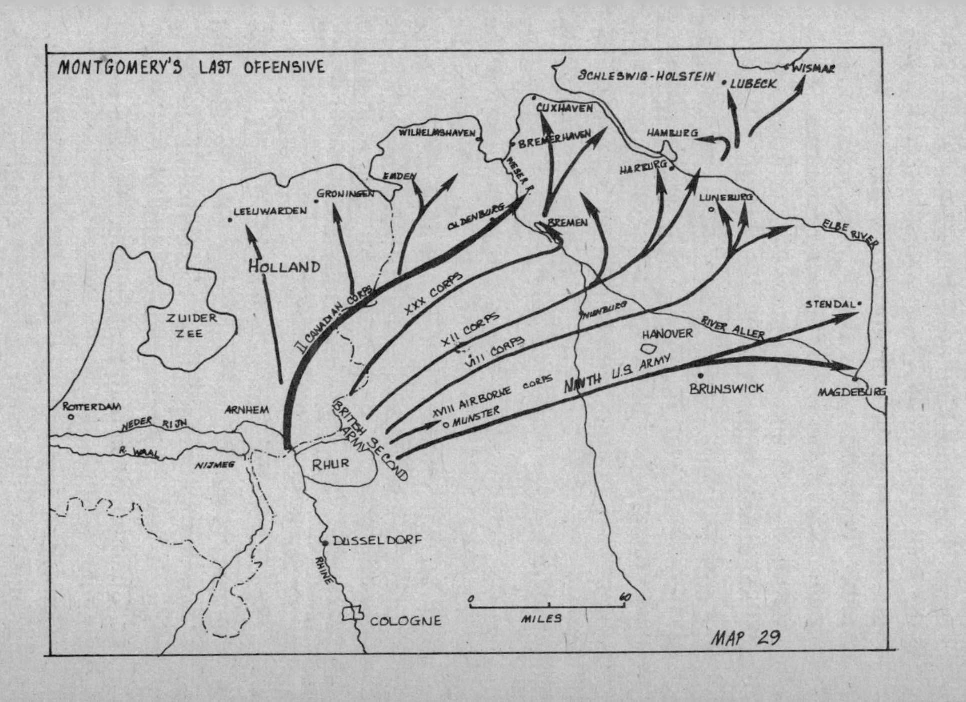
MONTGOMERY'S LAST OFFENSIVE
SCHLESWIG-HOLSTEIN
LUBECK
WISMAR
CUXHAVEN
WILHELMSHAVEN
BREMERHAVEN
HAMBURG
HARBURG
EMDEN
GRONINGEN
WESER R.
LEEUWARDEN
OLDENBURG
BREMEN
LUNEBURG
ELBE RIVER
HOLLAND
II CANADIAN CORPS
XXX CORPS
ZUIDER ZEE
STENDAL
NIENBURG
XII CORPS
VIII CORPS
HANOVER
RIVER ALLER
NINTH U.S. ARMY
BRUNSWICK
MAGDEBURG
XVIII AIRBORNE CORPS
ROTTERDAM
ARNHEM
BRITISH SECOND ARMY
MUNSTER
NEDER RIJN
R. WAAL
NIJMEG
RHUR
DUSSELDORF
RHINE
0
60
MILES
COLOGNE
MAP 29

Ruhr and was allowed to retain Simpson's Ninth Army for use in this campaign.

The Bulge had upset Montgomery's timetable during December. As a result, the Germans still clung to the western bank of the Rhine in southern Holland. Before advancing into Germany, the Allies would have to clear this opposition. The Battle of the Reichswald was one of the final great battles of the European theatre and tailor-made for a commander of Montgomery's talents: a set piece battle against a weakened foe. (See Map 29)

Plans were drawn up for a dual-pronged offensive to clear the approaches to the Rhine, Germany's final natural obstacle. "Operation Veritable" was designed to strike out of the Allied bridgehead at Nijmegen and drive south behind the defenses of the Siegfried line and through the heavily wooded area of the Reichswald, a series of thick forests. Gen. Henry Crerar's First Canadian Army was assigned the key role. His forces, bolstered by Horrock's XXX Corps on loan from Dempsey's Second Army, would surge forward and link up with Ninth Army advancing northward (Operation Grenade).

Montgomery and Crerar had relied on the use of the frozen roads and terrain over which to send their armour and mobile columns. Unfortunately, a week before the attack was scheduled to commence, warm weather set in bringing with it heavy rains. The resultant thaw turned the roads and countryside into flooded quagmires. Undeterred, Crerar launched the attack on schedule. Cleve, a key town in the German defensive line was leveled by the Allied air forces.

As usual, the British attack was preceded by

massive artillery which had become Montgomery's trademark. Led by the "funnies," tanks designed to clear minefields spit fire, and conduct amphibious operations, the attack moved from Nijmegen on February 8. By this time, the mud was so deep that mobility was reduced to an absolute minimum. Vehicles were unable to move forward and the flooded countryside prevented units from maintaining contact with each other; severe traffic jams were the order of the day. The entire battle soon degenerated into one of individual companies and regiments. The higher command was helpless to intervene as the final outcome rested in the hands of the individual troops. It was a soldier's battle and there was little the generals could do to influence the course of action.

The weather and flooded countryside also delayed the beginning of Grenade. Scheduled for jump off on February 11, Simpson's attack did not get moving until almost two weeks later. The delay proved fortuitous. By the time Ninth Army managed to get rolling, most of the German defenders had been drawn northward against Crerar's front. Three American corps drove up the front and rear of the Siegfried line defenses and along the bank of the Rhine. Early in March, the Canadians and Americans linked up.

The Battle of the Reichswald was a disaster for the Germans. Montgomery's army group had inflicted over ninety thousand casualties and destroyed the last German army in its path. Montgomery was right, Hitler was mad to fight west of the Rhine.

Now that virtually all opposition opposite Twenty-first Army Group had ceased to exist, Eisenhower finally gave permission for a strong thrust by Montgomery into the heart of Germany towards the Baltic. Ninth Army and Hodges' First Army were to encircle the Ruhr while Montgomery's other two armies surged forward to liberate Denmark and destroy the final German resistance in the north.

In the first week of March, the Allied armies were poised all along the Rhine, except for Patton whose momentum had been delayed by his efforts in the Ardennes and that once more Eisenhower had authorized the bulk of supplies to go to Montgomery for his attack. The Britisher scheduled his attack for March 23. But on March 7, the American Ninth Armoured Division of Hodges' First Army captured an intact bridge over the Rhine at Remagen. Hodges quickly pushed a few more divisions over the river and prepared to exploit the coup. Eisenhower quickly put an end to Bradley's and Hodges' ambitions. Loyal to his promise to Montgomery, that authorized the main thrust to come on his front, the supreme commander ordered Bradley not to expand the bridgehead until Montgomery crossed the line.

A great deal of planning and attention went into Montgomery's preparation for launching the attack. In the British camp the offensive was being ballyhooed as the first major amphibious assault over a major river in history. A great deal of publicity and attention was focused on Montgomery's army group and its forthcoming offensive. The field marshal relished the attention and buildup.

On March 24, as the official announcement of Montgomery's great feat was being circulated in England, a broadcast came through announcing that Patton had accomplished the very same thing over twenty-four hours earlier. The lustre was removed from Montgomery's magnificent feat and the American general had finally bested his rival.

Undaunted, Montgomery moved steadily forward through the great northern plain of Germany. While Simpson and Hodges encircled and reduced the Ruhr, the balance of Twenty-first Army Group drove relentlessly forward. Preceded by his armour, Montgomery headed for the Elbe and the Baltic coast. The German collapse was total. Hordes of enemy units streamed into the British lines anxious to surrender.

On April 25, Hitler committed suicide and left the country in the hands of Admiral Doenitz. The Germans were as yet unwilling to submit to unconditional surrender so decided to sound out the Allied High Command through Montgomery. On May 3, a deputation arrived at Montgomery's headquarters and attempted to surrender those units fighting the Allies but requested permission to continue the fight against the Russians. Montgomery turned them down flat. He informed the German delegation that he would accept nothing less than the total surrender of all German forces along his front, in Denmark, and Norway. Finally, he informed his visitors that if they refused his terms, "I shall carry on the war and be delighted to do so."[24] Doenitz wired his permission for capitulation.

Montgomery's active career did not end with the German surrender. After supervising the British occupation of northern Germany, Montgomery returned to England and assumed the position as chief of the Imperial General Staff. Then, from 1951 to 1958 he was deputy commander of NATO until his retirement. Settling down to retirement was the most difficult episode in his life. For almost forty years the army had been his life. Thanks to his abrasive personality, he had few friends to share reminiscences with and spent most of his time writing his memoirs and performing ceremonial functions. In recognition of his contribution to the war, he was elevated to the peerage as Montgomery, First Earl of Alamein.

How does one objectively evaluate Montgomery? Even his bitterest rival, George Patton, grudgingly showed a measure of respect, referring to him as a good soldier and no fool. But he also said that "I can outfight the little fart anytime."[25] But Montgomery did not reciprocate. He seemed to delight in going out of his way to antagonize Patton and constantly maneuvered behind the scenes to prevent the American from sharing the headlines. Was Montgomery jealous or envious of Patton's dash and willingness to throw caution to the wind or did he merely consider the latter's methods to be risky, rash, and foolhardy? In any event, his obvious attempts to seize the limelight and glory alienated him from his American colleagues, who almost to a man, were openly hostile and critical. Only the passive and easy going Simpson refused to embroil himself in the controversy. Could Simpson perhaps have fallen under the brilliant leadership spell of the Englishman? Of course, Montgomery too must shoulder some of the responsibility for the poor relationship between himself and the Americans. The field marshal never mislaid the impression that the Americans were amateurs at war and either consciously or subconsciously was unable to conceal his attitude. As a result, not until the final months of the war did he become a true team man.

As for his own countrymen, only Brooke seemed able to control Montgomery. The latter's memoirs are dotted with apologetic passages as a result of rebukes by Brooke. Even the great leader Alexander admits to an inability to control the headstrong Montgomery.

Montgomery relished the limelight. He constantly insisted on being the foremost or having the most prestigious assignments given to his army. Publicity was savored, as evidenced by a cultivated press corps and a well-oiled public relations section.

By the time the Americans entered the war, Britain's manpower levels were reduced to dangerously low levels. This may account for Montgomery's unwillingness to squander his resources. However, other considerations also entered into his refusal to accept unnecessary casualties. From his World War I days he learned to treat his men as tools to be used by a commander. Without these tools, no officer could hope to be successful. The British "Tommy" returned this respect twofold. Wherever their beloved "Monty" went, he was besieged and surrounded by admiring troops. The vanity and arrogance was lacking when he was in the company of troops or subordinates.

Then there were his little eccentricities. His obsession in North Africa with selecting the proper headgear before settling on the beret festooned with two cap badges, and his attire, primarily consisting of a pair of slacks and a turtle neck sweater. With these, he developed his own image. His refusal to deal with staff officers from different commands, his headquarters van on whose walls were hung the photographs of his opponent at the time—be it Rommel, Model, or von Rundstedt, the habit he developed of retiring early on the eve of battle and leaving the conduct of operations to his subordinates, and finally, his famous lectures and situation conferences during which no one was allowed to smoke or cough, all added to the legend that was Montgomery.

One thing about Montgomery unquestionably stands out. He was without doubt a good picker of men, something he had accused Auchinleck of not being. He insisted on having only his own handpicked men in key positions. The working relationship between him and his chief of staff, Gen. Freddie de Guingand, was flawless and one of the secrets of his success. Brian Horrocks and Miles Dempsey were certainly among the outstanding commanders of the war and they in turn were absolutely devoted to their chief. Montgomery even managed to obtain yeoman service from the unfairly treated Neil Ritchie, who benefited from the field marshal's tutelage. All these men were personally selected by Montgomery for their particular roles.

Vanity was one of Montgomery's worst enemies. He repeatedly demonstrated nothing short of contempt for any plan that was not of his own making, and when his own plans did go awry, he refused to admit that all had not gone according to plan. Market Garden was the only exception. He even managed to convince himself that the successful plans of others were in fact his own. This may not indicate selfishness on his part but instead, a delusion from which he suffered and was unable to overcome.

Readers must draw their own conclusions of Montgomery's talents. Certainly the historians have been of little help. All they have done is present the evidence, but American writers have presented this evidence with an American outlook and are therefore somewhat prejudiced. On the other hand, British historians have fallen under the mystical spell of the man's personality and have presented a picture with a distinct British flavor, one that glorifies his achievements. Thus, the verdict of history remains split.

Bernard Montgomery, Earl of Alamein, has been called England's greatest soldier since the days of Wellington. But if one pauses to think, in the nearly century and a half between the career of Wellington and that of Montgomery, what other British general has demonstrated enough talent to justify his claim of accepting the mantle of the great Iron Duke. When one reflects on the history of that period, Montgomery naturally is the obvious nominee.

Field Marshal Sir William Slim

Chapter 6

Field Marshal Sir William Slim conducted probably the most tenacious and strategically decisive campaign of the British army during World War II. From an army that produced such illustrious figures as Alanbrooke,* Alexander, O'Connor, Auchinleck, and Wavell, Slim's exploits stand out. But the strict caste system, so prevalent throughout the British army until its inglorious demise on the battlefields of the Somme, at Ypres, and in the Meuse-Argonne, nearly prevented Slim's rise to fame. This system could not, however, reckon with his tenacity and determination.

Bill Slim was born in Bristol, England in 1891. As a child growing up in Victorian Britain, it was young William's fondest desire to become an army officer. Unfortunately, Slim's family could ill-afford to send their son to one of the military polishing schools or the military college at Sandhurst. Even had sufficient funds been available, the private income that was so necessary to sustain the career of a junior officer was totally out of the question. Consequently, upon graduation from school he was obliged to obtain a position in private industry with the steel firm of Stewart and Lloyds, in Birmingham. While in their

*Alan Francis Brooke

employ, Slim managed to wrangle an appointment to the Birmingham University's Officer Training Corps. This appointment was highly unusual in light of the fact that Slim was not a student at the university.

Nevertheless, his talent was recognized early and he quickly rose through the ranks of the unit. Shortly after the outbreak of World War I, Slim was commissioned into the regular army as a second lieutenant in the Royal Warwickshire Regiment.

The young officer's introduction to the battlefield took place during the ill-fated Gallipoli campaign against the Turkish controlled Dardanelles. During the campaign he was seriously wounded in the shoulder while leading his company against a strongly held Turkish position and was eventually invalided home. During his convalescence a fellow officer informed him that periodic openings were available in the Indian army and that one need not have a private income to afford service in that country. Sensing a method whereby he could fulfill his lifelong ambition, Slim duly applied for and was granted a commission in the West Indian Regiment.

Before joining this unit however, he was reposted to his old regiment, the Warwickshires, and fought with them in Iraq and the Middle East where he distinguished himself by his leadership ability. Finally in 1922, he joined the Indian army as a captain in the Sixth Gurkha Rifles. Slim had fought alongside this regiment during the campaign in the Dardanelles and had come to respect its ability as a fighting formation.

Settling down to life as an officer on the Indian frontier, Slim's leadership and administrative ability did not go unnoticed by his superiors, and when an opening occurred for an Indian officer to instruct at the British army Staff College at Camberley in 1934, Major Slim was selected to fill the position. After three years in this assignment, he was chosen to attend the annual course of study at the Imperial War College. As the prospect of war became more acute, Slim rejoined the Indian army as commander of the Sixth Infantry Brigade in the Fifth Indian Division.

In the fall of 1940, Fifth Indian Division was ordered to the Sudan to participate in the campaign against the Italians in Ethiopia and Eritrea. While in Africa, he made the acquaintance of a young, rather intense officer by the name of Orde Wingate. Both were destined to make a major contribution to the war in the Far East as fellow officers in Burma. During the campaign against the Italians, Slim saw action in the battles of Gallabat and Keren, being slightly wounded again during the latter. He returned to India and after a brief convalescent period was promoted to major general and given command of the Tenth Indian Division. Soon after, this division was ordered to Syria to secure that area from the turmoil resulting from conflicts between the Vichy and free French. Slim remained in Syria until 1942 when British fortunes in Burma took a drastic turn for the worst.

On December 7, 1941, Japan struck a lethal blow toward the establishment of the Greater East Asia Co-Prosperity Sphere. The commander in chief of the Combined Fleet, Adm. Isoroku Yamamoto, hoped that an attack on the American naval base at Pearl Harbor would buy for Japan the necessary time to

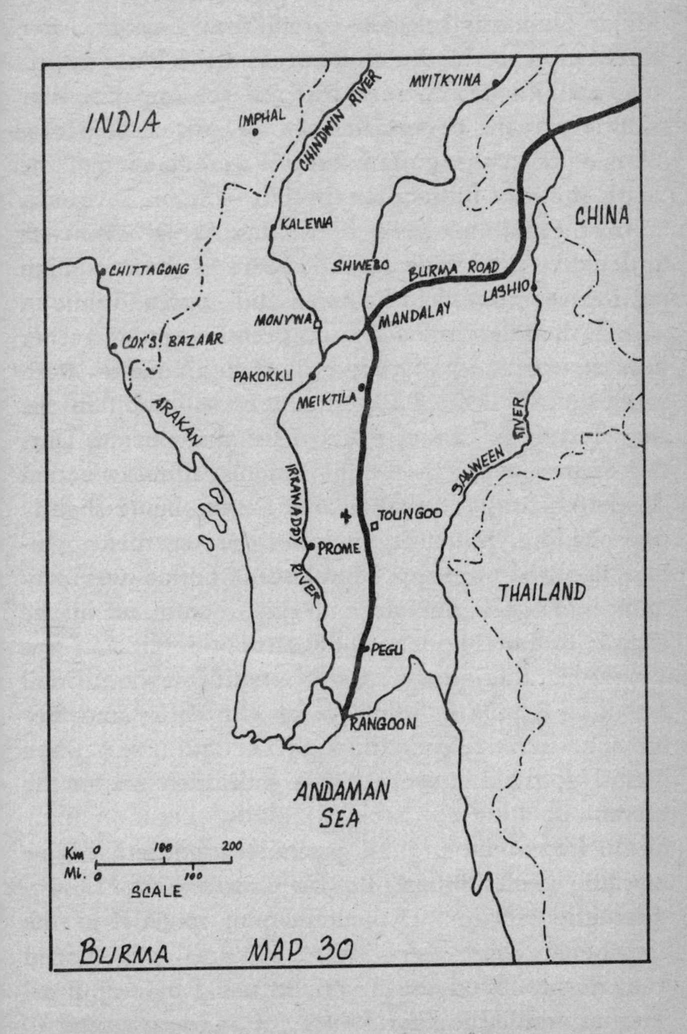
INDIA
IMPHAL
CHINDWIN RIVER
MYITKYINA
KALEWA
CHINA
CHITTAGONG
SHWEBO
BURMA ROAD
LASHIO
MONYWA
MANDALAY
COX'S BAZAAR
PAKOKKU
MEIKTILA
ARAKAN
SALWEEN RIVER
IRRAWADDY RIVER
TOUNGOO
PROME
THAILAND
PEGU
RANGOON
ANDAMAN
SEA
Km 0 100 200
Mi. 0 100
SCALE

BURMA MAP 30

establish an impenetrable barrier around her empire before America could develop the resources to strike back.

Simultaneous with the attack on Hawaii, the Japanese struck to the south against the Philippines, the Dutch East Indies, and into the rich Malay peninsula. This area contained the raw materials which Japan so desperately needed if she were to survive the heavy strain of industrialization.

From 1937, four years before launching her strike against the United States and Great Britain, Japan had been embroiled in a costly and devastating war with China. During this time Japan's resources had been strained to the limit in trying to conquer that vast country. Though forced to retreat to its interior, the Chinese government was determined not to give in. Japan realized that China had been able to continue the struggle because of the war materials supplied by the United States and transported over the two-thousand-mile-long road from Burma into Yunnan, in China. Therefore, if Japan were to defeat China, this lifeline would have to be severed. Thus Burma became a target for Japanese conquest. Control of this country would serve a threefold purpose for the warriors from the Land of the Rising Sun. First, it would sever China's link with the West thereby isolating the latter. Secondly, the occupation of Burma would protect Japanese conquests to the east and south. Finally, Burma possessed oil and vast quantities of rice with which Japan could fuel and feed her war machine. (See Map 30)

The Japanese invasion of Burma had begun as early as mid-December of 1941, when a small detachment of the Fifteenth Army moved across the Burmese border from Thailand, their primary targets being the capture of strategically located airfields. Control of these bases would protect their army as it advanced down the Malay peninsula toward the pearl of the British Far Eastern possessions, Singapore. The airfields could also be used to launch raids on Rangoon, which the Japanese did on December 23 and 25, sending both Burmese and British into a state of panic.

The main assault against Burma commenced on January 20, 1942, with Rangoon as its immediate target and by March 8, the city found itself in Japanese hands. Shortly after the fall of Rangoon, Slim arrived in Burma. Few commanders could have been faced with a more unfavorable situation than was Bill Slim, when on March 19, 1942, he assumed command of what was designated Burcorps.* His orders were to hold out as long as possible and if necessary, organize an orderly retreat.

As corps commander he was faced with determining the overriding intention of the campaign. Should he stand and fight? Should he advance and attempt to retake areas already captured by the Japanese? Or, was withdrawal to the safety of India the most prudent thing?

Slim inspired confidence as he made his presence felt among his subordinates. He wished to stand and fight and if possible, drive the invaders out of Burma. In his book *Defeat Into Victory*, he emphasizes the necessity of taking the initiative away from the

*Burma Corps

Japanese at this stage of the campaign. The only way to accomplish this was to attack. He therefore decided that the objective of Burcorps:

> should be to concentrate our two divisions with a view to counterattacking at the earliest possible opportunity.[1]

However, Slim faced many obstacles. The intelligence agency was not well organized. His troops were ill-trained and poorly equipped for jungle warfare. He found combat units well below acceptable strength and local inhabitants unable to provide help, as well as being totally unreliable. Worst of all, morale was at an extremely low ebb. Though desiring to avoid retreat at all costs, little by little the Japanese advanced in force, and with the disappearance of the Royal Air Force, retreat appeared to be the inevitable solution for Slim.

On March 28, Gen. Sir Harold Alexander, who was newly placed in command of all British forces in Burma, was urged by Chiang Kai-shek, the Chinese generalissimo, to demand that Slim take the offensive immediately in order to relieve pressure on the Chinese forces fighting in the north desperately attempting to keep the Burma Road open for traffic. The attack proved futile and Slim was forced to call a halt to the offensive. On April 15, he issued orders for the demolition of the oil fields, not wanting them to fall into Japanese hands intact.

Gen. Joseph Stilwell, Chiang's chief of staff and the United States' theatre commander, attempted to sustain the Chinese offensive in the north, but like Slim's Burcorps, his attacks were in vain. With the failure of

Stilwell's efforts and the collapse of Slim's offensive,

> realism demanded that we should now decide to get out of Burma as intact as we could.[2]

On April 28, Alexander gave Slim authorization to withdraw. The problems facing the latter were immense. A withdrawal would necessitate moving his command more than two hundred miles over terrain that could be considered some of the worst found on earth: thick tropical rain forests, malarial swamps, and steep jungle-clad mountains. Burcorps also faced the danger of supply shortages which could conceivably leave thousands to die of starvation in the verdant forests of death. There also was a race against time, for the monsoon was due in May and if it were to arrive early, before India was reached, the streams would be swollen and impassable causing many to die of drowning. Lastly, the Japanese, licking at the flanks of the retreating forces, threatened to cut off the retreat entirely. Slim was indeed faced with a most difficult and virtually impossible task.

Thanks to his inspirational leadership and determination, Burcorps made it with but one week to spare before the arrival of the monsoon. The cost however, had been heavy. Slim's bedraggled command had lost most of their equipment, all of their tanks, and their casualties were unacceptably heavy, 13,500; three times that of the enemy. The fact that they did get away however, could be viewed as a significant accomplishment. But now the Japanese were able to seal off China, and Burma became the western terminus of the heralded Greater East Asia Co-Prosperity Sphere. The Japanese star was indeed rising. They seemed unbeatable.

Upon arrival in Assam, India, Slim turned what was left of his troops over to IV Corps. He then modestly admitted that the Allies had been outmaneuvered, outfought, and outgeneraled. The long, hard retreat had given him time to evaluate the reasons why the Allied effort had suffered so costly a defeat. Slim concluded that the terrain was a prime cause and ill-preparedness to fight a war of this nature was another. The lack of roads connecting India to Burma, which hampered resupply, definitely had a negative effect. The forces in Burma were inadequate to defend the roads, and lack of sufficient air protection as well as inept intelligence all proved to handicap the prosecution of a strong defense let alone a successful offensive. Slim did credit a Japanese tactic, the "hook," as a superior tactic which wrought havoc and greatly enhanced their conquest. By use of this tactic, the Japanese found themselves able to send mobile forces on a wide turning movement around the enemy flank through the jungle, thereby cutting into the enemy line and severing communications, effectively isolating terrified units.

With the Japanese consolidating their conquests, the British planned for a comeback as soon as the dry season arrived to make any effort plausible. Many difficulties faced the British command at whose head was the Combined Chiefs of Staff who placed Burma low on the order of priority. The amount of shipping and supplies allocated for India were only one-third of what was essential if India was going to be built up into a major springboard for offensive action. Furthermore, there were internal problems within India itself which hindered serious preparations. Political unrest fomented by Mohandas K. Gandhi, who desired immediate independence for his country, caused many Indians to follow Gandhi's tactic of civil disobedience, resulting in a lack of cooperation with the British as they prepared to take the offensive.

In time, when settled conditions returned in the wake of Indian nationalistic uprisings and the aftermath of the retreat from Burma ended, Slim settled down to the critical job of training new divisions for the forthcoming battles. Applying the lessons learned during the previous fighting, he created a soldier capable of fighting in the horrible conditions of the jungle atmosphere.

While Slim was deeply involved in this all-important task, in July of 1942, General Headquarters planned a modest offensive into the Arakan with the goal of clearing the Mayu Peninsula and the seizure of Akyab Island. The Mayu Peninsula is about ninety miles long and twenty miles wide at its northern end, tapering to a point just short of Akyab Island. Down its center runs a razor sharp ridge of mountains, the Mayu Range, whose jungle-covered peaks average between one to two thousand feet in height. Control of this area would give the British excellent airfields which they could use to support a future advance of forces into central Burma. (See Map 31)

Not until mid-December did the Arakan offensive begin, with the British attacking on both sides of the Mayu Range, along the seacoast, and astride the Mayu River. By the beginning of the next year, the British found themselves just short of Donbaik, ap-

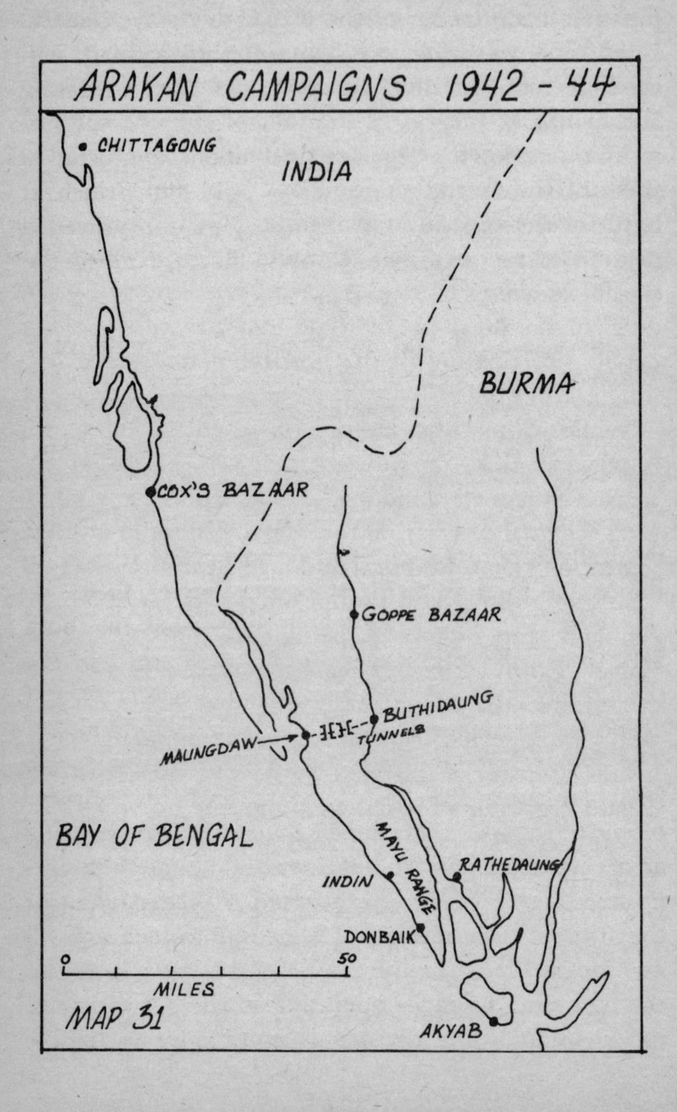
ARAKAN CAMPAIGNS 1942 - 44
CHITTAGONG
INDIA
BURMA
COX'S BAZAAR
GOPPE BAZAAR
BUTHIDAUNG
TUNNELS
MAUNGDAW
BAY OF BENGAL
MAYU RANGE
RATHEDAUNG
INDIN
DONBAIK
0
50
MILES
MAP 31
AKYAB

proximately ten miles from the tip of the peninsula. Here they paused until January 6, allowing the Japanese commander of the Fifteenth Army, General Iida, time to bring up reinforcements which successfully repulsed the British attacks at Rathedaung and Donbaik. With only a battalion and a handful of reserve troops, the Japanese defenders conducted a skillful defense and managed to hold the British at bay. Bunkers constructed by the Japanese proved a nemesis to the attackers. General Slim described the typical bunker.

> This was a small strong point made usually of heavy logs, covered with four or five feet of earth, and so camouflaged in the jungle that it could not be picked out at even fifty yards without prolonged searching.[3]

These bunkers were sited in groups so that they mutually supported each other and made it next to impossible for supporting troops to destroy them.

Attack after attack was sent into Donbaik, both men and tanks, but each one failed in turn. In the second week of March, Slim was summoned to Calcutta by General Irwin, the army commander. The latter requested that Slim go to Arakan to see what could be done about the failure of the British offensive to date. Slim hoped that he would be going as a corps commander but Irwin said that there was no need for a corps headquarters in the Arakan at that time, all he desired of Slim was to look around and report back on the overall situation. He found that the nine brigades operating in the Arakan were too awkward for a divisional commander to handle and that morale among the troops was very low.

On April 5, 1943, Slim was awakened from his sleep and told that a corps headquarters was to be sent to the battlefront. He was to assume operational command in the Arakan. While he was in the process of establishing his corps headquarters in Chittagong, the Japanese struck the British line. Slim had estimated that the lateral road between Maungdaw and Buthidoung would be the target of the attacking Japanese. Just as anticipated, the Japanese struck the road in force and quickly captured it. With the road in enemy hands, the British troops in Buthidoung were forced to escape via jungle tracks; it had the appearance of 1942 all over again. The tunnels on the western part of the lateral road were, however, still in British hands with the forces in Maungdaw vitally depending on them. Again the Japanese struck and by May 11, Maungdaw had to be evacuated. The British were forced to retreat back to where they had begun the offensive. Liddell-Hart sums up the accomplishments of this offensive.

> In sum, the British attempt to recapture Akyab and its airfields by an overland advance and without seaborne aid had proved a complete and dismal failure. The Japanese had shown their skill in flanking moves and infiltrations through the jungle, while the British had damped the spirit of their troops by costly frontal attacks and blundering disregard.[4]

The British forces were in desperate need of revitalization. One step in this direction was the appointment of Slim to command the Fourteenth Army on May 15, 1943. Another was the appointment of Sir Claude Auchinleck to command the Indian army. Accompanied by his headquarters staff, Slim traveled to Calcutta at the end of May for a round of talks on the Arakan situation. Upon conclusion of this round of discussions, he resumed training troops for combat in the jungle atmosphere.

During August 1943, events were taking place on the other side of the world that would radically alter the command structure of the Burma-India theatre. Meeting at the plush Chateau Frontenac Hotel in Quebec, Roosevelt, Churchill, and the Combined Chiefs of Staff discussed among other important topics, the main objectives for a 1944 Burma offensive. It was agreed that the opening of a road and pipeline route from Ledo in Assam, via Moguang and Myitkyina in Burma, to Kunming in China, the old terminus of the Burma Road, must receive a high priority. The command structure was also changed. A new theatre designation was created with the name South East Asia Command and the man appointed to command this theatre was the dashing and brilliant naval hero, Adm. Lord Louis Mountbatten of England.

For the forthcoming campaign, the plan called for a major role to be played by Orde Wingate, a semibiblical character whose force of irregulars, known as the Chindits, would cut deep into Japanese lines and cut the communications running from the south to the forces opposing Stilwell's Ledo forces. The latter would in turn, launch an attack from the north.

Slim's Fourteenth Army was designated to play but

a limited role for the balance of the year. His primary assignment was to support the Chindits. But, the Japanese were about to alter the entire situation.

During the summer and fall of 1943, Slim was confronted by three major antagonists; supply, health, and morale. He knew it was necessary to build up a logistics system that would insure that when his forces attacked deep into the jungle, ample supplies could reach them. In addition, he deemed it critical to drastically improve health services and foremost of all, restore the badly shaken morale of his troops.

Slim felt that chances for a successful offensive would be greatly improved if the Japanese army were weakened before commencement of battle. A weakened enemy would place favourable odds on the British side. He stated:

> The only way this could be done was, at an early stage to entice the enemy into a major battle in circumstances so favourable to us that we could smash three or four of his divisions.[5]

Slim's hope would soon be fulfilled, though perhaps not in the way he imagined.

The Japanese conducted a high level strategy meeting in June of 1943. Among the items discussed was how the British Chindit operation had demonstrated the vulnerability of their own communications. Thus they concluded that the best way to defend Burma was to attack, cut off the vulnerable British line of communications, and destroy the British Indian divisions based in the Imphal-Kohima region of Assam. In effect, hit the British before the British could hit them. As a prelude, they planned to launch a diversionary attack into the Arakan in order to draw off Fourteenth Army reserves before launching the main offensive directed at Imphal and Kohima. The latter would be the jumping-off point for an eventual invasion of India itself.

The Japanese offensive into the Arakan was labeled Operation Ha-Go, whose primary objective was to cut off the Indian Fifth and Seventh Divisions under the command of Gen. Frank Messervy, late of the western desert, and destroy these two formations. If successful, these divisions would be prevented from interfering with the main assault further north.

In December of 1943, the Japanese attack was launched in all its fury. Initially, all went according to plan as they managed to capture many British strongpoints and isolate groups of enemy troops. Fighting in the surrounded strongpoints was fierce, at times hand-to-hand. But neither Indian, British, nor Gurkha would yield ground. The Japanese command had established a rigid timetable and now found themselves falling behind. The British were showing no sign of panic or retreat, a result that the Japanese had relied on. Instead, the attackers found themselves bogged down in heavy fighting and suffering irreplaceable and unacceptable losses. Thanks to a heroic stand by the Seventh Indian Division, the entire Japanese offensive lost its momentum. Then, British troops from the north attacked in force.

Up to this point in the war, the Burmese theatre had been treated as the backwater of the war effort, resulting in a low priority for equipment and reinforcements. Indeed, the lack of these vital items had played a major role in contributing to the earlier defeat in Burma. Under Mountbatten, the situation began to take a drastic change. Lord Louis' influence and outstanding qualities of leadership managed to increase the flow of supplies and an efficient organization was established to insure prompt delivery of this material to the front.

By the middle of February 1944, the Japanese had shot their bolt in the Arakan. Various scattered Japanese troops were observed retreating into the jungle. Buithidoung was retaken on March 11, and the Japanese were left to defend the tunnels. By May 3, the Arakan was cleared of Japanese. Slim had called the Arakan battle:

> One of the historic successes of British arms. For the first time a British force had met, held and decisively defeated a major Japanese attack and followed this up by driving the enemy out of the strongest possible natural position that they had been preparing for months and were determined to hold.[6]

Although Messervy's gallant stand had proved decisive, the ultimate triumph was all Slim's.

> It was mainly his determination which made the divisions stand firm in face of what appeared to be disaster.[7]

Though the Japanese Arakan offensive demanded the major portion of Slim's attention, he realized that this was not the main effort. He was convinced that it was but a preliminary to a major attack on the IV Corps area near Imphal. This astute observation was soon to pay significant dividends.

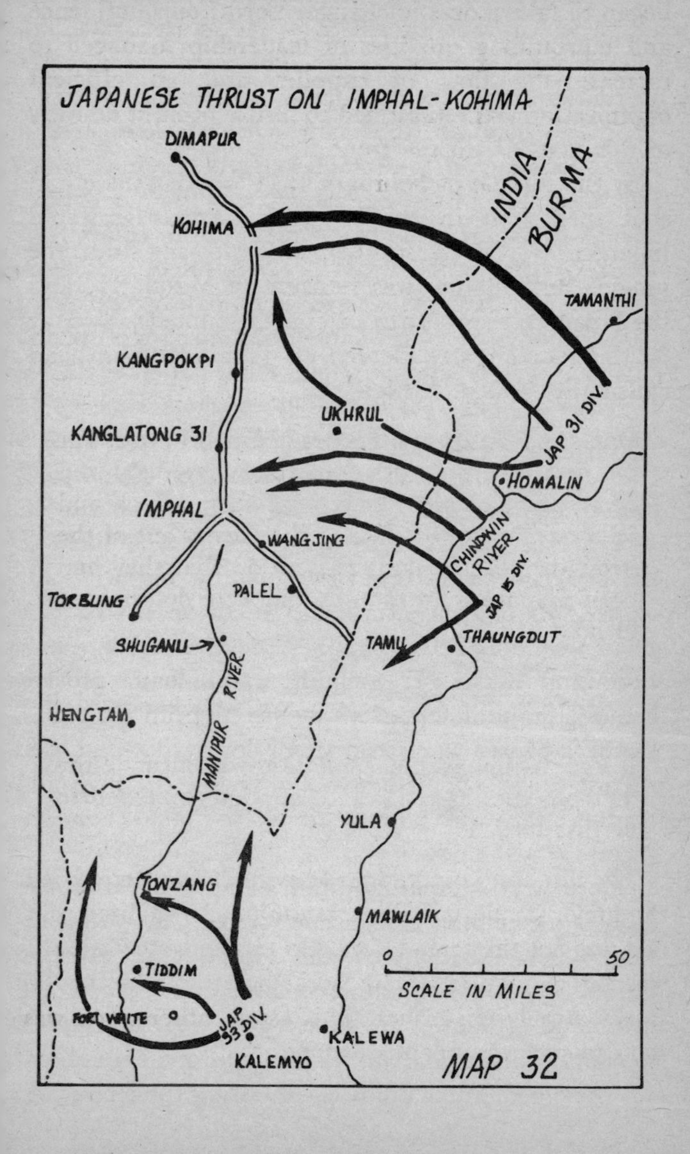
JAPANESE THRUST ON IMPHAL-KOHIMA
DIMAPUR
KOHIMA
INDIA
BURMA
TAMANTHI
KANGPOKPI
UKHRUL
KANGLATONG 31
JAP 31 DIV.
HOMALIN
IMPHAL
WANG JING
CHINDWIN RIVER
PALEL
JAP 15 DIV.
TORBUNG
SHUGANU
TAMU
THAUNGDUT
MANIPUR RIVER
HENGTAM
YULA
TONZANG
MAWLAIK
0
50
SCALE IN MILES
TIDDIM
FORT WHITE
JAP 33 DIV.
KALEWA
KALEMYO
MAP 32

Ha-Go was officially abandoned on February 24, but it was in Operation U-Go that the Japanese had placed their greatest hopes. The final conquest of Burma and the defeat of India was vital to Japanese efforts to continue the war. Without these crucial areas, Japan's fortunes would suffer a severe setback. (See Map 32)

As a decoy, Ha-Go did compel Slim to commit his reserves, troops that would be desperately needed at Imphal and Kohima. Now, anticipating the main Japanese offensive, Slim had three alternatives opened to him. First of all, he could order all three of his divisions to hold their extended positions while being supplied by air. Then he would be able to launch a counterstroke from the area of Dimapur. The second option open to Slim was to have his forces counterattack before the Japanese did, thus beating them to the punch. The third option, and the one he finally chose, was to concentrate his forces on the Imphal plain where airfields, supplies, reserves of ammunition, and tanks were readily available. This area could then be defended as a fortress until such time as the Japanese wore themselves down and weakened themselves to a point that would enable the British to counterattack with a better than reasonable chance of success.

Along with preparing for the Japanese offensive, Slim found himself responsible for the Chindit operation which was handed the objective of assisting Stilwell's Ledo forces who also came under the overall command of Slim. Wingate's units were also directed to capture Myitkyina with its strategic airfield and cut Japanese communications by harassing their rear and preventing their reinforcement.

While the Chindits were moving into position, Stilwell was ordered to attack from the north with his Chinese units and an American force trained especially for the jungle known as Merrill's Marauders after their commander, Gen. Frank Merrill.

The Japanese offensive against IV Corps, Operation U-Go, began in the second week of March with Lt. Gen. Mutaguchi Renya in overall command of the operation. His plan of attack called for a three-pronged offensive. In the south, the Japanese Thirty-third Division was to surround the British Seventeenth Division and cut off its communications with Imphal. In the center, the Fifteenth Division, after crossing the Chindwin River, was to infiltrate south of Ukhrul and north of Imphal. In the north, the Thirty-first Division was to cross the Chindwin between Tamanthi and Homalin and make for Kohima.

Slim had already decided to fight the battle on the Imphal plain and had every intention of winning. Piecing together all the information they could gather, the IV Corps commander, General Scoones, and Slim concluded that the Japanese offensive would begin on or about March 15. Scoones then organized his defenses on the Imphal plain by ordering a series of defended boxes to be placed around the supply dumps and airfields in the area.

By March 13, Scoones was convinced that the Japanese offensive had begun and gave General Cowan, commanding the Seventeenth Division, permission to begin a retreat to the Imphal plain. Slim realized that the order to retreat might not be popular and could lead the enemy into feeling that a great success had been achieved, but he was convinced that those hundreds of square miles of jungle and mountains mattered little when weighed against an opportunity to smash the enemy. In his own words Slim reiterated:

> There are three reasons for retreat, self-preservation, to save your force from destruction, pressure elsewhere which makes you accept loss of territory in one place to enable you to transfer troops to a more vital front, and last, to draw the enemy into a situation so unfavourable to him that the initiative must pass to you. It was for this third reason that I now voluntarily decided on a withdrawal.[8]

Reinforcements for the units entrenched on the Imphal plain were urgently required. Therefore, he proposed to pull the Fifth Division out of the Arakan and move it by air and rail from Chittagong to Dimapur and Imphal.

Unfortunately, General Cowan was slow in issuing the retreat order to his Seventeenth Division. By the time he did, the enemy had already blocked most exits to the Imphal plain except for the one via the Manipur River bridge. Nevertheless, Seventeenth Division finally made good their withdrawal and reached Imphal by April 5, maintained enroute by supply drops from the air.

Slim however, held serious reservations over the long and precarious line of communication to Kohima and beyond to Dimapur where sat forty-five thousand administrative troops. Should the Japanese descend into the Brahmaputra valley, they would not only cut off IV Corps, but Stilwell's forces as well. Thus, General Stopford's XXXIII Corps was concentrated at the Dimapur railhead.

General Mutaguchi allotted his forces three weeks to achieve their objective. He had grossly underestimated the enemy's resistance and his own difficulties.

In reviewing his strategy, Slim reduced it down to four simple phases; concentration of force, attrition where the forces would be worn down, counteroffensive, and finally, pursuit of the fleeing enemy. However, Slim had grossly underestimated the Japanese strength. Within a week of the start of the offensive, it was obvious that the situation in the Kohima area was likely to be even more precarious than at Imphal. Slim himself flew to Dimapur and identified the gravity of the situation. Fierce fighting ensued around Kohima. Fortunately for the British, Japanese rigidity to orders resulted in Major General Ito concentrating on Kohima even though he was more favourably situated for a move against Dimapur where he could have achieved greater results.

During the first week of April, the hard-pressed British found themselves fighting desperately on the rim of the Imphal plain. Dimapur was still being threatened and the Kohima garrison was in dire peril as the Japanese cut the Kohima-Imphal road and isolated them. On April 18, the siege of Kohima was finally lifted, primarily due to the cooperation and efficiency of the air forces who were able to supply the besieged garrison. The Japanese however, continued to fight to the death.

At Imphal the fighting became synonymous with

ferocity and brutality. Despite this, by the middle of May Slim's worst anxieties were past. The Japanese had been thrown onto the defensive at Kohima and at Imphal the British were ready to strike back. The time had now come for the Fourteenth Army to pass over to the offensive with the prime objective being the destruction of the Japanese Fifteenth Army.

By the end of June, though the battles were still raging, the British began to anticipate victory. The blood was in Slim's eyes as he now prepared to destroy the Japanese. He stated:

> If we could drive the enemy over the Chindwin, establish bridgeheads on its east bank, and be ready to push a considerable force into the plains of central Burma immediately after the Monsoon ended, we could strike Kawabe's* main force in front of Mandalay before it had recovered.[9]

By July 13, the Japanese were in full retreat towards the Chindwin River. The maneuver was a nightmare of horror and suffering. On the long, treacherous trek over the mountains in the pounding, driving rain, men savagely fought one another for the slightest crumb of food. Thousands of sick and wounded fell out of the march and rather than be captured or die in agony, killed themselves with grenades. The rains turned the paths they traveled to seas of mud and when a man stumbled he became half-buried in the gooey slime. The trail was littered with anything too useless for men to carry: light machine guns, rifles, helmets, gas masks. Of course everywhere one looked the gruesome sight of bloated bodies and rotting flesh

*Commanding General, Burma Area Army

assailed the eyes and nostrils of the fleeing. Only the desire to live propelled the survivors, some men hobbling along on anything that could hold them up. Many died by drowning while trying to capture some sleep when the constant, heavy downpour created streams which engulfed those too weak and unable to raise their head. At last, after months of endless torture, the Chindwin was sighted, the last obstacle to safety. But the incessant rains had swollen the river and its current claimed the lives of hundreds more. It must have been a terrible fate: to struggle through endless months of sheer hell only to succumb with the final goal in sight.

In all the Japanese lost sixty-five thousand men during Operation U-Go, more than two and one-half times the number lost at Guadalcanal. It proved a loss of the greatest magnitude. The Japanese would be unable to recover from the depths of this debacle.

Slim had won a great victory and achieved his stated objective of letting the Japanese bash their heads against a wall far from their base. Just as planned, he wore the Japanese down and the time was now ripe to turn and destroy them.

In analyzing the abortive Japanese offensive, Slim realized that the British had committed some serious errors. The mistiming of the withdrawal of Seventeenth Division was one that could have resulted in the destruction of this formation. The underestimation of the strength of the Japanese thrust at Kohima was another error that might have had serious consequences, but thanks to air reinforcements, the day was eventually saved. Errors notwithstanding, the Fourteenth Army had achieved a great victory and was now prepared to exploit it. They were proud and true and had proven beyond doubt that they were more than a match for the Japanese. Accordingly, morale soared.

Even while the Japanese were fleeing towards the Chindwin, Slim was planning his next move. Many plans were considered but the one that finally was adopted was codenamed Capital. It called for an advance across the Chindwin east to the Irrawaddy River with the objective of capturing Mandalay. In conjunction, the Chinese forces were to strike from the north while the XV Corps conducted a limited offensive in the Arakan with a possible sea and airborne assault on Rangoon scheduled for March of 1945. That operation was codenamed Dracula and would be attempted only if enough reinforcements were available to insure victory.

Slim was aware that much prestige was to be gained by capturing cities but his keen military instinct demanded that the destruction of the Japanese forces in the field take precedence. With final defeat of the enemy, the cities and towns would automatically fall into British hands. Though Mandalay was his stated target, Slim's true aim was to force a major battle with the Japanese.

Looking over the Burmese map, Slim deduced that the Shwebo Plain would be an ideal area to force this battle. It was a dry flat plain between the Chindwin and Irrawaddy Rivers and was excellent terrain for maneuvering armour and taking advantage of air power. He stated:

We must, therefore, get as many divisions and as

much armor as possible quickly into the Shwebo Plain and there fight an army battle.[10]

Slim therefore formulated a plan based on three foundations. First of all, he was firmly convinced that the Japanese commander was committed to fight for Mandalay. Secondly, he was confident that the other forces in the Burma theatre would be able to hold off at least four or five Japanese divisions, and thirdly, he could rely on the air force to supply his units.

The Fourteenth Army offensive began on December 3, 1944. The Japanese were taken totally by surprise by the British thrust as it swept eastward towards the Irrawaddy. However, Slim was dismayed by the Japanese refusal to come into the Shwebo Plain and do battle, as he had anticipated.

The cause of this refusal to stand and fight was that Gen. Kimura Hitaro* realized that his troops were exhausted and knew that his army would be at a distinct disadvantage on the open plain. He therefore ordered his forces to withdrew gradually behind the Irrawaddy, leaving only light covering forces to delay the British advance while he prepared to battle them on the river itself, hoping to destroy them as they attempted to cross this water course.

Consequently, Slim decided to redirect his main force to attempt a capture of the Japanese administration base at Meiktila, across the Irrawaddy but about seventy miles south of Mandalay. This city was the key administrative center for both the Japanese Thirty-third and Fifteenth Armies. (See Map 33)

*New commander of the Burma Area Army

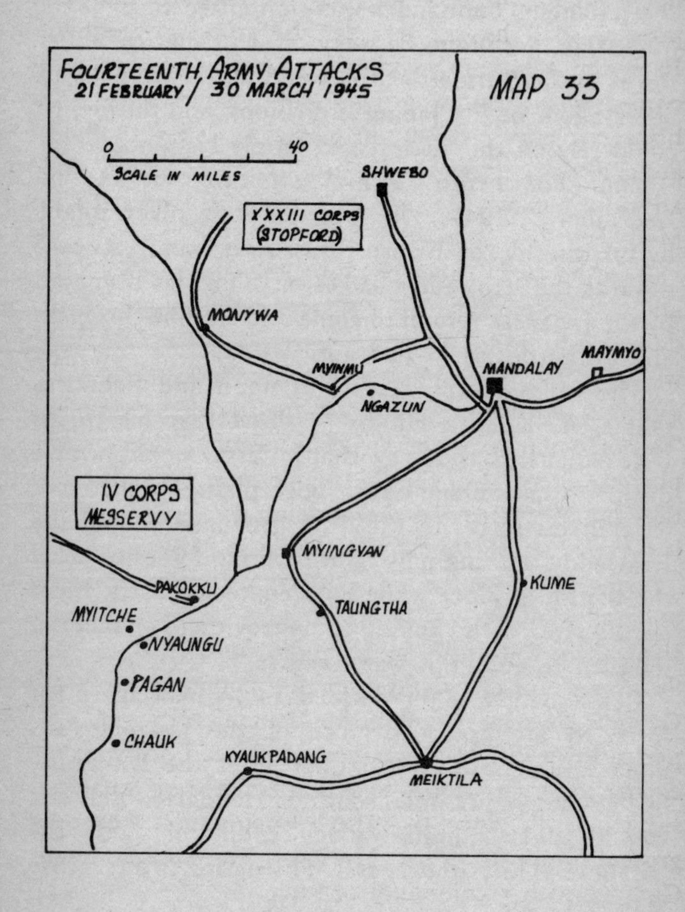
FOURTEENTH ARMY ATTACKS
21 FEBRUARY / 30 MARCH 1945
MAP 33
0
40
SCALE IN MILES
XXXIII CORPS
(STOPFORD)
SHWEBO
MONYWA
MYINMU
NGAZUN
MANDALAY
MAYMYO
IV CORPS
MESSERVY
MYINGYAN
KUME
PAKOKKU
TAUNGTHA
MYITCHE
NYAUNGU
PAGAN
CHAUK
KYAUKPADANG
MEIKTILA

This change of plan was typical of Slim and a true masterpiece in concept. He designated it "Extended Capital." Slim knew that for his plan to be successful, he would have to maintain the charade of attacking north of Mandalay and giving the Japanese the impression that the city was still the primary objective. In doing this, it was hoped to keep the enemy occupied with preventing a northerly attack while half his army moved down the Gangaw Valley to Pauk and Pakokku, cross the Irrawaddy at this point, and advance rapidly through the wide open country to Meiktila.

In order to convince the Japanese that the XXXIII and IV Corps were poised to strike north of Mandalay, a dummy IV Corps was created complete with wireless sets that sent out signals from a dummy headquarters at Tamu giving orders to the advancing "forces" north of Mandalay. Success of this deception plan was crucial to the entire operation. Meanwhile, the true IV Corps was maintaining wireless silence as it traveled south for its rendezvous at Meiktila.

In January, while IV Corps was on its long march to Pakokku, XXXIII was moving toward the Irrawaddy vigorously clearing all opposition in the Shwebo Plain. IV Corps ran into stiff opposition at Gangaw and its commander, General Messervy, experienced a difficult time because he did not wish to expose too many troops to action and arouse Japanese suspicions. Thanks to superb cooperation between ground and air units, Messervy was able to take Gangaw with a minimum of force.

Although he knew all along that he would have to eventually ford the Irrawaddy, Slim's forces were woefully short of the basic tools necessary for river crossings. Thus, he was forced to rely on the protection afforded by the air forces and by a successful deception of the Japanese. Only the latter could delude the enemy into thinking the major effort was elsewhere and therefore draw off troops that would have contested the river crossing. By persuading Kimura that any serious opposition would be north of Mandalay, the IV Corps could actually cross in the south, giving hope for success as relatively high.

The initial crossings north of Mandalay took place on January 11 in the face of strong opposition. Meanwhile, Slim moved his headquarters to Monywa in order to be nearer to the apparent action at Mandalay. Kimura fought with grim determination but fortunately for Slim, the Japanese commander had totally bought the deception scheme. As far as he was concerned, this was the main British attack and he was committed to stopping it.

While the fighting continued in the north, IV Corps had continued its secret march toward Pakokku. Via photographic air reconnaissance, Slim was provided with a complete intelligence assessment of the area. Though the Japanese would still be at Pakokku, they did not occupy this position in force and had no idea that a major crossing was about to take place in their front yard.

The IV Corps approached the river in a three-pronged advance. Slim directed that after the river was successfully crossed, Meiktila be hit fast and hard. The Seventh Division crossed on February 13 in the face of a spirited opposition by the few Japanese left to contest the crossing. Although the enemy fought tooth and nail for every foot, a bridgehead was eventually achieved. After the crossing Slim remarked:

> This sudden success after a shaky beginning was something of a surprise as well as a relief. It was owning, first to the fact that the enemy command was concentrating on the crossing of XXXIII Corps to the north and regarded all riverbank activities from Pakokku southward as mere demonstrations.[11]

In time the Japanese awoke to the fact that the crossing at Pakokku was in strength, so the local Japanese commander concentrated against the bridgehead in an effort to drive the British forces back across the river. Messervy, realizing that he could soon expect enemy reinforcements to arrive, wanted to strike quickly. Under heavy opposition he pushed across another division and ordered yet another to cross the river further south, at Pagan. Despite heavy opposition, both crossings proved highly successful.

By February 21, while troops were still crossing the Irrawaddy, the British advanced on Meiktila and pushed aside what little opposition was encountered. Although he received prompt reports of the crossings at Pakokku, Kimura still maintained that the entire Fourteenth Army was facing him north of Mandalay and he chose to ignore the threat to his rear as he prepared to repel the British offensive in the north.

With his forces driving rapidly on Meiktila, Slim now hoped that his opponent would direct reinforcements to move south from Mandalay. Should this happen, then Kimura would be caught in a vise between XXXIII Corps striking towards Mandalay while the IV Corps was firmly established in the south.

By February 28, the Seventh Division had made contact with the western defenses of Meiktila. The next day, Slim visited the battlefield where he was able to witness firsthand the ferocity of the battle. By March 3, the enemy was being driven through the city, street by street and house by house. The Japanese clung tenaciously to their positions and by late afternoon on the third, the city finally fell, to be followed two days later by the airfield.

The fate of the Japanese army was now virtually sealed. Conscious of the battle of Meiktila, Kimura abandoned his plan to concentrate against XXXIII Corps and moved all available reinforcements from Mandalay to Meiktila. Lieutenant General Honda with his Thirty-third Army was ordered to retake the city, but his forces approached piecemeal and the British were able to attack each Japanese column as it approached. The airfield became the focal point of major confrontations as the landing strips became no-man's-land between the fighting forces. Finally, by March 29, the Japanese were completely driven out with the exception of a handful holding out on the road to Meiktila, effectively closing the road temporarily. This road was vital to the interests of IV Corps, for without it supplies could not be brought forward. After a brief but furious assault, the area was finally secured by month's end and supplies began to flow along the road.

While the battle for Meiktila was in full sway,

Mandalay was in flames and the XV Corps campaign was making excellent headway in the Arakan. By April then, both banks of the Irrawaddy from Mandalay to Chauk, including the main road and railway to Rangoon as far south as Wundwin, were in British hands. (See Map 34)

The only hope remaining for the Japanese was to flee south to Rangoon. Because he desired to have Rangoon in British hands before the monsoon which was due shortly, Slim was required to race against time. His major concern was that should the Japanese elect to defend Rangoon as stubbornly as they had resisted at Meiktila, the British would be forced to await the arrival of decent campaigning weather.

This concern convinced Slim to resurrect Dracula, the amphibious assault of Rangoon, to coincide with a ground attack. Gen. Oliver Leese, the army group commander, vetoed the plan forcing Slim to attempt the capture of Rangoon from the north. The advance towards Rangoon was conceived as a dual-pronged attack with one prong advancing down the railroad tracks while the other column moved down the Irrawaddy Valley. Both advances would be mutally supportive even though the latter was considered to be the subsidiary advance.

Kimura knew that he must halt the British before Rangoon and realized that by taking advantage of the coming monsoon and using it as an ally, victory was still within his grasp.

Slim's worst fears were realized when the Japanese did indeed put up a stiff resistance thereby slowing the British advance. Because of this determined opposition and the weather forecasters predicting the

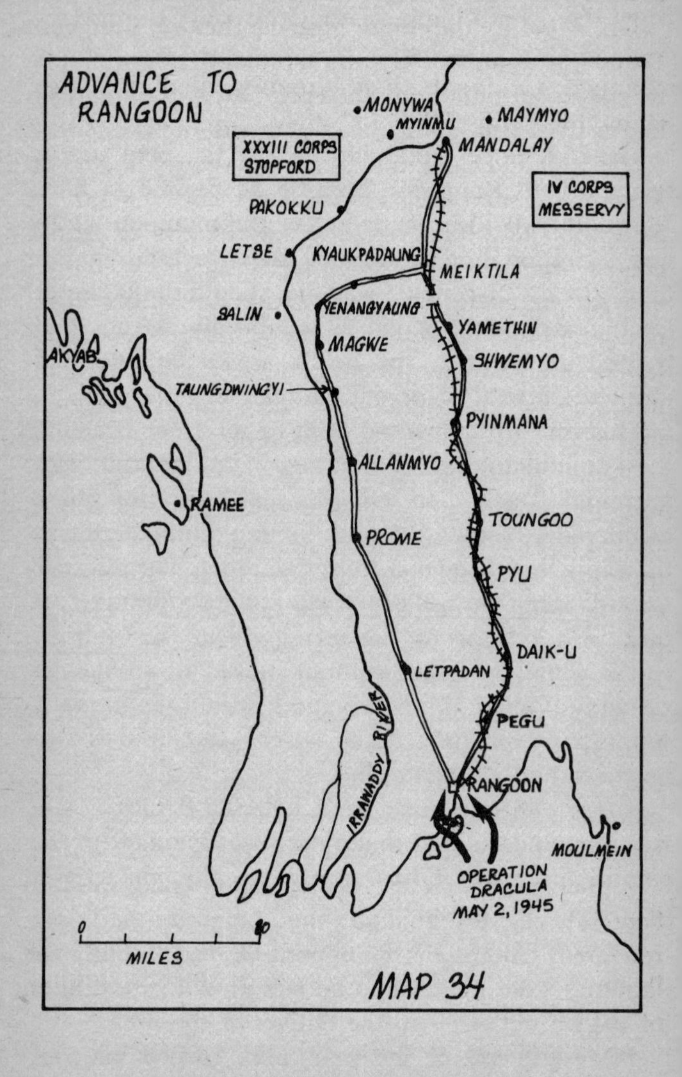
ADVANCE TO RANGOON
MONYWA
MYINMU
MAYMYO
MANDALAY
XXXIII CORPS
STOPFORD
IV CORPS
MESSERVY
PAKOKKU
LETSE
KYAUKPADAUNG
MEIKTILA
SALIN
YENANGYAUNG
YAMETHIN
MAGWE
SHWEMYO
AKYAB
TAUNGDWINGYI
PYINMANA
ALLANMYO
RAMEE
TOUNGOO
PROME
PYU
DAIK-U
LETPADAN
IRRAWADDY RIVER
PEGU
RANGOON
MOULMEIN
OPERATION
DRACULA
MAY 2, 1945
0
MILES
MAP 34

monsoon at any time, Admiral Mountbatten overruled Leese and ordered Dracula to commence.

On May 1, the final obstacle before Rangoon, Pegu, was assaulted. On the same day, a terrible torrential storm burst over the entire area; the monsoon had arrived two weeks ahead of schedule. The British forces were too close to final success, however, and on May 2, a successful landing was made south of Rangoon. The following day saw the city in British control with the Japanese in full retreat.

With the fall of Rangoon, two major tasks still remained. First, was the expulsion of all remaining Japanese forces from Burma and secondly, the planning, reequipping, and regrouping for an imminent invasion of Malaya and the recapture of Singapore.

"Office politics" now played a major part in determining the future of the command arrangement in Asia. Leese, under the guise of insisting that Slim required a rest after almost three years of constant campaigning, ordered him to take a leave and replaced him with one of his own favorites, General Roberts. Upset over being passed over as commander of "Operation Zipper," the projected invasion of Malaya, Slim, newly appointed full general, appealed the decision. His appeal was upheld and he was appointed overall commander, replacing Leese at whose hands he had received such shabby treatment.

Zipper was launched during the second week in September even though the Japanese had surrendered. Although no opposition was found, the landings were planned to be merely a demonstration of British authority to the natives of the area.

Near the end of the year, Slim turned his command over to Gen. Sir Miles Dempsey and returned to England to assume command of the Imperial Defense College. He remained there for two years until he had had his fill of the chief of the Imperial Staff, Montgomery. In 1947, he retired from the army.

A year later, he was recalled and replaced Montgomery as chief of staff and remained in this post until his final retirement in 1952. His promotion to field marshal came during his tenure as CIGS. He later served as governor general of Australia but retired from active life permanently in 1958. The remaining years were spent in full retirement writing his memoirs and offering assistance to historians of the Second World War. Death finally claimed the gallant warrior at the age of 79, shortly before the end of 1970.

Slim's major claim to fame is that he was an outstanding leader whose concern for the welfare, health, and morale of his troops was vividly demonstrated by his willingness to share these hardships. Immediately upon assumption of command of Fourteenth Army, he turned his attention to restoring decent levels of these important items. In the steaming jungles of Burma, he made the British soldier confident that he could fight on equal terms with the vaunted Japanese jungle fighter, and even lick him. At Imphal and Kohima, he denied the Japanese the opportunity to exploit their successes into India itself, a nation that was torn by internal strife and ripe for invasion. Finally, his bulldog like tenacity and determination refused to allow for resting on his laurels after Imphal and this trait resulted in the annihilation of his opponent by the refusal of Slim to let the enemy escape unscathed. By following up his victory with a determined pursuit, the Japanese were decisively defeated and driven out of Burma once and for all.

Notes

Introduction

1. Ralph Bennett, *Ultra in the West,* p. 1.
2. Anthony Cave-Brown, *Bodyguard of Lies,* p. 15.
3. *Ibid.,* p. 21.
4. *Ibid.,* p. 22.

Chapter 1 Notes

1. Corelli Barnett, *The Desert Generals,* p. 27.
2. Stephen Sears, *Desert War in North Africa,* p. 15.
3. Alan Moorhead, *The March to Tunis,* p. 75.
4. Barnett, *op. cit.,* p. 40.
5. *Ibid.,* p. 53.
6. Moorehead, *op. cit.,* p. 114.
7. Winston S. Churchill, *The Grand Alliance,* p. 204.
8. John Connell, *Wavell, Soldier and Scholar,* p. 392.
9. John Smyth, *Leadership in War 1939–1945,* pp. 87-88.
10. *Ibid.,* pp. 87-88.
11. Barnett, *op. cit.,* p. 27.

Chapter 2 Notes

1. Robert Wright, *The Man Who Won the Battle of Britain,* p. 29.
2. *Ibid.,* p. 31.
3. *Ibid.,* p. 48.
4. *Ibid.,* p. 59.
5. *Ibid.,* p. 94.
6. Peter Townsend, *Duel of Eagles,* p. 227.
7. *Ibid.,* p. 240.

8. *Ibid.*, p. 240.
9. *Ibid.*, p. 240.
10. Paul Brickhill, *Reach for the Sky,* p. 154.
11. *Ibid.*, p. 157.
12. *Ibid.*, p. 157.
13. Len Deighton, *Fighter,* p. 148.
14. Edward Bishop, *Their Finest Hour,* p. 160.
15. Robert Wright, *op. cit.*, p. 137.
16. *Ibid.*, p. 138.
17. Peter Townsend, *op. cit.*, p. 352.
18. *Ibid.*, p. 394.
19. *Ibid.*, p. 395.
20. Robert Wright, *op. cit.*, p. 147.
21. Peter Townsend, *op. cit.*, p. 364.
22. Robert Wright, *op. cit.*, p. 258.
23. *Ibid.*, p. 239.
24. *Ibid.*, p. 238.
25. *Ibid.*, p. 280.

Chapter 3 Notes

1. Roger Parkinson, *The Auk,* p. 13.
2. *Ibid.*, p. 29.
3. *Ibid.*, p. 51.
4. Bernard L. Montgomery, *Memoirs,* p. 71.
5. Parkinson, *op. cit.*, p. 86.
6. J.L. Scoullar, *Battle for Egypt,* pp. 372-373.
7. Parkinson, *op. cit.*, p. 94.
8. *Ibid.*, p. 102.
9. Winston Churchill, *The Grand Alliance,* p. 405.
10. Montgomery, *op. cit.*, p. 93.
11. Corelli Barnett, *The Desert Generals,* pp. 73-74.
12. Parkinson, *op. cit.*, p. 108.
13. Ronald Lewin, *The Life and Death of the Afrika Korps,* p. 77.
14. Barnett, *op. cit.*, p. 75.
15. *Ibid.*, p. 87.
16, I.S.O. Playfair et al., *The Mediterranean and the Middle East,* Vol. III, p. 46.
17. Parkinson, *op. cit.*, p. 125.

18. Barnett, *op. cit.*, p. 113.
19. John Connell, *Auchinleck*, p. 369.
20. Ronald Lewin, *Rommel as Military Commander*, p. 112.
21. B.H. Liddell-Hart, ed., *The Rommel Papers*, p. 172.
22. Winston Churchill, *The Hinge of Fate*, p. 295.
23. Ronald Lewin, *Rommel as Military Commander*, p. 145.
24. Winston Churchill, *op. cit.*, pp. 370-371.
25. Anthony Cave-Brown, *Bodyguard of Lies*, pp. 96-97.
26. Playfair, *op. cit.*, p. 286.
27. *Ibid.*, p. 295.
28. Arthur Bryant, *The Turn of the Tide*, p. 338.
29. Ronald Lewin, *Rommel as Military Commander*, p. 170.
30. Barnett, *op. cit.*, p. 218.
31. *Ibid.*, p. 237.
32. Winston Churchill, *The Hinge of Fate*, pp. 459-460.
33. Montgomery, *op. cit.*, p. 94.
34. John Strawson, *The Battle for North Africa*, p. 121.
35. Parkinson, *op. cit.*, p. 237.
36. William Slim, *Defeat Into Victory*, pp. 175-176.

Chapter 4 Notes

1. Michael Carver, *The War Lords*, p. 332.
2. W. G. F. Jackson, *Alexander of Tunis*, p. 52.
3. Arthur Bryant, *The Turn of the Tide*, p. 82.
4. Harold Alexander, *The Alexander Memoirs*, p. 79.
5. Winston Churchill, *The Hinge of Fate*, p. 146.
6. Jackson, *op. cit.*, p. 119.
7. Joseph Stilwell, *The Stilwell Papers*, p. 60.
8. Harry Butcher, *My Three Years With Eisenhower*, p. 43.
9. I.S.O. Playfair et al., *The Mediterranean and the Middle East*, Volume IV, p. 369.
10. Churchill, *op. cit.*, p. 537.
11. Jackson, *op. cit.*, p. 188.
12. *Ibid.*, p. 195.
13. *Ibid.*, p. 204.
14. *Ibid.*, p. 238.
15. Martin Blumenson, *Salerno to Cassino*, pp. 311-312.
16. Jackson, *op. cit.*, p. 252.
17. Alexander, *op. cit.*, p. 124.

18. *Ibid.*, p. 121.
19. *Ibid.*, p. 121.
20. Mark Clark, *Calculated Risk*, p. 367-68.
21. Alexander, *op. cit.*, pp. 41-44.
22. Jackson, *op. cit.*, p. 319.

Chapter 5 Notes

1. David Irving, *The War Between the Generals*, p. 268.
2. Ronald Lewin, *Montgomery as Military Commander*, p. 26.
3. *Ibid.*, p. 28.
4. Arthur Bryant, *The Turn Of The Tide*, p. 111.
5. Lewin, *op. cit.*, p. 47.
6. Harold Alexander, *The Alexander Memoirs*, p. 53.
7. Basil Liddell-Hart, *History of the Second World War*, p. 301.
8. Bryant, *op. cit.*, pp. 418-19.
9. Bernard Montgomery, *El Alamein to the River Sangro*, p. 133.
10. Irving, *op. cit.*, p. 42.
11. Mark Clark, *Calculated Risk*, p. 19.
12. Liddell-Hart, *op. cit.*, p. 565.
13. Charles MacDonald, *The Mighty Endeavor*, p. 332.
14. Brian Horrocks, *Corps Commander*, p. 132.
15. Irving, *op. cit.*, p. 281.
16. Cornelius Ryan, *A Bridge Too Far*, p. 88.
17. *Ibid.*, p. 88.
18. *Ibid.*, p. 88.
19. Irving, *op. cit.*, p. 350.
20. *Ibid.*, p. 350.
21. *Ibid.*, p. 328.
22. *Ibid.*, p. 329.
23. MacDonald, *op. cit.*, p. 404.
24. Alan Moorehead, *Eclipse*, p. 284.
25. Irving, *op. cit.*, p. 43.

Chapter 6 Notes

1. Field Marshal Sir William Slim, *Defeat into Victory*, p. 21.
2. *Ibid.*, p. 60.
3. *Ibid.*, p. 124.
4. Basil Liddell-Hart, *The History of the Second World War*, p. 366.
5. Slim, *op. cit.*, p. 186.
6. *Ibid.*, p. 213.
7. Michael Clavert, *Slim*, p. 81.
8. Slim, *op. cit.*, p. 250.
9. *Ibid.*, p. 296.
10. *Ibid.*, p. 316.
11. *Ibid.*, p. 358.

Bibliography

Chapter 1 Bibliography

Arnold-Forster, Marc, *The World at War*, Stein and Day, New York, 1973.
Barnett, Corelli, *The Desert Generals*, The Viking Press, New York, 1961.
Cave-Brown, Anthony, *Bodyguard of Lies*, Harper and Row, New York, 1975.
Churchill, Winston, *The Grand Alliance*, Houghton Mifflin Co., Boston, 1950.
Connell, John, *Wavell, Soldier and Scholar*, Harcourt Brace and World, New York, 1964.
Jablonski, David, *The Desert Warriors*, Lancer Books Inc., New York, 1972.
Jackson, W.G.F., *The Battle for North Africa, 1940–43*, Mason/Charter, New York, 1975.
Macksey, Kenneth, *Beda Fomm*, Ballantine Books, New York, 1971.
Moorehead, Alan, *The March to Tunis*, Harper and Row, New York, 1965.
Parrish, Thomas, ed., *Encyclopedia of World War II*, Simon and Schuster, New York, 1978.
Playfair, Major General I.S.O. et al., *The Mediterranean and Middle East*, Vol. 1, Her Majesty's Stationery Office, London, 1954.
Salmaggi, Ceasere, and Pallavisini, Alfredo, *2,194 Days of War*, Windward, New York, 1979.
Sears, Stephen, *The Desert War in North Africa*, American Heritage Publishing Co., New York, 1967.
Smyth, John, *Leadership in War 1939–1945*, St. Martin's Press, New York, 1974.

Chapter 2 Bibliography

Bekker, Cajus, *The Luftwaffe War Diaries*, Doubleday & Co., New York, 1968.
Bishop, Edward, *Their Finest Hour*, Ballantine Books Inc., New York, 1968.
Brickhill, Paul, *Reach for the Sky*, W.W. Norton & Co., New York, 1954.

Churchill, Winston, *Their Finest Hour,* Houghton Mifflin Co., Boston, 1949.
Deighton, Len, *Fighter,* Alfred A. Knopf, New York, 1977.
Douglas, Sholto, *Combat and Command,* Simon and Schuster, New York, 1963.
Forrester, Larry, *Fly For Your Life,* Bantam Books, New York, 1956.
Galland, Adolf, *The First and the Last,* Henry Hull & Co., New York, 1954.
Johnson, Air Vice Marshal Johnnie, *Full Circle,* Chatto & Windus Ltd., London, 1964.
Johnson, Air Vice Marshal Johnnie, *Wing Leader,* Chatto & Windus Ltd., London, 1956.
Lewin, Ronald, *Ultra Goes to War,* Hutchinson & Co., Ltd., London, 1978.
Parkinson, Roger, *Summer 1940,* David McKay & Co., New York, 1977.
Townsend, Peter, *Duel of Eagles,* Simon and Schuster, New York, 1970.
Wright, Robert, *The Man Who Won the Battle of Britain,* Charles Scribners Sons, New York, 1969.

Chapter 3 Bibliography

Barnett, Corelli, *The Desert Generals,* Ballantine Books Inc., New York, 1960.
Brownlow, Donald Grey, *Checkmate at Ruweisat, Auchinleck's Finest Hour,* Christopher Publishing House, North Quincy, 1977.
Bryant, Arthur, *The Turn of the Tide,* Doubleday & Co., New York, 1957.
Carver, Michael, ed., *The War Lords,* Little, Brown & Co., Boston, 1976.
Cave-Brown, Anthony, *Bodyguard of Lies,* Harper & Row, New York, 1975.
Churchill, Winston, *The Grand Alliance,* Houghton Mifflin Co., Boston, 1950.
Churchill, Winston, *The Hinge of Fate,* Houghton Mifflin Co., Boston, 1950.
Connell, John, *Auchinleck,* London, 1959.
Lewin, Ronald, *Rommel as Military Commander,* Ballantine Books, New York, 1968.

Lewin, Ronald, *Montgomery as Military Commander*, Stein and Day, New York, 1971.
Lewin, Ronald, *The Life and Death of the Afrika Korps,* B.T. Batsford, Ltd., London, 1977.
Lewin, Ronald, *Ultra Goes to War,* McGraw Hill, New York, 1978.
Liddell-Hart, B. H., ed., *The Rommel Papers,* Harcourt Brace & Co., New York, 1953.
Lucas, James, *Panzer Army Africa,* Presidio Press, San Rafael, 1977.
Montgomery, Bernard L. *The Memoirs of Field Marshal the Viscount Montgomery,* Collins, London, 1958.
Moulton, J . L., *Warfare in 3 Dimensions,* Ohio University Press, Athens, 1967.
Parkinson, Roger, *The Auk,* Granada Publishing, London, 1977.
Playfair, I. S. O. et al., *The Mediterranean and Middle East,* Her Majesty's Stationery Office, London, 1960.
Scoullar, J. L., *Battle for Egypt,* War History Branch, Dept. of Internal Affairs, Wellington, 1955.
Slim, William, *Defeat Into Victory,* David McKay Co., New York, 1961.
Smyth, V. C., Sir John, *Leadership in War 1939–1945,* St. Martin's Press, New York, 1974.
Strawson, John, *The Battle for North Africa,* Bonanza Books, New York, 1969.
Winterbothem, F. W., *The Ultra Secret,* Harper & Row, New York, 1974.

Chapter 4 Bibliography

Alexander, Harold, *The Alexander Memoirs 1940–1945,* McGraw-Hill Book Co., New York, 1961.
Blumenson, Martin, *Salerno to Cassino,* Office of the Chief of Military History, Wash., D.C., 1969.
Bryant, Arthur, *The Turn of the Tide,* Doubleday & Co. Inc., New York, 1957.
Butcher, Capt. Harry C., *My Three Years With Eisenhower,* Simon and Schuster, New York, 1946.
Carver, Michael, ed., *The War Lords,* Little, Brown and Co., Boston, 1976.
Cave-Brown, Anthony, *Bodyguard of Lies,* Harper & Row, New York, 1975.

Churchill, Winston S., *The Hinge of Fate,* Houghton Mifflin Co., Boston, 1950.
Clark, General Mark, *Calculated Risk,* Harper & Bros., New York, 1950.
Fisher, Ernest F., *Cassino to the Alps,* Center of Military History, Washington, D.C., 1977.
Garland, Albert N. et al., *Sicily and the Surrender of Italy,* Office of the Chief of Military History, Wash., D.C., 1965.
Howe, George F., *Northwest Africa: Seizing the Initiative in the West,* Office of the Chief of Military History, Wash., D.C., 1957.
Jackson, W. G. F., *The Battle for Italy,* Harper & Row, New York, 1967.
Jackson, W. G. F., *Alexander of Tunis,* Dodd Mead & Co., New York, 1967.
Kesselring, Albert, *Kesselring: A Soldier's Record,* Greenwood Press Reprint, 1970.
Macksey, Kenneth, *Kesselring: The Making of the Luftwaffe,* David McKay Co. Inc., New York, 1978.
Nicolson, Nigel, *Alex,* Atheneum, New York, 1973.
Parrish, Thomas, ed., *The Encyclopedia of World War II,* Simon and Schuster, New York, 1978.
Playfair, I.S.O. et al., *The Mediterranean and Middle East,* Volume III, Her Majesty's Stationery Office, London, 1960.
Playfair, I.S.O. et al., *The Mediterranean and Middle East,* Volume IV, Her Majesty's Stationery Office, London, 1966.
Slim, William, *Defeat into Victory,* David McKay Co. Inc., New York, 1961.
Stilwell, Joseph, *The Stilwell Papers,* William Sloane Associates Inc., 1948.
Tuchman, Barbara, *Stilwell and the American Experience in China 1911–45,* The Macmillan Co., New York, 1970.
Winterbotham, F. W., *The Ultra Secret,* Harper & Row, New York, 1974.

Chapter 5 Bibliography

Alexander, Harold, *The Alexander Memoirs,* McGraw Hill, New York, 1962.
Allen, Peter, *One More River,* Charles Scribner's Sons, New York, 1980.
Barnett, Correlli, *The Desert Generals,* Viking, New York, 1961.

Bauer, Cornelius, *The Battle of Arnhem*, Stein & Day, Briarcliff, 1967.
Bennett, Ralph, *Ultra in the West*, Charles Scribner's Sons, New York, 1979.
Bradley, Omar, *A Soldier's Story*, Rand McNally, Chicago, 1978.
Bryant, Arthur, *The Turn of the Tide*, Doubleday, New York, 1957.
Butcher, Harry, *My Three Years With Eisenhower*, Simon & Schuster, New York, 1946.
Chalfont, Alun, *Montgomery of Alamein*, Atheneum, New York, 1976.
Churchill, Winston, *The Hinge of Fate*, Houghton Mifflin, Boston, 1950.
Clark, Mark, *Calculated Risk*, Harper Brothers, New York, 1950.
Einsenhower, Dwight, *Crusade in Europe*, Doubleday, New York, 1948.
Elstob, Peter, *Battle of the Reichswald*, Ballantine Books, New York, 1970.
Essame, H., *The Battle for Germany*, Charles Scribner's Sons, New York, 1969.
Essame, H., *Normandy Bridgehead*, Ballantine Books, New York, 1970.
Farago, Ladislas, *Patton — Ordeal and Triumph*, Ivan Obelensky, New York, 1963.
Farago, Ladislas, *The Last Days of Patton*, McGraw Hill, New York, 1980.
Farrar-Hockley, Anthony, *Airborne Carpet — Operation Market Garden*, Ballantine Books, New York, 1969.
Florentin, Eddy, *The Battle of the Falaise Gap*, Hawthorn Books, New York, 1967.
Grigg, John, *1943—The Victory that Never Was*, Hill & Wang, New York, 1980.
Horrocks, Brian, *A Full Life*, Collins, London, 1960.
Horrocks, Brian, *Corps Commander*, Charles Scribner's Sons, New York, 1977.
Irving, David, *The War Between the Generals*, Congdon & Lattes, New York, 1981.
Jackson, W. G. F., *The Battle for Italy*, Harper & Row, New York, 1967.
Jackson, W. G. F., *The Battle for North Africa*, Mason/Charter, New York, 1975.
Lewin, Ronald, *Montgomery as Military Commander*, Stein & Day, Briarcliff, 1971.

Lewin, Ronald, *Ultra Goes to War,* McGraw Hill, New York, 1978.
Liddell-Hart, B. H., *History of the Second World War,* G.P. Putnam's Sons, New York, 1971.
MacDonald, Charles, *The Mighty Endeavor,* Oxford University Press, New York, 1969.
Majdalany, Fred, *The Battle of El Alamein,* J.P. Lippincott Co., Philadelphia, 1965.
Majdalany, Fred, *The Fall of Fortress Europe,* Doubleday, New York, 1968.
Mason, David, *Breakout — Drive to the Seine,* Ballantine Books, New York, 1968.
McKee, Alexander, *Caen — Anvil of Victory,* Souvenir Press Ltd., London, 1964.
Montgomery, Bernard, *Normandy to the Baltic,* Hutchinson & Co. Ltd., London, 1947.
Montgomery, Bernard, *El Alamein to the River Sangro,* Hutchinson & Co. Ltd., London, 1948.
Moorehead, Alan, *Eclipse,* Harper & Row, New York, 1968.
Moulton, J. L., *The Battle for Antwerp,* Hippocrene Books, New York, 1978.
Ryan, Cornelius, *The Longest Day,* Simon & Schuster, New York, 1959.
Ryan, Cornelius, *A Bridge Too Far,* Simon & Schuster, New York, 1974.
Sheppard, S. L. A., *The Italian Campaign,* Frederick A. Praeger, New York, 1968.
Smyth, J., *Leadership in the War,* St. Martin's Press, New York, 1974.
Stock, James, *Rhine Crossing,* Ballantine Books, New York, 1973.
Thompson, R. W., *Montgomery,* Ballantine Books, New York,
Thompson, R. W., *D-Day,* Ballantine Books, New York, 1968.
Urquhart, Roy, *Arnhem,* Cassell, London, 1958.
Whiting, Charles, *Battle of the Ruhr Pocket,* Ballantine Books, New York, 1970.
Whiting, Charles, *The End of the War,* Stein & Day, Briarcliff, 1973.
Wilmot, Chester, *The Struggle for Europe,* Harper & Row, New York, 1952.

Chapter 6 Bibliography

Alexander, Field Marshal H., *The Alexander Memoirs,* McGraw Hill Book Co., 1962.
Calvert, Michael, *Slim,* Ballantine Books, 1973.
Calvert, Michael, *Chindits,* Ballantine Books, 1973.
Carver, Michael, ed., *The War Lords,* Little, Brown and Co., 1976.
Kirby, S. Woodburn et al., *The War Against Japan,* Volume III, Her Majesty's Stationery Office, 1961.
Kirby, S. Woodburn et al., *The War Against Japan,* Volume IV, Her Majesty's Stationery Office, 1965.
Liddell-Hart, B. H., *History of the Second World War,* G.P. Putnam's Sons, New York, 1970.
Slim, Field Marshal William, *Defeat Into Victory,* David McKay Co. Inc., 1961.
Smith, E. D., *Battle for Burma,* B.T. Batsford Limited, London, 1979.
Stilwell, Joseph W., *The Stilwell Papers,* William Sloane Associates Inc., 1948.
Swinson, Arthur, *The Battle of Kohima,* Stein and Day, 1967.

A TERRIFYING OCCULT TRILOGY
by William W. Johnstone

THE DEVIL'S KISS (1498, $3.50)
As night falls on the small prairie town of Whitfield, red-rimmed eyes look out from tightly shut windows. An occasional snarl rips from once-human throats. Shadows play on dimly lit streets, bringing with the darkness an almost tangible aura of fear. For the time is now right in Whitfield. The beasts are hungry, and the Undead are awake . . .

THE DEVIL'S HEART (1526, $3.50)
It was the summer of 1958 that the horror surfaced in the town of Whitfield. Those who survived the terror remember it as the summer of The Digging—the time when Satan's creatures rose from the bowels of the earth and the hot wind began to blow. The town is peaceful, and the few who had fought against the Prince of Darkness before believed it could never happen again.

THE DEVIL'S TOUCH (1491, $3.50)
The evil that triumphed during the long-ago summer in Whitfield still festers in the unsuspecting town of Logandale. Only Sam and Nydia Balon, lone survivors of the ancient horror, know the signs—the putrid stench rising from the bowels of the earth, the unspeakable atrocities that mark the foul presence of the Prince of Darkness. Hollow-eyed, hungry corpses will rise from unearthly tombs to engorge themselves on living flesh and spawn a new generation of restless Undead . . . and only Sam and Nydia know what must be done.

Available wherever paperbacks are sold, or order direct from the Publisher. Send cover price plus 50¢ per copy for mailing and handling to Zebra Books, Dept. 1753, 475 Park Avenue South, New York, N.Y. 10016. DO NOT SEND CASH.